John Lawrence, John Lawrence

The History Of The United Brethren In Christ

Vol 1

John Lawrence, John Lawrence

The History Of The United Brethren In Christ
Vol 1

ISBN/EAN: 9783743355071

Manufactured in Europe, USA, Canada, Australia, Japa

Cover: Foto ©ninafisch / pixelio.de

Manufactured and distributed by brebook publishing software (www.brebook.com)

John Lawrence, John Lawrence

The History Of The United Brethren In Christ

THE HISTORY

OF THE CHURCH OF THE

UNITED BRETHREN IN CHRIST.

BY JOHN LAWRENCE.

IN TWO VOLUMES.

VOL. I.

DAYTON, OHIO:
PUBLISHED AT THE UNITED BRETHREN PRINTING
ESTABLISHMENT.
VONNIEDA & SOWERS, PUBLISHERS.

1860.

PREFACE

UNITED BRETHREN history is, for the most part, a history of spiritual religion in opposition to carnal ecclesiasticism. If the question be asked, what is it that most distinctly marks the history of the Waldenses, the United Brethren, the earlier Mennonites, the Church of the United Brethren, the Renewed United Brethren, and the United Brethren in Christ, it must be answered, *it was the spiritual life which they cherished and diffused abroad.* It was for the religion of the heart,—the religion of the Holy Spirit,—that they turned their backs upon the parade and glitter of great worldly churches, earnestly contended, cheerfully suffered, and bravely died. The same Spirit which was poured out upon the disciples, on the day of Pentecost, made an evangelist of Peter Waldo, endued the Brethren at Lititz with power in 1457, sat upon the lips of Menno Simonis, and fired, with missionary ardor, the builders of Herrnhut. And, about one hundred years ago, a revival, originating in a baptism of the Spirit, was commenced in the heart of a German minister at Lancaster, in Pennsylvania, which has been deepening and widening ever since; and now, as a result, a church, composed of converted persons, approximating a hundred thousand souls, confesses that the Gospel is, indeed, "the power of God unto salvation to every one that believeth." WILLIAM OTTERBEIN, the minister referred to, although but little known to the present generation, had, during the last half of the eighteenth century, and the first decade of the nineteenth, few, if any, superiors in the American pulpit; and, as an evangelist, he has not been excelled in this country. The church to which his evangelical labors, and the labors of the good men who co-operated with him, gave rise—known as the "*United Brethren in Christ*"—although not the smallest member of the Christian family recognized by the common Father, has attracted but little public notice; yet, adhering firmly to the fundamental facts and truths of the Gospel, and zealously proclaiming them, it has been, and is now, adding, every year, no inconsiderable number to the hosts of the redeemed on earth and in heaven. This church has, under its care, an extensive printing establishment, several good institutions of learning, and it supports more than two hundred missionaries. It exists in the Eastern, Middle, Southern, and Western States, in most of the territories, and in Canada; and, in several of the Western States, it is amongst the largest denominations.

It has been very properly remarked, that there are two methods of writing the history of a denomination. One is, to trace the cropping out of its principles, through ecclesiastical history, from the time of the New Testament to the present time. Another is, to look for the earliest time when its present organization took its form and shape, and thence trace its progress. I have attempted to combine both these methods; and, in pursuance of this plan, the volume now offered to the public is divided into two parts.

Part First, which is introductory, contains a sketch of the antecedents of the United Brethren in Christ, by which term I refer to those older religious bodies to which our's is related in history, doctrine, spirit, and name. Some account will be found, in this part, of the Renewed United Brethren; of the Mennonites, who are related to the United Brethren; of the Church of the United Brethren; of the primitive United Brethren, and of the Waldenses, from whom the United Brethren descended. A proper understanding and application of the facts noticed in this part of the work, would do something, I think, toward the abatement of that high-church pride which manifests itself in very lofty pretensions, and is wont to scorn the United Brethren in Christ as a "sect," using that term in its most offensive sense. High-churchmen have their antecedents, and the United Brethren in Christ have their's; and, if I have a proper understanding of the facts of history, the latter need not shrink from a comparison with the former.

The Second Part contains a history of the rise and progress of the United Brethren in Christ, up to the death of William Otterbein, near the close of the year 1813. With the death of Boehm, Guething, and Otterbein, properly closes an important period of United Brethren history. A second volume, now in course of preparation for the press, will bring the history down to the present time.

In the preparation of Part First, I have been very materially aided by the excellent history of the United Brethren, written by REV. JOHN HOLMES, and published in London, England, in 1825. It is now, I believe, entirely out of print; but, through the kindness of the Brethren at Bethlehem, Pa., a copy was placed in my hands.

In the preparation of the Second Part, I have drawn largely upon the history of the United Brethren in Christ written by REV. H. G. SPAYTH, and published at Circleville, in 1851. In many cases, I have followed Mr. Spayth's idea closely without using his language; in other cases, I have transferred whole pages, making slight changes in the language. Indeed, Mr. S.'s history is indispensable to a proper understanding of the rise of the United Brethren in Christ; and the Church, in all time to come, will be indebted to him for the most valuable contribution to her early history.

The likeness which accompanies this volume, was obtained from a painting executed for Peter Hofman, one of the elders of Mr. Otterbein's church in Baltimore.

I submit this work to the public, desiring that it may contribute something to the cause of experimental religion.

JOHN LAWRENCE.

CONTENTS

PART FIRST.

CHAPTER I.
THE WALDENSES.

Union with Christ essential to religious life and fellowship. Character of the primitive church. Development and power of the Man of Sin. The true church never destroyed. The Waldenses. Character described by an inquisitor. Peter Waldo—conversion, character, labors, and death. Character of the Waldenses. Waldensian ministers. A Waldensian Confession of Faith... ...... 17—37

CHAPTER II.
UNITED BRETHREN.

Sketch of the religious history of Bohemia. The Waldenses taking refuge there, and establishing numerous churches. Their number in 1315. John Huss—early history, conversion, conflicts with Romanism, appearance at Constance, trial and martyrdom. The long war following. Compromise of the Calixtines. Overthrow of the Taborites. Organization of the United Brethren. Synods in dark forests. Views of ordination. Ordination obtained from a Waldensian bishop. Bloody persecutions. A picture of Christendom a few years prior to the reformation of the 16th century. The reformation. Conferences between the Brethren and Luther. Views of the Brethren entertained by the reformers. The church of the United Brethren. The Brethren not recognized in the treaty of Westphalia. Sad results. Lamentation of Comenius. Doctrine, discipline, and usages, of the primitive United Brethren.................. 38—65

CONTENTS.

CHAPTER III.

THE MENNONITES.

A harvest from Waldensian sowing. Menno Simonis—conversion, talents, labors, sufferings, success, and death. Character and doctrine of the Mennonites. Persecutions and wrongs. Immigration to America.. 66—73

CHAPTER IV.

THE RENEWED UNITED BRETHREN.

Influence of the Protestants, before the reformation, in producing that revolt. Failure of the reformation to mold the churches to which it gave birth according to the apostolic pattern. Spener and the Pietists. Revival among some remnants of the primitive Brethren—Christian David leads a few of them to Herrnhut. Count Zinzendorf. Gathering of the people at Herrnhut. Rules adopted. Wonderful outpouring of the Spirit, August 13th, 1727........ 74—92

CHAPTER V.

UNITED BRETHREN IN ENGLAND.

State of religion in England when the Brethren commenced their missionary labors there. The Oxford club. Mr. Wesley, on his way to America, learning of the Brethren. Mr. Wesley an inquirer at their meetings, and a member of the Brethren society at Fetter Lane, London. Charles Wesley's conversion. Wesley at Herrnhut. Whitfield and Wesley at Fetter Lane. Wonderful outpouring of the Spirit. Mr. Wesley's withdrawal from the Brethren. The labors of the Brethren in England. Missionary society organized in 1741 .... 93—103

CHAPTER VI.

UNITED BRETHREN IN AMERICA.

State of religion in this country, in 1736. Lutherans, German Reformed, Mennonites, and others. Saltzbergers—Gronau and Bolzius. Bachtel, Antes, and Spangenberg. Union convention. Zinzendorf. Congregation of God in the Spirit. Bright hopes blasted. Muhlenberg and Schlatter. The Congregation dissolved. 105—120

PART SECOND.

CHAPTER I.
PHILIP WILLIAM OTTERBEIN.

Mr. Otterbein's parentage, birth, education, ordination, and entrance upon the ministry. His zeal excites opposition. Is selected as a missionary to America. Separation from his mother. Examination and outfit. Letter of salutation. Sails for the New World .... 123—134

CHAPTER II.
MR. OTTERBEIN'S MINISTRY AT LANCASTER.

Character of the congregation at Lancaster. Mr. O.'s devotion to the work. Severe trials. An inquirer asks what he must do to be saved. Mr. O. sent to his closet. Enters into the new life. Opposition commences. Efforts to bring the church at Lancaster up to the Gospel standard. Frederick Schaeffer, and other living converts. Resignation of his charge....................... 135—143

CHAPTER III.
MR. OTTERBEIN AT TULPEHOCKEN.

The country and congregations. Mr. O. preaching from house to house. Prayer-meetings. Class-meetings. Many souls awakened and converted. Remarks on prayer-meetings. The aid they afforded... 144—151

CHAPTER IV.
MARTIN BOEHM.

God's plan of selecting preachers recognized. Interesting facts concerning Boehm's ancestors. His birth, education, and selection, by lot, to be a preacher. Attempts to speak, and failures. Is awakened and converted. A relation of his experience in his own words. Visit to Virginia. Whitfield's converts. Miss Keller a sad mourner. Boehm's conversation with her parents. A family prayer-meeting. Miss K., and others of the family, converted. Others led into the good way. Boehm returns to Pennsylvania, strengthened. Enlarges the sphere of his influence. Introduces meetings during the week................................... 152—169

CONTENTS.

CHAPTER V.
GREAT UNION MEETING—"WE ARE BRETHREN."

Otterbein and Boehm brought together. Great union meeting at Isaac Long's. God's people, of various denominations, flowing together as in days of old. Otterbein folds Boehm to his bosom, and cries out, "We are brethren." Impression upon the congregation. The result another United Brethren church.................. 170—175

CHAPTER VI.
OTTERBEIN AT FREDERICK.—GEORGE ADAM GUETHING.

Dr. Zacharias on Otterbein as a pastor. Opposition at Frederick. Preaching in the graveyard. Preaching at Antietam. G. A. Guething's nativity, education, and conversion. Reading sermons. The book taken from him. Guething as a preacher. Otterbein, Boehm, and Guething, viewed together. Great meetings. Guething's house, Otterbein's home .... 176—186

CHAPTER VII.
OTHER LABORERS—CHRISTIAN NEWCOMER.

A God-called ministry. Necessity of more laborers. How that necessity was created. A living church will always furnish living ministers. Sketch of the life, Christian experience, and character, of Christian Newcomer. Acquaintance with Otterbein and Guething. Entrance upon the ministry. Great success as an evangelist .... 187—204

CHAPTER VIII.
CO-LABORERS—HENDEL AND OTHERS, AND THE METHODISTS.

Mr. Otterbein at York. Every year adding to the reasons for his virtual separation from the Reformed church. State of the Reformed church, and composition of the cœtus of Pennsylvania. Hendel, Wagner, Stahlschmidt, and Hantz. Rise of the Methodists. Co-operation with them. Schwope, Asbury, and Otterbein. Character of early Methodist preachers, and the reasons why they were welcomed by the Brethren. Otterbein assisting in the ordination of Asbury... .205—223

CONTENTS. xi

CHAPTER IX.

OTTERBEIN AT BALTIMORE.

Otterbein organizing an independent church in Baltimore. History of the movement. Church book of this new church. Regulations. Remarks on the constitution and ordinances of the new church. God smiles upon Mr. O.'s labors in Baltimore and elsewhere. A description of Mr. O. in his pulpit at Baltimore. Sorrow at his separation from the Reformed church. A farewell visit to the cœtus.. 224—262

CHAPTER X.

CONFERENCES OF 1789-1791.—DRAKSEL, PFRIMMER, NEIDING, AND OTHERS.

War of the Revolution. Informal conferences. First special conference. Sketches of Kreider, Grosh, Draksel, and Baker. Second conference. Sketches of Pfrimmer and Neiding......... 263—277

CHAPTER XI.

THE WORK ADVANCING—INCIDENTS—CONFERENCE OF 1800.

Persecutions. Churches closed against the evangelists. Interesting meetings. Singular power of grace. A quarterly meeting in 1796. Three days meetings. The Brethren ministry of this period men of the apostolic stamp. Co-laborers. Conference of 1800. "In Christ" added to the denominational name. Election of superintendents. A fresh impetus given to the work.......... 278—295

CHAPTER XII.

CONFERENCES OF 1801-1802—GREAT MEETINGS—LOVE-FEASTS.

Conference of 1801. Conference address. Itinerancy. Resolutions on class-meetings and brevity in preaching. A sermon by Otterbein. Conference of 1802. Registry of members discussed. Manner of dealing with offending preachers prescribed. Provision in case of the death of a superintendent. Bible doctrine to be preached. Times of refreshing in Rockingham county, Virginia. Numerous great meetings. Stirring love-feast experiences.. 296—314

CONTENTS.

CHAPTER XIII.

CONFERENCES OF 1803-1804.—PENTECOSTAL MEETINGS—
THE BENEFITS.

Resolution relating to awakened souls. Meeting at Shopps' The work west of the Alleghany mountains. Meeting at Schwope's. Newcomer. Results of revival meetings considered. The United Brethren church identified with a blessed revival of religion. Notices of meetings in various places in Pennsylvania, Maryland, and Virginia... 315—326

CHAPTER XIV.

A GLANCE AT THE CONFERENCES, FROM 1805 TO 1812.
—FIRST CONFERENCE IN OHIO.

Re-election of superintendents. Regulations respecting the itinerant preachers, and the administration of the ordinances. The last conference attended by Otterbein. At the conference of 1806, the preachers all united in love. Preachers, who wish to enter the conference, to be previously examined and licensed at a great meeting The subject of a closer union with the Methodists considered, and a letter from the Baltimore church, on the subject, received. Letter from the M. E. conference. The conference in Ohio. Fifteen preachers present. Pioneers. Salaries of preachers fixed. List of preachers who were authorized to administer all the ordinances .... 327—339

CHAPTER XV.

THE FRIENDLY CORRESPONDENCE WITH THE METHODISTS.

Welcome to the first Methodist preachers by the United Brethren. Newcomer meets Whatcoat. Sneithen, Roberts, Otterbein, and Enoch George. Roberts, Sneithen, and Cooper, in Otterbein's pulpit. Union camp-meetings. Friendly conference between George, Newcomer, and Guething, at Antietam. Newcomer at a Methodist conference. Letters of correspondence, and exchange of messengers. Terms of co-operation agreed upon. The terms abrogated. Rigid enforcement of Methodist rules........................ 340—367

CONTENTS. xiii

CHAPTER XVI.

"THE SO-CALLED ALBRIGHTS."—ANOTHER PROPOSED UNION.

Rise and progress of the "so-called Albrights, now known as the Evangelical Association. Newcomer visits an Evangelical conference. Discussion of the subject of union, at Herre's. Meeting of a committee on union in 1813. Another meeting in 1816. Failure to agree. Alleged reasons.................................. 368—376

CHAPTER XVII.

P. KEMP, JOHN HERSHEY, MARTIN BOEHM, AND GEO. A. GUETHING—THEIR LAST TESTIMONY.

Happy death of P. Kemp and John Hershey. Last hours of Martin Boehm. Sings and prays in a clear voice, and then sinks to rest. A preacher 54 years. Review of an account of M. Boehm found in Dr. Bang's History of the M. E. Church. An error sifted out and exposed. Last days of G. A. Guething. At the conference of 1812. Visits Otterbein. Is taken ill, and returns toward home. Triumphant death. A preacher forty years. Tribute to Guething, from Henry Smith...................................... 377—390

CHAPTER XVIII.

CLOSE OF MR. OTTERBEIN'S LIFE.

Otterbein "happy in God." Is written to from the West. Is visited by Newcomer and Hoffman. Ordains Newcomer, Hoffman, and Schaffer. Certificate of ordination. Farewell words to the church. Dr. Kurtz at his bedside. "Lay my head upon my pillow, and be still!" Funeral solemnities. Sermon by Dr. Kurtz. Sermon by bishop Asbury. Brunner's singular dream. Otterbein's grave. Sixty-two years a minister. Otterbein no partisan,—life pure,—as a Christian, evangelical,—remarkably humble,—benevolence unbounded,—plain in reproof—as a preacher, scarcely excelled. Conference sermons. Dr. Kurtz's notice of Otterbein and his co-laborers. Questions by Asbury, and answers in the hand-writing of Otterbein. The characteristic humility of Otterbein reflected in the answers given to Mr. A.'s inquiries..................... 391—410

CHAPTER XIX.

END OF THE FIRST PERIOD—A RESUME.

Nearly a half century had passed since the union meeting at Isaac Long's. The gradual developement of the work. Death of the earliest fathers. Asbury's estimate of the labors of Otterbein and his cotemporaries, and of the number of preachers and members in the communion of the United Brethren. . ... 411—416

PART FIRST.

CHAPTER I.

THE WALDENSES.

Union with Christ is essential to religious life. This is a fundamental doctrine of the Christian religion. It is distinctly asserted, and impressively illustrated, by the Lord himself, in the parable of the vine and the branches; and it is the central thought in the writings of all the apostles. The most wonderful mystery of the universe,—the mystery which was hid from ages and generations, and into which the angels desired to look,—is solved and summed up in the brief sentence—"Christ in you the hope of glory."

Union with Christ is also the condition of Christian fellowship. That pure, fervent, disinterested love, which is its essence, is a pulsation from the heart of Jesus. They, and they only, who live in Christ, who is the Life,—who walk in Christ, who is the Light, —have fellowship one with another; and, therefore, union with Christ is indispensable to the very existence of a Christian church;

for it will hardly be maintained, by any one, that a Christian church can exist where there is no Christian fellowship.

The PRIMITIVE CHURCH was, without doubt, composed, exclusively, of men and women who had personally renounced all sin, and accepted of Jesus as the only Savior and Mediator. The Gospel came to them, not in word only, but in power; and, therefore, each member of the church could relate a stirring, personal experience, and magnify the grace of God, rejoicing in a happy consciousness of pardon and peace, purity and power, arising from an intimate and endearing union with Christ.* In a word, it was a living church, united in Christ the living head.

Its worship consisted in the singing of psalms, hymns, and spiritual songs; in reading the Holy Scriptures; in sermons and exhortations; in the relation of Christian experience; and in the celebration, in the simplest

---

* Many are the marks which the learned have given us of the true church: but, be that as it will, no man, whether learned or unlearned, can have any mark or proof of his own true church membership, but his being dead unto all sin, and alive unto all righteousness. This can not be more plainly told us than in the words of our Lord, "He that committeth sin is the servant of sin;" but, surely, the servant of sin can not, at the same time, be a living member of Christ's body, or that new creature which dwelleth in Christ, and Christ in him.—*William Law.*

possible manner, of the ordinances established by the Lord. It had no stately liturgy, no imposing forms. These were introduced at a later period, when the power of godliness had somewhat declined.

The government of the church was simple as its worship. No one was called Rabbi, Doctor, His Grace, or His Holiness; while all acknowledged the one Divine Lord and Savior. The most perfect equality reigned. Whoever believed the Gospel with the heart, and, with the mouth, made confession unto salvation, was solemnly baptized, immediately received into the church, and recognized as a fellow-citizen of the household of faith. To the rich and the poor, to persons of rank, and to slaves, the endearing and leveling term, "brethren," was applied without distinction. No traces, whatever, of a pompous and lording hierarchy can be discovered in the constitution of the apostolic church.*

Simple as this church was in its organization and mode of worship, and little as it possessed of wealth, learning, or any human

---

* There reigned among the members of the Christian church, however distinguished by wordly rank and titles, not only an amiable harmony, but also a perfect equality.—*Mosheim:* Applegate & Co.'s Ed. p. 21.

means of success, it proved to be, nevertheless, a moral force, unequalled and irresistible. Into all the accessible and known habitations of the world, the plain and earnest messengers of salvation went abroad, preaching a crucified and risen Savior, making no compromises with evils, giving no quarter to errors, cheerfully enduring all manner of reproaches and persecutions, tortures and deaths; and, every-where, numerous converts were made, and living churches planted. During the first three centuries millions of people, of various and diversified languages and climes, heard and received the glad tidings. Paganism, although honored in thousands of magnificent temples, presiding in all the seats of learning, embalmed in immortal poetry, diffused through every species of literature, interwoven with the social state, and entrenched behind all the civil and military powers of the earth, fell before the onward march of the Gospel; and so gloriously did the light shine forth that the universal reign of righteousness seemed near.

But "the mystery of iniquity," foreseen by the apostle, and delineated with remarkable faithfulness in the glowing pages of the Revelation, began to develop its amazing power within the ecclesiastical pale itself. The conversion to the Christian faith of the Roman emperor, Constantine, was every-where hailed by the church as an event of great promise to Christianity. Long had the Christians endured every species of wrong and suffering in defense of the Gospel; but now they were promised rest, and nobility began to smile on them. The Christian church became a popular institution. Wealth poured into it. Its original simplicity of worship, doctrine and government, was essentially modified to render it more consonant to the high views of the imperial convert and his court, and more agreeable to the appetites and fashions of a corrupt age. Hence, the chief ministers or bishops were elevated to seats of princely power; lordly ecclesiastical titles were invented and conferred; new doctrines were promulgated, and pagan mysteries were either associated with the simple rites of the Gospel, or substituted in their place. The touching simplicity of worship gave place to an empty ceremonial, pleasing enough to the unspiritual eye, and sufficiently attractive to the carnal mind. The word of God, so long the only authority in all matters of faith and practice, was subordinated to the decisions of councils, and ceased to be the touchstone of truth. The mild and strict discipline of the apostolic times, was partially or wholly abandoned. The strait gate was widened, the narrow way made broad, for the convenience and comfort of the fashionable, the proud, the ambitious, and even the immoral. The boundaries, marked out by the Lord, between the church and the world, one by one, were removed, until all had at last disappeared.

While this transformation of the popular church was going forward, for it was a work of centuries, the dark ages came on. The Roman empire, which had long been decaying, unable to withstand the powerful assaults of the hardy barbarians with whom it had long warred, and having fulfilled its prophetic destiny, fell. Whole nations of barbarians poured into it from the North, and in the East Mohammedanism arose and began its bloody conquests. Amid the confusion and darkness, the strife and blood, the Man of Sin —the papal hierarchy—grew up with wonderful rapidity, and attained amazing power. Before it kings and emperors bowed in the most slavish submission. The pope, as God, seated himself in the temple of God, and, for ages and ages employed his almost unlimited civil and ecclesiastical power in the gratification of the worst vices, and in shedding the blood of the saints of the Most High.

But it must not be inferred from the foregoing facts, that the gates of hell had prevailed against the church; for, *the history of a living church, adhering unswervingly to Christ's word, filled with the Spirit, distinguished for all practical virtues, and protesting against all departures from apostolic faith and discipline, is coeval with the history of papal usurpation and depravity.* It is a fact universally admitted, that, during every period of the middle ages, Jesus had numerous witnesses in the dark bosom of the church of Rome itself. But entirely outside of that church, distinct from it, and protesting boldly against it, we find, in every age, vigorous and powerful bodies of Christians, who maintained the doctrine, discipline, and spirit of the apostolic church. Toward this church the anger of Rome never cooled; and the blood of its confessors, however freely poured out, never satiated her cruel thirst.

The most painfully exciting portion of ecclesiastical history is that which describes the extraordinary efforts of the papal power to extirpate the true and only church of Christ on earth. But the dungeon, scaffold, gibbet, rack, fire, and every instrument of torture which infernal ingenuity could invent, failed to accomplish the desire of that great and malignant power, because Jesus had said,— "Upon this rock I will build my church; and the gates of hell shall not prevail against it."

The Vaudois or Waldenses (Men of the Valleys) existed at a very early period. They have a tradition among them, which is not altogether unworthy of credit, that their fathers, offended at the liberality with which Constantine endowed the church, and especially at the eagerness with which the imperial favors were received by Sylvester and the leading bishops, seceded from ·the popular church, and organized societies for the promotion of genuine religion, and to keep alive the holy flame of love; and, that they might be less exposed to annoyance and persecution, they retired into Alpine solitudes, where, for a long period, they flourished in comparative quietude. It is evident that the Cathari, or Puritans in the West, who arose in the third century, and the Paulicians in the East, who flourished in the seventh, separated from the prevailing church on account of its increasing errors of doctrine and practice, and that they agreed, in all essential matters, with the Leonists, Piccards, Albigenses, Vaudois, and Waldenses.*

Reinerius Sacho, a Romish inquisitor, who was, at one period of his life, a member of the Waldensian church, has left upon record a valuable testimony in relation to the Waldenses. He says:—"Among all sects or religious parties separated from the Romish church, there is not one more dangerous than the Leonists or Waldenses, for the following reasons: first, because this sect is older than any other. It existed, according to some, in the days of pope Sylvester, in the fourth century, and, according to others, even in the days of the apostles. Secondly, because it is widely spread; for there is scarcely a country into which it has not found its way. Thirdly, because, while other sects create disgust by their blasphemous doctrines, this has a great appearance of piety, as its members lead a righteous life before men, believe the truths concerning God and divine things, and retain all the articles of the apostolic faith, *only hating the Romish church and clergy.*"

---

* History of the Protestant Church of the United Brethren, by Rev. John Holmes. Printed in London, 1825.

About the year 1160, Peter Waldo, an opulent merchant of Lyons, in France, awakened by a startling providence* from the sleep of sin, commenced the study of the Holy Scriptures. It was not long before the way of salvation, by faith in Jesus, was made plain to his mind, and verified by a happy experience of sins forgiven. Henceforth he devoted himself and all his possessions to the service of God. With the assistance of some learned men, he translated the four Gospels into the French language. "This was the first translation of any part of the Bible into a modern tongue." He also organized a society for the promotion of religious knowledge, and the circulation of the Scriptures in the language of the common people. Many persons heard and received the glad tidings of salvation from the lips of Waldo; and those living converts were not long separated from their brethren of like faith and experience,—the Vaudois or Waldenses,—in the vallies of Piedmont; and, although known by different names in different countries, their history uniformly flows in one channel.

From the commencement of his evangel-

---

* One evening after supper, while enjoying the society of his friends, one of them fell down and instantly expired.

ical labors at Lyons, Waldo was opposed by the Romish ecclesiastics. The leader of the opposition was the archbishop. That a layman should profess a knowledge of sins forgiven, translate and circulate the Scriptures, preach, and awaken the people to a sense of their sins, was an unpardonable offense in the eyes of his grace, the archbishop of Lyons. Hence, stringent measures were adopted to prevent the circulation of the Scriptures, to close the mouth of Waldo, and destroy his influence. "But the purity and simplicity of the religion which" he and his co-laborers "taught, the spotless innocence which shone forth in their actions, and the noble contempt of riches and honors manifested in the whole of their conduct and conversation, appeared so engaging to all such as had any sense of true piety, that the number of their societies increased from day to day."*

Unable to check the revival, the archbishop appealed for help to the pope of Rome. Alexander III. issued a terrible bull against the heretics, as he affected to regard them. "We, therefore," said he, "subject to a curse both themselves and their defenders and harborers, and, under a curse, we prohibit all

---

* Moshiem, p. 291.

persons from admitting them into their houses, or receiving them upon their lands, or cherishing them, or exercising any trade with them. * * Let them not receive Christian burial." Liberal indulgences were granted to soldiers who should slaughter them without pity; and, to facilitate the work of death, the Inquisition, horribly prominent in later ecclesiastical history, was invented. Deprived of all civil, social, and religious rights and privileges, the poor Waldenses were pursued with unrelenting fury for a period of seventy-three years—from 1180 to 1253. "But such was their invincible fortitude, that neither fire nor sword, nor the most cruel inventions of merciless persecution, could dampen their zeal, or entirely ruin their cause." God was with them, and, in spite of all opposition, the good seed of the word was extensively sown, "an incredible number" of converts were made; and, although every-where proscribed, and "killed all the day long," they stood up for Christ and his word, and bore a testimony against Rome which cast a shadow upon the papal throne itself.

In the early part of the struggle, Peter Waldo was driven from Lyons into Piccardy; thence into Germany; and at last he closed his evangelical labors and his life among the brave Bohemian mountaineers,—the ancestors of John Huss. After sowing in those mountains the imperishable seed, he died peacefully in 1180.* Of the fruits of his labors we shall see hereafter.

In relation to the character of the Waldenses, the general purity of their lives and the soundness of their doctrine, we have the most satisfactory proofs. Even those who esteemed it their duty to kill them without pity, bear testimony to the excellence of their lives. Of them St. Bernard says:—"There is a sect which calls itself after no man's name, which pretends to be in the direct line of apostolical succession, and which, rustic and unlearned though it is, contends that the church (Roman Catholic) is wrong, and that itself alone is right. If you ask them of their faith, nothing can be more Christian-like; if you observe their conversation, nothing can be more blameless, and what they speak they make good by their actions. * * As to life and manners, he (the Waldensian) circumvents no man, overreaches no man, does violence to no man. He fasts much, and eats not the bread of

---

* Waddington, p. 356.

idleness, but works with his hands for his support." An inquisitor says of them: "They are orderly and modest in their behavior. They avoid all appearance of pride in dress; they neither indulge in finery of attire, nor are they remarkable for being mean and ragged. They get their living by manual industry. They are not anxious about amassing riches, but content themselves with the necessaries of life. Even when they work they either learn or teach."*

In piety and zeal, in humility and patient endurance for Christ's sake, and in all the elements of a New Testament minister, the WALDENSIAN PREACHERS were the truest representatives and successors of the apostles on earth. They were not lovers of filthy lucre, nor did they aspire to places of power. Raised up from among the working people, and moved to preach by the Holy Ghost, they aimed singly at the glory of God; and such was their interest in the cause, that they thought it no hardship, when necessity required, to earn a part, or the whole, of their support at the loom. Although pre-eminently qualified to "win souls," and to feed the flock of God, they were held in great con-

* Jones' Church History, Vol. II., p. 64.

tempt by the Romish ecclesiastics; and it was regarded as especially disgraceful that they were "tradesmen." To this the Waldensians usually replied: "We do not think it necessary that our pastors should work for bread. They might be better qualified to instruct us, if we could maintain them without their own labor, but our poverty has no other remedy."*

In DOCTRINE the Waldenses never swerved from the apostolic teaching. The reader will pardon us for inserting in this place, without abridgment, a confession of faith put forth by this church in 1544. It contains the substance of, and is in perfect concord with, the older confessions; and it is a very clear expression of that truth which was from the beginning, and was never lost nor corrupted by the true church:—

CONFESSION.

1. WE believe that there is but one God, who is a Spirit—the Creator of all things—

---

* Referring to the reproach cast upon the Waldensian ministry because they were tradesmen, John Milton says: "But our ministers [referring to the English clergy] scorn to use a trade, and count it a reproach of this age that tradesmen preach the Gospel. It were to be wished they were all tradesmen; they would not then, for the want of another trade, make a trade of their preaching: and yet they clamor that tradesmen preach, though they preach, while themselves are the worst tradesmen of all."

the Father of all, who is above all, and through all, and in us all; who is to be worshiped in spirit and in truth—upon whom we are continually dependent, and to whom we ascribe praise for our life, food, raiment, health, sickness, prosperity, and adversity. We love him as the source of all goodness, and reverence him as that sublime being who searcheth the reins and trieth the hearts of the children of men.

2. We believe that Jesus Christ is the Son and image of the Father—that IN HIM all the fullness of the Godhead dwells, and that BY HIM alone we know the Father. He is our Mediator and Advocate; nor is there any other name given under heaven by which we can be saved. In HIS name alone we call upon the Father, using no other prayers than those contained in the Holy Scriptures, or such as are in substance agreeable thereunto.

3. We believe in the Holy Spirit as the Comforter, proceeding from the Father and from the Son; by whose inspiration we are taught to pray; being by him renovated in the spirit of our minds; who creates us anew unto good works, and from whom we receive the knowledge of the truth.

4. We believe that there is one holy church,

comprising the whole assembly of the elect and faithful, that have existed from the beginning of the world, or that shall be to the end thereof. Of this church the Lord Jesus Christ is the head. It is governed by his word, and guided by his Holy Spirit. In the church it behooves all Christians to have fellowship. For her he (Christ) prays incessantly, and his prayer for it is most acceptable to God, without which, indeed, there could be no salvation.

5. We hold that the ministers of the church should be unblamable both in life and doctrine; and, if found otherwise, that they ought to be deposed from their office, and others substituted in their stead; and that no person ought to presume to take that honor unto himself, but he who was called of God as was Aaron; that the duties of such are to feed the flock of God, not for filthy lucre's sake, or as having dominion over God's heritage, but as being examples to the flock in word, in conversation, in charity, in faith, and in chastity.

6. We acknowledge that kings, princes, and governors, are appointed and established ministers of God, whom we are bound to obey, [in all lawful and civil concerns]; for they

bear the sword for the defense of the innocent, and the punishment of evil doers; for which reason we are bound to honor them and pay them tribute. From this power and authority no man can exempt himself, as is manifest from the example of the Lord Jesus Christ, who voluntarily paid tribute, not taking upon himself any jurisdiction of temporal power.

7. We believe that, in the ordinance of baptism, the water is the visible and external sign, which represents to us that which, by virtue of God's invisible operation, is within us—namely, the renovation of our minds, and the mortification of our members through [the faith of] Jesus Christ. And by this ordinance we are received into the holy congregation of God's people, previously professing and declaring our faith and change of life.

8. We hold that the Lord's Supper is a commemoration of, and thanksgiving for, the benefits which we have received by his sufferings and death; and that it is to be received in faith and love—examining ourselves, that so we may eat of that bread, and drink of that cup, as it is written in the Holy Scriptures.

9. We maintain that marriage was instituted of God—that it is holy and honorable,

and ought to be forbidden to none, provided there be no obstacle from the divine word.

10. We contend that all those in whom the fear of God dwells, will thereby be led to please him, and to abound in good works [of the Gospel] which Gôd hath before ordained that we should walk in them—which are love, joy, peace, patience, kindness, goodness, gentleness, sobriety, and the other good works enforced in the Holy Scriptures.

11. On the other hand, we confess that we consider it to be our bounden duty to beware of false teachers, whose object is to divert the minds of men from the true worship of God, and to lead them to place their confidence in the creatures, as well as to depart from the good works of the Gospel, and to regard the inventions of men.

12. We take the Old and New Testament for the rule of our life, and we agree with the general confession of faith contained in [what is usually termed] the apostles' creed.*

The soundness of their doctrinal views finds expression also in the condemnation which they passed upon the principal errors of the Roman Catholic church. The Centurators of Magdeburg, in their History of the Christian

---
* Perrin. See Jones, Vol. II., p. 46.

Church, under the twelfth century, recite from an old manuscript, an epitome of the opinions of the Waldenses of that age; and in relation to the errors referred to, they quote the following from the MS.:

"Masses are impious; and it is madness to say masses for the dead.

"Purgatory is the invention of men; for they who believe go into eternal life; they who believe not, into eternal damnation.

"The invoking and worshiping of dead saints is idolatry.

"The church of Rome is the whore of Babylon.

"We must not obey the pope and bishops, because they are the wolves of the church of Christ.

"The pope hath not the primacy over all the churches of Christ; neither hath he the power of both swords.

"That is the church of Christ, which hears the pure doctrine of Christ, and observes the ordinances instituted by him, in whatever place it exists.

"Vows of celibacy are the inventions of men, and productive of uncleanness.

"So many orders (of the clergy), so many marks of the beast.

"Monkery is a filthy carcass.

"So many superstitious dedications of churches, commemorations of the dead, benedictions of creatures, pilgrimages, so many forced fastings, so many superfluous festivals, those perpetual bellowings, [alluding to the practice of chanting,] and the observations of various other ceremonies, manifestly obstructing the teaching and learning of the word, are diabolical inventions."

As the Waldenses wrote but few books, being distinguished more for their deeds than for their words, some portions of their history are involved in obscurity, and the principal part of what we have has been preserved in the writings of their adversaries; yet enough of it has come down to our times to satisfy the enlightened enquirer that, from the rise of popery to the fifteenth century, they constituted by far the purest church of Christ on earth, and, in fact, the only considerable body which can be regarded as a true Christian church. Their numbers in Europe, during the early part of the fourteenth century, were computed at eight hundred thousand. They were most numerous in France, Italy and Piedmont; and they collected large congregations in Bulgaria, Croatia, Dalmatia, and Hungary.

CHAPTER II.

UNITED BRETHREN.

WHILE the Waldenses in France, and in the countries adjacent which had submitted entirely to the papal yoke, were passing through scenes of persecution, the bare recital of which chills the blood; and while the evangelical fire, which had burned for many centuries so brightly upon their altars, seemed about to be quenched in blood, God was preparing a way for his people in another country, where the light of salvation began to shine forth upon the surrounding darkness.

Christianity had been introduced into Bohemia and Moravia, from the East; but those countries, having, by conquest, been added to the western empire, the Roman pontiffs exerted all the power of both their swords to subject them to the papal yoke. This, however, proved to be a most difficult task. After a struggle of a hundred years, a brave Bohemian king sent a deputation to pope

Gregory VII., asking a confirmation of the religious liberties of Bohemia, and, especially, that divine worship might be performed in the language of the common people. To this very reasonable request, the arrogant pontiff replied by a bull which reads as follows:—

"Gregory, bishop and servant of the servants of God, sends greeting and benediction to the Bohemian prince Wrastislas. Your highness desires that we should give permission to your people to conduct their church service according to the old Sclavonian ritual. But know, my dear son, that we can by no means grant this your request; for, having frequently searched the Holy Scriptures, we have discovered that it hath pleased Almighty God to direct his worship to be conducted in a hidden language, that not every one, especially the simple, should understand it. For, if it were to be performed in a manner altogether intelligible, it might easily be exposed to contempt and disgust; or, if imperfectly understood by half-learned persons, it might happen that, by hearing and contemplating the word too frequently, error might be engendered in the hearts of the people, which would not be easily eradicated. Let no one pretend to quote, as a precedent, that formerly exceptions were in favor of new converts and simple souls. True it is that, in the primitive church, much was conceded to upright and well-meaning people; but much injury and many heresies were thereby created: insomuch that, when the Christian church spread more and more, and became better grounded, it was plainly perceived that, from the root of such ill-timed indulgence, many errors had sprouted up, which it required great labor and pains to stop. Therefore, what your people ignorantly require can in no wise be conceded to them: *and we now forbid it, by the power of God, and his holy* APOSTLE PETER, and exhort you, for the sake of the honor of Almighty God, that you oppose such levity of sentiment by every possible means, in conformity to this our command."

This audacious document was issued in 1079, and its publication was followed by the infliction of the most relentless cruelties upon those who continued to pray and praise God in their own tongue, and to protest against image and saint worship, purgatory, and kindred Romish inventions. Many churches were closed, great numbers were despoiled of their possessions, and others were put to death.

Thus passed another century, and yet large numbers of the inhabitants of Bohemia and Moravia openly or secretly resisted the claims of Romanism, and sighed for deliverance from its heavy yoke, and for a pure religion.

About this time some Waldenses, flying from their persecutors, found their way into Bohemia. Peter Waldo, as we have seen in a previous chapter, there closed his evangelical labors and his life in 1180; and, about that period, many other Waldenses found among the same honest, liberty-loving people, a temporary home and refuge. Carrying with them into this, as into every place whither they were dispersed, the uncorrupted word of God, they found a soil well prepared for its reception; and an abundant harvest was the result. It has been ascertained, from a reliable source, that, in 1315, the Waldenses numbered, in Bohemia, and in the country of Passau, eighty thousand members; and that, thirty-five years later, they had two hundred churches in Bohemia alone. When we take into account the tyranny under which they lived, the strictness of their discipline, and, especially, the fact that they received and retained in their communion only such persons as gave evidence of a renewed heart, these statistics indicate remarkable religious prosperity.

Early in the fifteenth century a series of events occurred in Bohemia, interesting in themselves, and important in their influences upon the church of God, which resulted in the organization of the church of the *United Brethren*—a church which possessed the pure theology and sound evangelical life of the Waldenses; and which must be regarded, indeed, as a part of the same church under a different name. To these events we will now call attention.

JOHN HUSS, the most prominent actor in the great religious drama of the fifteenth century, was born in a small village in Bohemia, in 1373. He studied at Prague, and was appointed Professor of Theology in that University. Through the liberality of a wealthy citizen, a church, called Bethlehem, was erected in Prague, where the Gospel was to be freely dispensed to all the people in both the German and Bohemian languages. Huss was appointed preacher, and, in 1402 he commenced his public ministry. Previous to that time the writings of Wickliffe,—the "Morning Star of the Reformation,"—had been extensively read in Bohemia; and, although Huss could not subscribe to all the views of the English reformer, he reverenced him as a great religious teacher, and his mind was so far enlightened that he rested his faith upon the word of God alone, and was made savingly acquainted with Christ. His eloquent, bold, and evangelical sermons were attended by throngs of hearers.

But during the first year of Huss' public ministry, pope Alexander V. issued a bull condemning the doctrines and writings of Wickliffe, and forbidding all persons to recieve or promulgate them; and the archbishop of Prague caused upwards of two hundred costly-bound volumes of the proscribed books to be publicly burned in the streets of the city. Against this act, as also against many other crimes and corruptions of the papacy, the eloquent preacher of the Bethlehem church lifted up his voice. He was soon summoned to appear before the pope at Bologne, but, refusing to answer, was excommunicated and cursed, and Prague was laid under interdict. Huss appealed from the pope to God; and, enjoying the protection of the royal family, and being supported by the enlightened masses of the people, he was in little immediate danger. Meantime he saw in a clearer light the abominations of Romanism, and condemned them in stronger and more emphatic terms.

In 1414, the celebrated Council of Constance was convened, and Huss was summoned to appear before it. That he might do so without personal risk, a safe conduct, which pledged the word and honor of the emperor Sigismund, was furnished him. As soon, however, as he had reached Constance, he was thrust into a loathsome prison, and even chained to the floor. No regard whatever was paid to the safe conduct. The forms of a brutal trial were passed through, at the close of which the pious, learned, and eloquent preacher, in the prime of his days, was led out of the city and burned to ashes, and his ashes were cast into the Rhine! Nobly did he stand up for Jesus in the Council, and in the flames. The year following, his dear, manly friend, Jerome of Prague, was condemned to die by the same Council; and, at the stake he also witnessed a glorious confession for Christ.

These high-handed measures excited great sorrow and indignation in Bohemia. The nobility and the University united in a remonstrance to the Council, complaining of the murder of Huss as a wrong and an insult to the whole nation. Disdaining to reply, the Council issued a circular, calling upon the friends of the church in Bohemia to aid in exterminating all heretics; and wherever a Hussite could be seized, he was thrown into prison, drowned, burned, or "cast into the deep shafts of the mines near Huttenberg." As an illustration of the spirit and practice of the Romish church, a single incident, selected from numerous heart-rending details, may be noticed: "An upright clergyman, after suffering many cruelties, was, together with three farmers and four boys, placed on a pile of wood. Being once more exhorted to abjure all heresy, the clergyman replied,— 'God forbid! We would, if it were possible, endure death not only once, but a hundred times, rather than deny the truth of the Gospel, solemnly revealed in the Bible.' While the fire was kindling, the clergyman, clasping the children in his arms, began a hymn of praise, in which all joined till they were suffocated by the flames."*

The Council of Constance was convened in 1414, and was not dissolved until 1418. It settled the dispute between the rival popes,

* Holmes' History, U. B. p. 18.

burned Huss and Jerome, condemned the memory of Wickliffe, and ordered that his bones be dug up and cast upon a dunghill; but nothing was done to conciliate the aggreived and excited Bohemians. On the contrary, two years later, pope Martin V. issued an edict accusing the adherents of Huss "of the most damnable heresies, and calling upon emperors, kings and princes, *for the sake of the wounds of Jesus, and their own eternal salvation*, to assist in their extirpation."

This virtual declaration of war by the pontiff, backed by the emperor, involved the country in a terrible civil conflict, which raged for a period of thirteen years. The Bohemians, under the leadership of the courageous Count John Ziska, who regarded himself as "the sword of the Lord," successfully resisted, and, at length, repelled their enemies, and obtained complete control of the whole country. The emperor, at length, sent proposals of peace, but the brave leader of the Bohemians died while on his way to the conference. The war was again renewed, and continued for a number of years longer, under the leadership of Procop.

By far the greater portion of those who took up arms in this bloody contest understood but imperfectly the true principles and spirit of the religion which is on earth peace and good will to men, and they desired only a few very superficial reforms. They were known as *Calixtines*. Hence, in 1431, a council which assembled at Basle, made such concessions as were satisfactory to a very large majority of them; and, after making peace with the Pope, they turned their arms against the *Taborites*, who, on no terms, would yield to that ecclesiastical despot. As an inevitable result of this treaty, the latter were totally defeated; but the Calixtines, who had compromised with Rome and aided in the overthrow of the Taborites, were deceived in their expectations, "as the pope, in the sequel, totally disannulled the Bohemian compact." The prince of darkness is always proposing compromises with religious bodies, and he seldom, if ever, fails to outwit them in the end, and disappoint all their hopes. The cause of true religion has never gained any thing from compromises or compacts with sinners or sinful institutions.

A half century had passed since Huss commenced his reformatory labors,—a half century of persecution, strife and blood,—during which time the cause of vital religion had attracted but little attention in Bohemia. In the year 1457, however, "some of the stricter Hussites, purer Calixtines, scattered and peeled Taborites, and Waldenses," organized a society on the confines of Moravia and Silesia, at Lititz. They took the law of Christ for their guide, and the primitive church for their model. "They called themselves *Brethren* and *Sisters;* and assumed the general appellation of FRATRES LEGIS CHRISTI, i. e., BRETHREN OF THE LAW OF CHRIST. But, as this appellation was liable to be misunderstood, and convey the idea of a new monastic order, they exchanged it for that of FRATRES, (Brethren,) and, after many persons of similar religious views, in different parts of Bohemia, had joined their union, they adopted the name of UNITAS FRATRUM, i. e. *the Unity of the Brethren,* or *the United Brethren,* and this name has ever since been retained."* They adopted, as fundamental, the doctrine of the Waldenses and of Huss, "that the New Testament supplied the only infallible rule" for the constitution of a church; and "that all regulations not enjoined by the word of God, or fairly deducible from it, were to be viewed as mere matters of expediency, and might be

* Holmes, p. 44.

altered according to circumstances;" and they unanimously resolved, "*To suffer all for conscience sake, and not to use arms in defense of religion, but to seek protection from the violence of enemies, by prayer to God, and by dispassionate remonstrance.*" This resolution was never, in a single instance, violated.

For the space of three years they enjoyed peace; and the word of the Lord was spread abroad, and religious societies formed in many parts of Bohemia and Moravia. Then persecution fell to their lot. They were condemned as incorrigible heretics. Some of them were put upon the rack; and the greater portion of them were driven from their homes, and compelled to seek refuge in the deep recesses of mountains. Yet they persevered and prospered. Synods were frequently held in dark forests, where every precaution was necessary to prevent discovery.

At a synod or conference held in 1467, it was, upon mature deliberation, resolved that they would elect their own ministers from their own body; and that, in doing so, they would, in every case, seek immediate divine direction. Three brethren were accordingly chosen, and joyfully received as pastors and teachers, and the right hand and kiss of peace were extended to them.

"The Brethren, however, soon found that the work was not yet complete. In their own estimation the appointment of those men for the ministry of the Gospel, in the manner described, was sufficiently valid; but they knew it required something more to give it equal sanction with the religious public. They required regular ecclesiastical ordination. In order to discuss this important subject, another synod was convened before the end of the year. In this assembly, two questions were principally agitated.

"The first was, whether ordination by a number of Presbyters was equally valid with that performed by a bishop? The decision of the synod was to this effect:—That Presbyterian ordination was consonant to apostolic practice, (1 Tim. 4: 14,) and the usage of the primitive fathers; consequently the newly elected ministers might be ordained by those now exercising the sacred functions of the Gospel among them. * * But as, for many ages, no ordination had been deemed valid in the reigning church, unless performed by a bishop, they resolved to use every possible means for obtaining episcopal ordination; that their enemies might thus be deprived of every pretext for discrediting the ministry among them.*"

Accordingly, as soon as opportunity occurred, three United Brethren ministers,—one of whom had been a Romish priest, another a Calixtine clergyman, and the third a Waldensian preacher,—were sent into Austria, to a Waldensian bishop, named Stephen, by whom they were joyfully received, and, with the assistance of another bishop, ordained.

Shortly after this period a proposition was made, and favorably entertained, for a complete union of the Waldenses and United Brethren, who, in doctrine, discipline, and spirit, were essentially the same; but this proposition becoming known, the ever-vigilant church of Rome excited against the Waldenses a bloody persecution, by which large numbers of them were put to death in the most cruel manner; and, among many others, Stephen, their last surviving bishop, was burnt. Many of the refugees found an asylum among the United Brethren, and became identified with them.

From 1468 up to the era of the great reformation, the Brethren enjoyed but few

* Holmes Hist. United Brethren, pp. 51, 52.

seasons of respite from persecution. In the year above mentioned an edict was issued by the diet of Prague, "enjoining the different states to use their best endeavors for apprehending as many of the Brethren as they could, *leaving it optional with them to do with them what they pleased.*" The scenes of distress which followed this edict baffle description. All the prisons in Bohemia were quickly crowded with Brethren. Many perished with hunger. Those who escaped had, as on former occasions, to conceal themselves in the forests and caves, where they often endured extreme misery.* This persecution continued, with little abatement, for three years, when a mild and benevolent monarch succeeded to the throne, and they had a season of rest, which was well employed in the dissemination of the good seed, and in building each other up in the holy faith.

In 1474 a deputation was sent out, consisting of four prominent Brethren, with instructions "to make inquiry into the general state of Christendom, in order to discover whether there existed any where Christian congregations, who were free from popish errors, and lived conformably to the rule of Christ and

* Holmes, pp. 54, 55.

his apostles, that they might form a union with them." Having travelled separately, and by different routes, "through Greece and Dalmatia, visited Constantinople and Thrace, and several provinces of Russia and Sclavonia, and penetrated into Egypt and Palestine, they returned, after an absence of some years, and brought their brethren the melancholy intelligence that they had no where found what they had sought, and that nominal Christendom every-where seemed to be sunk in error, superstition and profligacy."* A similar deputation travelled through France and Italy, in 1486, which was fortunate to discover, here and there, "some upright souls, who secretly sighed over the prevailing abominations." "They likewise witnessed the burning of several noble confessors for the truth," but they found in neither of those countries "a church with which they could unite;" and at a synod held in 1489, they unanimously adopted the following resolution: "That if it should please God, in any country, to raise up sincere teachers and reformers, in the church, they would make common cause with them."†

What a dark and mournful picture is here

* Holmes, p. 63. † Ibid.

presented of the nominally Christian world, a few years prior to the reformation. There were, at that very period, in parts of Europe not visited by those deputations, Christians of the primitive stamp, to whom we shall refer in a succeeding chapter, who, like the Brethren, were sowing in tears, and moistening the good seed freely with their blood, patiently waiting for the long-expected harvest.

It ought to be mentioned that, in 1470, the United Brethren "published at Venice the first known translation of the whole Bible into any European language. The sale of the sacred volume, hitherto unknown, was so rapid, that in a short time two new editions were printed at Nurenburg. The Brethren afterwards established three printing offices at Prague and Buntzlau, in Bohemia, and at Kralitz, in Moravia, which, for some time, were solely occupied in printing Bohemian Bibles."*

The reformation, which was commenced in 1517, by Dr. Martin Luther, was hailed with joy by the United Brethren, who had not forgotten the prophetic words of Huss, addressed to his judges as he was going to the stake,—"*A hundred years hence you shall answer this to God and me;*" and in 1522 they sent a

* Holmes, p. 63.

deputation to the great reformer, "to present him with the sincere gratulations of their whole body; to express the cordial interest they took in his labors, and the lively joy they felt at the success with which it pleased God to crown his exertions, and to give him a faithful account of their doctrine and constitution. They were very cordially received, and Luther frankly informed them that his former prejudices against them had now been removed. The following year a letter was sent, which represented to him the necessity of combining scriptural discipline and Christian practice with sound doctrine." Luther replied—"With us things are not sufficiently ripe for introducing such holy exercises, both in doctrine and practice, as we hear is the case with you. Our cause is still in a state of immaturity, and proceeds slowly; but do you pray for us."*

After waiting for some time, and seeing little hope of the introduction of a scriptural discipline into the reformed churches, a second deputation was sent to Luther, from the Brethren, "urging the necessity of strict discipline, and complaining of the tardy manner in which this subject was pursued." This

* Holmes, p. 93, 94.

message was not so kindly received, and, for a short period, the communication between the reformer and the Brethren was interrupted. However, in 1532, the Brethren transmitted to him a copy of their confession of faith, which pleased him so well that he published it with a preface from his own pen, in which he said:—"While I was a papist, my zeal for religion made me cordially hate the Brethren, and consequently likewise the writings of Huss. * * * But since God hath discovered to me the son of perdition I think otherwise, and am constrained to honor those as saints and martyrs, whom the pope condemned and murdered as heretics, for they have died for the truth of their testimony. To these I reckon the Brethren, commonly called Piccards, for among them I have found what I deem a great wonder, and what is not to be met with in the whole extent of popedom, namely, that, setting aside all human traditions, they exercise themselves day and night in the law of the Lord; and though they are not as great proficients in Hebrew and Greek as some others, yet they are well skilled in the Holy Scripture, have made experience of its doctrines, and teach them with clearness and accuracy."

From this period onward to the death of Luther, in 1546, the good understanding between him and the Brethren continued without interruption. "Since the days of the apostles," wrote Luther, "there has existed no church, which, in her doctrine and rites, has more nearly approximated to the spirit of that age, than the Bohemian Brethren. Although they do not exceed us in purity of doctrine, * * yet they far excel us in the observance of regular discipline, whereby they blessedly rule their congregations, and in this respect they are more deserving of praise than we. This we must concede to them for the honor of God and the sake of truth; for our German people will not bend under the yoke of discipline."

Others of the reformers spoke of the Brethren in terms of the most profound respect and affection. Bucer addressed them a letter, in which he said: "It is the inmost wish of my heart, that you may never lose the precious gift you have received from God, but may rather, by your example, excite us to attain to the same, for you are at present the only people in Christendom, to whom

God hath given, not only sound doctrine, but also a pure, scriptural church-discipline, convenient and salutary, not painful but profitable." "John Calvin likewise cultivated a friendly intercourse with the Brethren, and embodied several of their regulations in the constitution framed by him for the church at Geneva.*

But the distracted state of Europe during the thirty years' war, which was commenced by Charles V. against the Protestants, in 1546, involved the Brethren in the greatest troubles, and finally consummated their total dispersion and disorganization.

In some instances, during this period, the reformed churches, which knew not the spirit of Luther, persecuted them in the true Romish spirit. At one time they were required to relinquish their own church constitution, or quit Prussia, which was at that time a Protestant state. Some Lutheran and Reformed divines were the instigators of this decree.

The great majority of the Brethren preferred to quit the country, and some returned to Moravia, while a large number of them found a refuge in Poland, where the doctrines

* Holmes, Vol. I, p. 99.

of the reformation had been propagated with success by some Swiss ministers. A friendly correspondence between the Brethren and the Reformed congregations resulted in the formation of friendly union, "consummated on the express condition, however, that the two churches should have separate places of public worship." At the close of the synod where this alliance was formed, the delegates gave each other the right hand of fellowship, and together celebrated the Lord's supper. John Calvin wrote to Poland concerning this union, to some of the reformed, as follows:— "From your agreement with the Waldenses (so he calls the Brethren), I hope much good will accrue; not only because God does always bless the communion of his saints, the members of the body of Christ, but also, because I believe that the experience of the Waldenses, who have been long tried in the Lord's service, will be very profitable to you in the beginning of the Christian warfare." In the following century all remains of dissension were removed in the synods holden at Ostrog, in the years 1620 and 1627; and the two churches were formed into one under the title —THE CHURCH OF THE UNITED BRETHREN.*

* Mosheim, p. 482.

This was the second church organization which took the name of "United Brethren."

To trace the history of the United Brethren from 1564 to 1648, would lead us beyond the limits allowed in this work. Many passages of their history, during that period, possess unusual interest. Seasons of rest and prosperity were brief, while storms of persecution were frequent and protracted. In 1627 all their property in Bohemia and Moravia was confiscated, and all their churches and schools closed forever. Every Bible and Protestant book that could be found was burned. The Brethren were, of course, scattered over Europe, in all directions.

The treaty of peace concluded at Westphalia, at the close of the thirty years' war, between the Catholics and Protestants, made no mention of the Brethren, and all hope of their reorganization in Bohemia and Moravia vanished. The learned and devoted John Amos Comenius, who had eloquently urged a recognition of their claims by the civil powers, after the treaty was concluded, published a pamphlet, in which he gave a most affecting description of the condition of his people.

"We ought, indeed," he said, "patiently

to bear the wrath of the Almighty; but will those be able to justify their conduct before God, whose duty it was to make common cause with *all* Protestants, but who, unmindful of former solemn compacts, have not come to the help of those who suffer oppression while promoting the common cause? Having procured peace for themselves, they never gave it a thought that the Bohemians and Moravians, who were the first opponents of popery, and maintained the contest for centuries, deserved to be partners in the privileges obtained, at least in so far as to prevent the extinction of Gospel light in Bohemia, which they were the first to kindle and set on a candlestick. Yet this extinction has now actually taken place. This distressed people, therefore, which, on account of its faithful adherence to the apostolic doctrine and practice of the primitive church, is now universally hated and persecuted, and even forsaken by its former associates, finding no mercy from man, has nothing left but to implore the aid of the eternally merciful Lord God, and to exclaim with his oppressed people of old: "For these things I weep; mine eye, mine eye runneth down with water, because the Comforter that should relieve my soul is far from me. But thou, O Lord, remainest forever; thy throne is from generation to generation. Wherefore dost thou forget us forever; and forsake us for so long time? Bring us back unto Thee, O Lord, that we may return to the land of our nativity; renew our days as of old."*

A few general remarks touching the doctrine, discipline and usages of the primitive United Brethren, and we must dismiss them, reluctantly, indeed, from farther notice.

In doctrine they agreed with the Waldenses, one of whose confessions we have already inserted at length.†

By reference to page 50, it will be seen that they regarded but one order of ministers as of divine appointment. As a matter of *expediency*, they had bishops, or superintendents; and, it is a remarkable fact, "that, of fifty bishops, who for two centuries had the oversight of the church, no one was deposed."

In the selection of ministers, they chose "men of acknowledged piety, well versed in the Scriptures, of sound natural understanding, 'apt to teach,' unimpeachable in moral conduct, and enjoying the esteem and confi-

---

* Holmes, Vol. I., p. 130.   † Page 31.

dence of their brethren," but few of whom had received a classical or scientific education. After the reformation, they established three colleges of their own, and their ministers were more liberally educated. But "they laid greater stress on piety, moral conduct, and knowledge of the Holy Scriptures, in persons sustaining the pastoral office, than on human learning; for, as small as their community was, they had made the melancholy experience, that a more enlarged acquaintance with literature and philosophy had, in some instances, paralyzed the zeal of ministers in promoting the edification of their flocks, and, by the false gloss of heathen philosophy, obscured the bright purity of Christian doctrine, which derives all its luster from Christ crucified."*

"The head of every family was required to send his children diligently to church, to instruct them at home in the truths of the Gospel, and to meet them in family devotion three times a day,—in the morning, at noon, and in the evening.

"The frequenting of theaters, and worldly amusements, of public houses, (without absolute necessity) and all places of idle resort,

* Holmes, vol. 1 p.

was strictly forbidden. Not only open vices, but vanity and immodesty in dress, licentious discourse, all "improper intimacy between the sexes, and clandestine courtships, were severely censured. All dishonest traffic and usury were prohibited. None were allowed to engage in a lawsuit without first endeavoring to settle their differences by brotherly arbitration.

"The ministers derived their income from the voluntary contributions of their respective congregations, consisting either in money or provisions. In Poland, small farms, besides a garden, were generally attached to their dwellings. Nor were they ashamed to earn something by the labor of their hands, when their congregations were poor, and they could spare the time from their pastoral duties; * * care was taken, however, that such employments did not trench on the hours which ought to be devoted to study. Whenever a minister's yearly income amounted to more than $200, he was exhorted to spend the overplus in charity. They were enjoined not to assume pompous titles, but to set the greatest value on the name of brother.

"They attached the greatest sanctity to the

Sunday, considering the sanctification of one day in seven not as a Mosaic enactment, but as forming a part of the moral law, and, consequently, of perpetual obligation, the first day of the week, emphatically designated the Lord's day, being substituted in place of the Jewish Sabbath.

"Their churches were unadorned, fitted up with plain seats, or forms, the men and women sitting apart. They do not appear to have used any prescribed form of prayer, or instrumental music in their worship. But they delighted in vocal music; the whole congregation joined in the singing led by a precentor."*

* For a complete account of the doctrine, discipline, and peculiarities of the United Brethren, the reader is referred to Holmes, vol. 1, from which most of the above facts have been gleaned.

CHAPTER III.

THE MENNONITES.

The Waldenses, as we have seen in a previous chapter, were, at different periods of their history during the Middle Ages, dispersed into every country of Europe where they could find temporary succor, or a home. But the object of their dispersion and inhuman treatment by the papal church, was totally defeated; because, like the church dispersed from Jerusalem, "they went everywhere preaching the word." Some of the rich fruits of their labors in Bohemia, Moravia, and Poland, have already been noticed in our sketch of the primitive United Brethren. But we should do injustice to our subject, and to one of the most respected antecedents of the United Brethren in Christ, did we omit to mention the MENNONITES.

It has been well observed by Mosheim, that, "before the rise of Luther and Calvin, there lay concealed, in all the countries of

Europe, * * * many persons who adhered tenaciously to the following doctrine, which the Waldenses, Wickliffites, and Hussites, had maintained, some in a more disguised, and others in a more open and public manner, viz.: 'That the kingdom of Christ, or the visible church which he established upon earth, was an assembly of true and real saints, and ought, therefore, to be inaccessible to the wicked and unrighteous, and also exempt from all those institutions which human prudence suggests to oppose the progress of iniquity, or to correct and reform transgressors.' "*

A very large number of those persons, who walked closely with God, amid the general darkness which preceded and, too soon, alas! followed the reformation, are known in history as Mennonites,—a name which they derived from a distinguished convert from Romanism, who, while Europe, led by the reformers, was struggling for emancipation from papal despotism, collected thousands of them into a single fold.

That the church might be a holy church, separate from the world, that the simplicity of its original constitution might be restored,

* Mosheim, p. 491.

and that the Christian character, as exhibited in the conduct and manners of the professed servants of God, "might recover its lost dignity and luster," were the objects of the never-failing hope, and unceasing prayers and labors, of the Mennonites,—as it was also of the Waldenses and primitive United Brethren.

MENNO SIMONIS, the remarkable man who was the honored instrument, in the hand of providence, of gathering, into a well-organized body, the people who are called after his name, was born in Friesland, in 1505. He was trained up for the clerical office in the Roman Catholic church; but, soon after he entered upon his duties as a priest, he was induced to apply himself diligently to the study of the Scriptures, by which means he was evangelically enlightened and converted. Immediately he conferred not with flesh and blood, but began to preach the Gospel of Christ according to the New Testament, and to expose the sins of Rome. Soon his life was in great peril; but, nothing daunted, he cast in his lot with the scattered and bleeding people of the Lord, before referred to, who, at this period, were literally "killed all the day long," by both

Catholics and Protestants, on account of the excesses of some miserable fanatics at Munster and elsewhere, with whom they were obstinately, and, it is feared, maliciously, identified in the public mind.

"From this period to the end of his life, that is during a space of twenty-five years, he traveled from one country to another, exercising his ministry under a series of pressures and calamities of various kinds, and constantly in danger of falling a victim to the severity of the laws."* He proclaimed the Gospel faithfully, and with evangelical power and effectiveness, in east and west Friesland, the province of Groningen, Holland, Brabant, Guilderland, Westphalia, the German provinces on the shores of the Baltic, and Livonia.

He was a man of learning, genius, eloquence, courage, and indefatigable perseverance. His prudence never failed him in the most trying periods. In doctrine, he was sound; in piety, sincere; and his zeal for Christ was a pure and quenchless flame. In a word, he was a missionary who counted not his life dear unto him, that he might win Christ.

* Moshiem, p. 494.

Under his powerful influence, great numbers of the Lord's scattered sheep were gathered into a well-organized church, whose doctrine and discipline were a nearer approach to those of the primitive church than those adopted by any of his cotemporary reformers.

Menno and his brethren would gladly have united with the reformers; but, as had been the case with the United Brethren,* the want of Gospel discipline in the reformed churches, was an insurmountable obstacle to union. Menno had an interview with Luther and Melancthon at Wittenberg, with Bulinger at Zurich, and at Strasburg with Bucer; but, such was the intolerance of the times, that he was unable to secure to his long-suffering brethren the free exercise of their religion even in the Protestant states.

After a life of noble self-sacrifice for Jesus, such as few men have lived, this apostolic minister and model missionary found a quiet retreat, and a peaceful death-bed, "at the country seat of a nobleman, who, moved with compassion at a view of the perils to which he was exposed, and the snares that were daily laid for his ruin,

---

* See page 55.

took him in and gave him an asylum."
He died in 1561.

The doctrines of the Mennonites were usually expressed, in their confessions of faith, in the exact words of the Holy Scriptures; and they are not tainted with the popish leaven which, unhappily, was retained in that noble symbol, the Augsburg Confession, nor with the acute and erroneous speculations of the great Genevan.* A summary of those doctrines, printed in various languages in 1632, affords a clear view of all the fundamental doctrines of the word, and contains very few points to which the slightest objections can be taken. On the subject of experimental religion, this summary is very explicit. Article VI. says—"Neither baptism, supper, church, nor any other outward ceremony, can, without faith, regeneration, change or reformation of life, enable us to please God. But we must go to God with sincere hearts, and true and perfect

* The Romish leaven, in the old symbolic books of the Lutheran church in Europe, has been rejected by the most influential body of Lutherans in America. An able writer, in the Lutheran Observer, specifies the following errors found in those books:—"Ceremonies of the Mass; Exorcism; Private Confession and Absolution; Denial of the Divine institution of the Christian Sabbath; Baptismal Regeneration; Real Presence in the Eucharist, and the special sin-forgiving power of the Lord's Supper.

faith, and believe on Jesus Christ, according to the testimony of the Scriptures. By this living faith, we obtain remission or forgiveness of sins, are justified,—nay, made children of God, partakers of his image, nature, and mind, being born again through the incorruptible seed."

The Mennonites would not take an oath, would not go to law, nor bear arms. They were remarkable for industry, honesty, meekness, plainness of dress and manners, and general inoffensiveness of conduct; and, yet, few churches can count a greater number of martyrs. The Duke of Alva, that bloodthirsty Spaniard, slaughtered these poor sheep of Christ without pity, during his rule of terror in the Netherlands; but it was in those countries that they first obtained complete toleration. William, Prince of Orange, "the glorious founder of Belgic liberty," bore an honorable tribute to the excellence of their character as citizens; and, in spite of the most obstinate opposition from doctors of theology of the reformed faith, he secured to them legal protection.

But, in many countries of Europe, they have always been a proscribed people. At the close of the thirty years' war, great numbers of them emigrated to America, and found homes in Lancaster, and adjacent counties, in Pennsylvania, where, in the providence of God, they became associated with the rise of the United Brethren in Christ.

CHAPTER IV.

THE RENEWED UNITED BRETHREN.

The number of enlightened Christians, in various parts of Europe, who, before the rise of Luther, adhered unswervingly to the doctrine and discipline of the church which Christ had established, was very great; and the unblenching testimony which they bore against popery, the evangelical light which they dispersed abroad by their preaching and the circulation of the Holy Scriptures, and the remarkable heroism displayed by so many thousands while suffering a cruel death, did far more to render the papal power odious, and to prepare the public mind to respond to the voice of the reformers, than is generally supposed.

Cardinal Hosius, president of the Council of Trent, perceived, in the reformation, a result of "the leprosy," as he termed it, "of the Waldenses," which had "spread its infection throughout all Bohemia;" and Landanus, Catholic bishop of Ghent, in a defense of Romanism, written as early as 1560, speaks of John Calvin as the "inheritor of the doctrine of the Waldenses."

But the reformation, marked and glorious as were the blessings which it secured to mankind, and terrible as was the blow which it gave to the great papal tyranny, failed to mold the churches to which it gave birth, according to the apostolic pattern. As seen in a previous chapter,* this great error was early perceived by the United Brethren, and others, and deplored by the reformers; but it was never corrected. Hence, although the light of God's own word broke forth like the rising sun, and millions of people were suddenly emancipated from Romish errors and tyranny; yet, after all, it is a sad fact that the masses simply exchanged one formal religion for another,—Romanism for Protestantism,—and continued to live "without God in the world." A few, compared with the whole number who embraced the Protestant faith, were inwardly enlightened and truly converted.

The discipline of the reformed churches was extremely defective; indeed, it can hardly

* See page 55.

be asserted that they had any thing approximating the discipline of the church of Christ. All who professed the Protestant faith, and conformed to certain easy forms, were recognized as members of the church; and that relation was maintained through life, although there might be no evidence of piety,—nay, although the proofs of impiety, and even immorality, might be notorious. All grades of sinners, and, at length, all classes of unbelievers, filled the churches, occupied the pulpits, and surrounded the communion tables. The church and state were also united—a thing which can never be done without a plain violation of our Lord's commands, and the infliction of unutterable injuries upon the cause of true religion. "Protestant persecuted Protestant; dissensions and disputes on idle questions, or on subjects of minor importance, engaged the attention of all; the religion of·the heart was neglected, and the fruits of the blessed reformation (which at first gave such fair promise) were nearly blasted. Men loved their creeds, but not God; they adhered to orthodoxy, but not to the Savior of repenting sinners. For creeds, oceans of human blood were shed, countries laid waste, cities destroyed, and their inhabitants reduced to poverty and want. This was especially the case in Germany. Rulers frequently changed their creeds; and, having done so, they demanded their subjects to follow their example."*

It is admitted on all hands, that, at the beginning of the seventeenth century, the state of religion in the reformed churches was deplorable indeed. But at that very period, the work of God, in the hearts of men, was promoted with great zeal and success, by the pure and spiritual Mennonites, who, as already seen, could not unite with the reformed churches, on account of the worldly elements which became incorporated with them. And, in this dark hour, the blessed Lord caused a reformation of vital religion to break forth in the bosom of the reformed churches, through the instrumentality of the PIETISTS, the salutary effects of which have reached our times, and exerted no inconsiderable influence upon United Brethren history.

PHILIP JAMES SPENER, who, under God, was the leader in this revival, was born in Upper Alsace, France, in 1635. He

* History of the American Lutheran Church, by Dr. Hazelius, p. 21.

commenced his public ministry soon after the peace of Westphalia had "given rest to distracted, and well nigh ruined Europe." He was a converted man, and devoted himself unintermittingly to the promotion of heartfelt, personal religion. Wherever he preached, a wide-spread religious concern was awakened, and great numbers began to inquire what they must do to be saved. To aid inquirers, to confirm and strengthen young converts, and to promote the good work generally, Bible meetings and prayer-meetings were held in private houses and in public halls, to which multitudes of the people flocked. It is believed that not less than forty thousand persons were converted to Christ through the instrumentality of this distinguished man. He died in Berlin, in 1705, happy in the Lord.

The Pietists "laid it down as an essential maxim, that none should be admitted into the ministry but those who, in addition to other qualifications, had hearts filled with divine love." Strange to say, this was regarded as a very unreasonable, and even wicked maxim! They also maintained that the divine influence was necessary to a right understanding of the Scriptures. "Another thing which gave great offense was, that they renounced the vain amusements of the world. Thus, dancing, pantomimes, public sports, theatrical diversions, the reading of humorous and comical books, with several other kinds of pleasure and entertainment, were prohibited by them, as unlawful and unseemly; and, therefore, by no means of an indifferent nature." These views gave great offense to the worldly-minded, pleasure-seeking church members of that period. But the most objectionable of all the views advanced by the Pietists was this, that no man was properly qualified for the sacred office of the ministry who was not himself a truly pious man! The carnal clergy were enraged at the simple enunciation of the doctrine!

Had the Pietists not been persecuted and resisted by the churches of which they were the salt; and had the leaven of godliness which they diffused, not been neutralized by a blinded clergy and state; and, on the contrary, had the revival which they promoted been encouraged throughout Germany, how vastly different would have been the religious condition of that great country this day! As it is, no Christian country on the globe more needs the evangelical missionary, animated by the spirit of Spener and Franke, than Germany. The land which has been hallowed by the blood of thousands and thousands of martyrs, is overspread with a thick mantle of spiritual darkness. But the good leaven of the Gospel disseminated by the Pietists, still works in the Lutheran church, especially in America; and in other directions its healthful influence has been felt. In the *renewal* of the United Brethren church, under the supervision of Zinzendorf, it performed important service, as we shall see presently.

After the total extinction of religious liberty in Bohemia and Moravia, in the early part of the seventeenth century, the United Brethren remained in a state of great depression for nearly a century. They were never, however, extirpated; and, in the early part of the eighteenth century, God, who had not been inattentive to their plaintive cries, nor insensible to their grievous bondage, came to their relief, broke their prison doors, and sent them forth as messengers of salvation to a lost world. At about the same time in 1715, a revival of religion broke out among a remnant of Brethren who still remained in Moravia and Bohemia, although there had been no communication between them. But, finding themselves hedged in on every side, denied all religious privileges, and completely at the mercy of their unfeeling and powerful enemies, they humbly besought the Lord for some asylum to which they might fly for protection. This was provided for them, through the agency of Christian David, on the estate of a pious young German nobleman, in Upper Lusatia, in 1722.

Christian David was raised a Roman Catholic, employed in youth as a shepherd, and afterward put to the trade of a carpenter. While working as an apprentice in Holeschau, he became acquainted with one of the scattered remnants of God's people, who, although they were confined in a cellar, by the authorities, were engaged, day and night, in singing and prayer. These people were the means of arresting him in his evil ways, and, finding a Bible, he read it, until his mind was fully enlightened, and his heart was filled with joy and peace in believing. He now determined to join the Lutheran church, and, that he might do so with safety, he traveled to Berlin, where he was admitted to the Lord's Supper. But, "observing that the generality of Lutherans led very careless and even wicked lives, and that any individual earnestly seeking the salvation of his soul, was exposed to taunts and reproach, he resolved to enlist as a soldier, fancying that he would have more leisure in that state to attend to spiritual things." In this he was, of course, disappointed. After his discharge from the army, and return to his occupation as a carpenter, he was induced, by the persecutions to which he was exposed, to remove into Upper Lusatia, where he became acquainted with some pious Lutheran preachers, and with Count Zinzendorf. After he had become settled, he was moved to make frequent journeys into Moravia, to preach the Gospel to such of his fellow-countrymen as he might in safety reach. During these journeys, he became acquainted with some of the United Brethren, who were as sheep without a shepherd, and, in 1722, succeeded in leading a little band of them out of their prison house to the estate of Count Zinzendorf, in Upper Lusatia. Not desiring to settle in the village on the estate, they went into the forest, about two miles from Berthelsdorf, and on a hill, called *Hutburg*, they commenced to build HERRNHUT,—a name which has a "double signification, and may be translated either *the object of the Lord's protection*, or *the watch of the Lord*, the place where his servants stand waiting to receive, and ready to execute his commands."*

NICHOLAS LEWIS, COUNT ZINZENDORF, on whose estate Herrnhut was built, and who is so intimately associated with the renewal of the United Brethren church, was born at Dresden, in A. D. 1700. When an infant six weeks old, he was carried, by his nurse, into the presence of his dying father, who said to him, "My dear son, they ask me to bless you, but you are more blessed than I am; though even now I feel as if I were already standing before the throne of Jesus." His mother marrying again, young Zinzendorf was placed under the care of his grandmother, Madame von Gersdorf, an elect lady, at whose house the godly Spener was a frequent guest. It is also a fact worthy of record, that a daily prayer-meeting—a thing then regarded as an ex-

* Holmes, vol. 1, p. 169.

hibition of fanaticism bordering on lunacy—was maintained at Madame Gersdorf's residence.

Under the genial spiritual influences of his grandmother's home, the susceptible nature of young Zinzendorf, at a very early period, became thoroughly imbued with the Spirit of Jesus. At Halle, also, where he was placed at school in his tenth year, he advanced rapidly in the knowledge and love of God. At the house of the celebrated Franke, co-laborer of Spener, lessons of holiness were indelibly imprinted upon his memory. Some of his noble friends, displeased with his zeal and devotedness to the Lord, had him removed, in his seventeenth year, to Wittenberg. But no circumstances with which he was surrounded, no worldly employments with which his time was engrossed, ever caused his love to grow cold, or, in the slightest degree, abated his ardor, or dampened his glowing zeal. After he had reached his majority, he was induced, by his friends, to accept of an important office under the government, the duties of which he discharged, with conscientious fidelity, for a period of about eleven years. During this term of public official life, he was very busily employed in advancing true religion by every practicable means; and on his estate, in Upper Lusatia, God was preparing an humble people, with whom he was soon to become fully identified in the great work of saving sinners. The liberality of his heart had prompted him to offer a retreat to the United Brethren refugees and exiles from Moravia and Bohemia. Returning home, after an absence of some time, his attention was attracted by the rude house erected in the wood by the roadside, and, being informed that it was inhabited by the Moravians, he alighted from his carriage, entered the humble abode, greeted the refugees in the most cordial manner, and, before leaving them, kneeled down, and prayed for the blessing of God upon them.

The hand of industry, and the smiles of providence, caused Herrnhut to grow rapidly into a flourishing and beautiful village. As opportunity served, other Brethren from Moravia and Bohemia, escaped from their cruel house of bondage, and, leaving all behind them for Christ's sake, they fled to Herrnhut. Godly people of other persuasions, also, sought and found an asylum in this retreat.

Some of these were Lutherans, others Reformed, and others still Mennonites. Though differing in regard to some things, they were all perfectly united in Christ, and generally agreed in regard to those things which are essential in both faith and practice. Zinzendorf's interest in the Brethren, and his affection for them, increased continually, until at length his heart was fully won, and he became heartily and permanently identified with them in the renewed church.

It became necessary, as we may well suppose, for the people who had settled at Herrnhut, to organize themselves into a society for the enforcement and preservation of sound faith and Gospel discipline. This was effected in 1727, two hundred and seventy years after the original United Brethren church had been organized on the confines of Moravia and Silesia.

The first three rules or resolutions, adopted without a dissenting voice at Herrnhut, in the re-organization of the Brethren church, contain the "fundamental principles" of the society:

I. "It shall never be forgotten *in Herrnhut*, that it is built on the living God, and is a work of his Almighty hand. It is not so much a *new* settlement as an institution formed for the *Brethren,* and on their account.

II. "Herrnhut, with those properly intended to be its inhabitants, (i. e. Moravian exiles) shall constantly maintain love with all God's children in every Christian denomination, shall judge none, and abstain from all contentious and unseemly behavior towards those with whom they may differ in opinion; and endeavor to preserve, among its own members, the purity, simplicity, and grace of evangelical truth.

III. "In Herrnhut, the Holy Scriptures shall be the only standard of faith and practice, by which our whole conduct ought to be regulated. Agreeably to the word of God, we can acknowledge such only for genuine members of the body of Christ, in whom the following marks of true faith are discernible:

"Whoever does not confess that he hath been apprehended solely by the grace of God in Christ, and that he needs this grace every moment of his life;—that the most perfect rectitude of conduct, (if it even were attainable) can be of no avail in the sight of God without the intercession of Jesus, pleading the merit of his blood, and can be rendered acceptable only through Christ; whoever does not make it clearly manifest that he is really in earnest to be delivered from sin, (for which Christ has suffered) to become, daily, more holy and more like the image of God, in which man was created, to be more and more purified from the remains of natural corruption, vanity, and self-will, to walk even as Jesus walked, and willing to bear his reproach—such a one is not a genuine brother. But whoever holds the mystery of faith in a pure conscience, though some of his opinions may be sectarian, fanatical, or otherwise erroneous, shall not, on that account, be despised by us, or, if he separate himself from us, be forsaken, or treated as an enemy; but we will bear and forbear with him in love, patience, and meekness. Such persons, though they do not dissent from the fundamentals of faith, yet do not steadfastly continue in them, shall be considered as weak and halting Brethren, and be restored in the spirit of meekness."

Prudential measures, in conformity to the spirit of these resolutions, were, from time to time, adopted. The year which marked the renewal of the United Brethren was also remarkable for the great revival with which Herrnhut was visited. Brotherly love was greatly increased; and preaching by the regular pastor, Rev. Mr. Rothe, and other ministers who visited the place, was attended with astonishing power and unction. Thousands flocked to the place of public worship from far and near, and the meetings were sometimes continued, without intermission, from six o'clock in the morning until three in the afternoon.

The 13th of August, 1727, was a day which should never be forgotten. On the 10th, the Brethren "continued together in prayer, singing hymns and spiritual discourse until late at night." Each one endeavored to "dedicate himself with full purpose of heart to the Lord," and "more than an earthly influence animated the whole assembly." On the 12th, Count Zinzendorf, who had not yet assumed the clerical office, and was still a high officer of state, paid a visit to each family in Herrnhut, and conversed with them in relation to the communion which was to be celebrated the next day. In the evening, every member of the congregation signed the statutes. The next day, while on the way to church, which was about one mile from the village, "those who had taken offense at each other mutually confessed their faults, became reconciled, and were united in love." That day, in God's house, every heart was full, and the singing was almost drowned by loud weeping, and other expressions of overpowering emotion. It is a remarkable fact, that two of the elders who were far distant in Moravia, felt, during the hours of this remarkable meeting, a strong impulse moving them to pray, and, retiring into a garret of the house, "they poured out their souls to God with an unusual degree of emotion."*

The revival manifested itself with great power among the children and youth; and many of tender age were made savingly acquainted with Christ, who, in after years, with a disinterestedness and devotion which has never been surpassed, carried the glad tidings of salvation into heathen lands. The earliest of these youthful converts was a little girl of about eleven years, who, when the light broke in upon her sorrowing heart, exclaimed, "Now I am a child

---

* See a full account of this revival in Holmes, Vol. 1.

of God!" The interest became so absorbing that, on the evening of the 29th of August, two meetings were commenced in the open air, and continued until the break of day.

In this way was the church of the United Brethren rescued from bondage, [when their enemies regarded them as dead] re-organized, baptized, and prepared to enter upon the great missionary work, among the dead and dying churches of the reformation, and among the heathen, which has rendered their name precious to every friend of evangelical religion.

The renewed United Brethren had no ecclesiastical connection with the original United Brethren, as the original United Brethren had none with the Waldenses; but they had what was far more important, a life connection with them through Jesus Christ, and, therefore, in the highest sense in which the term can be used, they were one and the same church. In some prudential measures they differed from the first Brethren, as the Brethren differed from the Waldenses; but in all things essential to the being and prosperity of a true Christian church they agreed perfectly.

It was an outpouring of the Spirit upon the disciples at Jerusalem, which quickened them into a living church, and sent them forth to preach. Similar outpourings of the same Spirit, in fulfillment of the same promise of the Father, kept alive the flame of evangelical fire among the Waldenses, through all the long night of the Middle Ages, insomuch that no earthly or satanic power could quench it. And, owing to an effusion of the same ever-blessed Spirit, the people of God, of various persuasions, were united into one body, as United Brethren, and prepared to accomplish the work assigned them in Moravia, in 1457, and after 270 years at Herrnhut; and, presently, our attention will be invited to a revival among the German people in the United States, similar to that experienced at Herrnhut, which, under the supervision of divine providence, resulted in the spread of evangelical religion in this country, through the agency of the United Brethren in Christ.

CHAPTER V.

UNITED BRETHREN IN ENGLAND.

SHORTLY after the Spirit had been poured out upon the United Brethren at Herrnhut, divine providence opened the way for the employment of that unquenchable missionary zeal which is an invariable accompaniment of every genuine revival, and missionaries were sent out into various countries of Europe; and, after a few years, into heathen lands also. In 1728, the year following the memorable meetings at Herrnhut, United Brethren missionaries visited England, where they were instrumental in commencing the most remarkable revival of religion among the English people, on record.

The state of religion in England, and, in fact, throughout Europe, as before stated, was deplorable indeed. Very few, even of the ministers of religion, had any practical acquaintance with Christ. Ten years later, and subsequent to John Wesley's conversion, he wrote to Zinzendorf that he knew of "ten truly enlightened ministers in England;" in addition to whom he adds, "I have found one Anabaptist, and one, if not two, teachers among the Presbyterians, who, I hope, love the Lord Jesus in sincerity, and teach the way of God in truth." How poorly prepared was such a blinded ministry, to withstand the influence of that bold, subtle, and widespread infidelity, which, at that period, was poisoning the literature, and corrupting the morals, of all classes of society.

One year after the United Brethren had visited England, a society, consisting of a few young men, among whom was John Wesley, was organized at Oxford. Sometime after, George Whitfield was enrolled among its members. The object of this society, or club, was the promotion of practical religion; but it does not appear that any one of its members had ever experienced a change of heart, or knew, experimentally, the way of life. They were, however, honest and earnest inquirers.

After completing his studies, Mr. Wesley was ordained a minister, and sent to America, as a missionary. Happily, on the vessel which brought him to the New World, there were twenty-six United Brethren, with whom he soon formed a very agreeable acquaintance. The safety of the vessel upon which they sailed, was greatly endangered by violent storms. But this was the means of bringing before Mr. Wesley's mind the very important truth, that perfect love casteth out fear. He had already been struck with the humility and excellent temper of the Brethren; but, when the sea broke over the vessel, poured in between the decks, and split the mainsail in pieces, they exhibited a happy composure of mind, which he was unable to understand; for, while the English passengers screamed in terror, and Mr. Wesley himself was in distressing fear of death, the Brethren, with entire presence of mind, continued to sing a psalm which had been commenced. After the storm had abated, Mr. Wesley said to one of the Brethren,—"Was you not afraid? He answered, I thank God, no! But, were not your women and children afraid? He replied, mildly, No, our women and children are not afraid to die."

Arriving at Savannah, Mr. Wesley soon had an interview with Spangenberg, a United Brethren bishop, of sound learning and deep piety, of whom he asked advice in respect to the missionary labors which he expected to undertake. The bishop replied, "My brother, I must first ask you two questions. Have you the witness within yourself? Does the Spirit of God bear witness with your spirit, that you are a child of God?" Mr. Wesley knew not what to answer, for he was, as yet, in his sins; but the simple piety and excellent manners of the Brethren, impressed him very favorably. He wrote:—"They were always employed, always cheerful themselves, and in good humor with one another." Of one of their ecclesiastical meetings, which he attended, he says:—"After several hours spent in conference and prayer, they proceeded to the election and ordination of a bishop. The simplicity, as well as solemnity, of the whole, almost made me forget the seventeen hundred years between, and imagine myself in one of those assemblies where form and state were not; but *Paul*, the tent-maker, or *Peter*, the fisherman, presided; yet with the demonstration of the Spirit, and power."

Closing his labors in Georgia, Mr. Wesley returned to England, ignorant still of the way of salvation. On the voyage he became fully convinced that he was not a true Christian; and, when nearing the coasts of his native land, he wrote, in the bitterness of his spirit: —"I went to America to convert the Indians; but Oh! who shall convert me? Oh! who will deliver me from this fear of death? What shall I do? Where shall I fly from it? What must I do to be saved?" Shortly after his return, he had an interview with Peter Bohler, and other United Brethren, who were then laboring with much success in England. He was amazed when they unfolded to him the way of life, through faith. This interview was followed by many others, which eventuated in the removal of the last doubt from his mind. At a Brethren meeting in 1739, the way of salvation by faith, became so plain to his mind, that he could only cry out,—"Lord, help thou my unbelief."

He now united with a United Brethren society in Fetter Lane, London,—a society which, to use the language of its constitution, "was organized, in obedience to the command of God, by St. James, and by the advice of Peter Bohler." Now his sense of sin, and need of a Savior, pressed still more heavily upon him, so that he wrote: "I feel that I am sold under sin. I know, too, that I deserve nothing but wrath, being full of all abominations. * * *

So that my mouth is stopped. I have nothing to plead. God is holy; I am unholy. God is a consuming fire; I am a sinner, altogether meet to be consumed." Not long after these agonizing words were penned, he was enabled to trust in Christ, Christ alone, for salvation; and an assurance was given him that his sins were taken away, and that he was saved from the law of sin and death.

Charles Wesley was converted about three days before his brother John. He had visited one of the small Moravian assemblies, and says: "I thought myself in a choir of angels." Soon after, while suffering from a fit of sickness, he was entertained at the house of a poor, pious member of the Brethren society, named Bray. This mechanic read and expounded the Scriptures to his gifted and learned guest, and directed his troubled mind into the way of life. Mr. C. Wesley says: —"God sent Mr. Bray, a poor, ignorant mechanic, who knows nothing but Christ; yet, by knowing him, knows and discerns all things." While at this man's house he was enabled to trust in Christ.

Soon after his happy conversion had occurred, Mr. John Wesley visited the Brethren at Herrnhut, and at Marienborn, where they had also planted a church. At Marienborn he met Count Zinzendorf. From this place he wrote: "God has given me, at length, the desire of my heart. I am with a church whose conversation is in heaven, in whom is the mind that was in Christ, and who so walk as he walked. * * * O, how high and holy a thing Christianity is! And how widely different from that—I know not what —which is so called, though it neither purifies the heart, nor renews the life, after the image of our blessed Redeemer." From Herrnhut he wrote: "I would gladly have spent my life here. O, when shall THIS Christianity cover the earth, as the waters cover the sea!" He returned to England, greatly strengthened in the Lord.

About this time Mr. Whitfield returned from America, and we find both these great evangelists at a United Brethren love-feast meeting, at Fetter Lane, lighting their torches, to use a figure, at the United Brethren altar. Of this memorable meeting, Mr. Wesley wrote, in his journal: "About three in the morning, as we were continuing instant in prayer, the power of God came mightily upon us, insomuch that many cried out for exceeding joy, and many fell to the ground.

As soon as we were recovered a little from that awe and amazement at the presence of his Majesty, we broke out with one voice, "We praise thee, O God, we acknowledge thee to be the Lord." This meeting occurred in 1739.

Mr. Wesley's connection with the United Brethren was suddenly broken off, in 1740, owing to some slight difference of opinion, which arose between him and Philip Henry Malther, who was pastor of the church at Fetter Lane, in regard to doctrine; and also because he disapproved of some of the rules of discipline, "which the Brethren deemed essential to the spiritual welfare of the Society." When he had made up his mind to withdraw from the Society, he read a paper to the congregation, at a public meeting, in which his reasons for withdrawal were stated. When the reading was finished, he said: "You who are of the same judgment, follow me." "I, then," he adds, "without saying any thing more, withdrew, as did eighteen members of the Society." Those who withdrew, met at the Foundry, where they organized the first Methodist society in the world.*

---

* For further information on this subject the reader is referred to Whitehead's Life of Wesley, Vol. II., p. 82. Also to Holmes' His-

Although Mr. Wesley withdrew from the Brethren, under a misapprehension, probably, of some of their views, yet he retained, himself, and carried into the Methodist societies which he formed, a large share of the United Brethren spirit; and he always regarded the Brethren with feelings of peculiar affection. "I marvel," said he, at one time, "that I refrain from joining these men; I scarce ever see any of them, but my heart burns within me; I long to be with them, and yet I am kept from them."

The labors of the Brethren, in England, were not confined to London. During 1738, the year of the conversion of the Wesleys, an extensive revival was in progress, under their labors, in Yorkshire, and many societies were organized there by John Toeltschig, a Moravian exile, in conjunction with Messrs. Ingham and Delamotte. Shut out of the churches, and bitterly persecuted, they resorted to the fields and barns, where they gathered vast congregations; "and such was the eagerness of the people to hear, and such the

tory of the United Brethren, Vol. I., pp. 311, 312, 313. Holmes vindicates Malther, and the church at Fetter Lane, from the errors which have been attributed to them, and which are reiterated in Steven's History of Methodism.

impression made on their minds by the doctrine of salvation through faith in the Lord Jesus, that they listened with silent and fixed attention to the discourses of Toeltschig, and other Germans, whose imperfect knowledge of the English language made them, indeed, speak with "stammering tongues." But the defects of the speakers were lost in the power which accompanied their testimony."* In 1740, Mr. Ingham, in his report, said: "There are now upwards of fifty societies, where the people meet for edification." At a public meeting held in 1742, a thousand members of the Brethren societies were convened. In 1741 a society, called "*The Brethren's Society for the furtherance of the Gospel among the heathen,*" was organized in London. "The members met once a month, for consultation, receiving missionary intelligence, and for prayer." Crantz, in his history of the Brethren, observes that "the very sight of these truly apostolic men, and their zeal for the conversion of the heathen, influenced neither by pride and vainglory, nor affected pharisaical piety, but accompanied by a humane, cheerful, and humble deportment, was

* Holmes, p. 316.

most edifying to us, and awakened an ardent desire in us to do our part in furtherance of this noble design."

We can not enter at length into the history of the United Brethren in England; but, from what we have stated, it is evident, we think, that the great religious movement, in England, at the beginning of which the Wesleys were converted, had its origin, under God, in the United Brethren who went out from Herrnhut, full of the Holy Ghost, and of faith, and intent on the conversion of the world to Christ. We have seen how these German Brethren, understanding the English language but imperfectly, opened the Scriptures to learned ministers, who had been educated at Oxford, prayed for them when they became penitent, and rejoiced with them when they found the pearl of great price.

Lighting their torches at the altars on which the evangelical fire had been kept burning brightly among the United Brethren, Mennonites, and Waldenses, through long, long ages of darkness and persecution, the Wesleys, and their coadjutors, went forth with apostolic faith and zeal, disseminating the light of salvation wherever the English language was spoken.

As we pursue our subject, we shall see how that, from the same sacred altar, the light of reformation burst forth as the morning, among the Germans in America. This will introduce us to another branch of United Brethren history.

CHAPTER VI.

UNITED BRETHREN IN AMERICA.

THE quenchless zeal for the salvation of men, kindled by the Holy Spirit at Herrnhut, moved the United Brethren to undertake the conversion of the American Indians, who, at that period, were the principal owners and inhabitants of this vast country. Accordingly, the first company of missionaries reached America in 1735; and, about the year 1736, bishop SPANGENBERG, a devoted evangelist and servant of God, spent some time in Pennsylvania, where he was the means of confirming and comforting some in the faith, and of leading others into the way of life.

Although there were, at that period, ministers and churches, and not a little denominational zeal, in this country, yet it is generally admitted that the life and power of godliness were almost unknown, both in the ministry and laity. Any one who professed a change of heart, and claimed "the witness of the Spirit," was the object of ridicule, if not of persecution; but any minister or member might frequent the tavern, visit the races, or participate in the promiscuous dance, without exciting remark, or subjecting himself to reproof.

However, between 1738 and 1770, multudes of the English-speaking people, in the older localities, between Georgia and Massachusetts, were favored with frequent visits from that flaming evangelist, George Whitfield, and through his influence great numbers, both of ministers and laymen, were aroused from the sleep of sin, and, through faith in Jesus, were introduced into a new spiritual life.

The people speaking the German language were, if possible, in a worse condition than the English. They were, with few exceptions, members of the Reformed, Lutheran, Mennonite, and Tunker churches; and, although ardently attached to the churches in which they had been trained, and even obstinately religious, in their way, yet very few of them had any clearer idea of the new birth than the Jewish ruler, who came to Jesus by night.

The Lutheran population numbered, in

1748, not less than 60,000 souls. Of them, Dr. Muhlenberg, who devoted his valuable life to their improvement, in a letter to Halle, said: "The spiritual state of our people is so wretched as to cause us to shed tears in abundance. The young people have grown up without any knowledge of religion, and are fast running into heathenism."* The population adhering to the Reformed faith, about the middle of the century, 1750, numbered between 30,000 and 60,000 souls,† and, as a body, were much like the Lutherans. The Mennonites, who also constituted a numerous and influential portion of the population of Pennsylvania, had lost the spirit of the noble confessors and martyrs who honor their earlier history; and the power of religion had declined among them to such a lamentable extent, that a truly converted person could with difficulty be found in many of their churches. They were, however, scrupulously honest and upright in their behavior, and adhered, with more than pharisaical exactitude, to certain forms of religion. The same may be said of the Tunkers and Amish.

* Life and Times of Muhlenberg, p. 68. † Schlatter's Life and Journal, p. 201.

But it must not be inferred from the foregoing facts, that all had departed from God, and were walking in the blindness of their own minds. Within the bosom of all the churches named, persons might have been found, widely scattered, it is true, who had experienced a change of heart, and were walking humbly with God. Some of these were fruits of the revival promoted by Spener; others had been brought to the knowledge of the truth, while in Germany, by the Brethren; others were a remnant, still surviving the general declension, of the once spiritual Mennonite societies; and, in 1734, a colony of Saltzbergers,—one of the remnants of the long-suffering Waldenses of Piedmont, driven from their homes by that papal power which in vain had sought their extirpation for a thousand years, settled in Georgia, under the patronage of General Oglethorpe. These last mentioned were a remarkably spiritual people, and their earliest pastors, BOLZIUS and GRONAU, were among the first candlesticks in the Lord's hand in this country. Ebenezer,—"Rock of Help,"—built by the Saltzbergers, in the wilderness, shed an humble light upon the surrounding darkness.

ISRAEL CHRISTIAN GRONAU, one of the pastors of these pious people, died in 1745. During his last sickness, "his heart continually enjoyed communion with his Redeemer." "Nothing," said his fellow-laborer, "troubled him, for he tasted the reconciliation with God, and the joy and peace of the Holy Ghost. * * * When one of his brethren took hold of his hand, which he had lifted up in praise to God, to cover it with the bed-clothes, he desired that the friend might support his arm in the uplifted position. This being done, he exclaimed, 'Come, Lord Jesus! Amen, amen!' With these words he closed his eyes and lips, and entered into the joy of the Lord, full of peace." In 1765, Bolzius also died. A little while before his death, he was visited in his solitary home by a Christian friend, to whom he said: "I can not describe how happy I am in my solitude, whilst I enjoy the presence and communion of my Savior! Happy! oh, indescribably happy!" His friend then recited to him the Lord's words, —"Father, I will that they whom thou hast given me, be with me, where I am, that they may see my glory, which thou hast given me." The dying witness for Jesus repeated the words, "*that they may see my glory,*" and added,—"Ah! how delightful it is in yonder heaven! how delightful to be with Christ! These men possessed true religion—the religion which sustained their brethren during the dark centuries, when they were hunted down like wild beasts for Christ's sake.

As early as 1726, JOHN BACHTEL, a truly converted man, and afterward minister of Jesus Christ, emigrated from Germany, and settled at Germantown, Pa., where he resided until 1746. He experienced a change of heart in Germany, in his youth; but afterward, while a traveling journeyman, he fell from grace. Through the mercy of God, however, he was re-awakened, and, with many tears, he sought and found forgiveness. Ever afterward he was an unswerving witness for Jesus.

HENRY ANTES was another clear light in that dark period. It is not known when he settled in America, when he was converted, nor when he commenced to preach; but he was, evidently, one of the most active and spiritual Christians of his day.

When bishop Spangenberg came into Pennsylvania, he soon formed an acquaintance with Bachtel, Antes, Stiefel, Gruber, and others of like precious faith, whom he confirmed and strengthened in the Lord. In an account of his life and experience, Mr. Bachtel relates that, in 1738, he became acquainted with Spangenberg when he resided at Schippach, Pa., to which place he, with others, were in the habit of going once a month. He says: "The sainted Brothers Antes, Stiefel, J. Adam Gruber, myself, and others from Germantown, enjoyed many blessed hours together" in association and worship with Spangenberg. These awakened and enlightened Christians very much desired to form a closer union with each other, that they might edify one another in love, and unite their labors to advance the cause of Christ; and at the meetings at Schippach, and at other times and places, the subject was discussed.

At length, in 1741, they issued a circular inviting all true Christians, of every name, to meet in a convention, in order to consider, in a fraternal spirit, what might be done. This circular read as follows:

"In the name of Jesus! Amen!
"My dear friend and brother:
"Since a fearful injury is done in the

church of Christ among those souls who are called to the Lamb, and this mostly through the mistrust and suspicion, and that often without foundation, which we entertain toward one another, by which every attempt to do good is frustrated,—and since, contrary to this, we are commanded to love one another,—the question has been discussed in the minds of some persons for two or more years, whether it would not be possible to bring about a general assembly, not for the purpose of disputing with one another, but to confer, in love, on the important articles of faith, in order to see how near all could come together in fundamental points, and in other matters that do not overthrow the ground of salvation, to bear with one another in charity, that thus all judging and condemning among the above-mentioned souls might be abated and prevented: since by such uncharitableness we expose ourselves before the world, and give it occasion to say: *Those who preach peace and conversion themselves stand against each other.* These facts have induced many brethren and God-fearing souls to take this important matter into earnest consideration, and to view it in the presence of the Lord; and they have concluded to assemble on the coming New Year's day in Germantown. Accordingly, you also are heartily entreated, with several others of your brethren who rest on good ground, and can give a reason for their faith, to assemble with us, if the Lord permit you so to do. Nearly all others have been informed of this by the same kind of letter as is here sent to you. It is believed that it will be a large assembly; but let not this keep you back; every thing will be done without much rumor. The Lord Jesus grant his blessing to it.

"From your poor and humble, but sincere friend and brother.

"HENRY ANTES.

"Frederick Tp., Phila. Co., Dec. 15, 1741."*

Shortly after this call was issued, Count Zinzendorf reached Philadelphia, animated with the blessed spirit which reigned at Herrnhut. He soon became the leader of those who had a knowledge of the Savior, in the forgiveness of sins. Mr. Bachtel, in speaking of this visit, says:

"In 1742, when the dear, departed dis-

---

* I am indebted to the "Fathers of the German Reformed Church" for this circular, and for many of the facts in relation to this movement.

ciple, Count Zinzendorf, came to Pennsylvania, I became acquainted with him and other Brethren. My heart, at once, felt a tender inclination towards them, and I loved them sincerely. When I, for the first time, heard the Count preach, in the church at Germantown, I said in my heart: Yes, this is truly the only and true ground of salvation—Jesus Christ and his merits and sufferings. Other foundation can no man lay; through his death alone has life been secured to us. From this time on the Brethren (Moravian) were the pleasantest society at my house; and when hatred and bitterness in the country against them began, I also received my honest share."

The contemplated union convention met at Germantown, January 1st, 1742, ten years previous to Mr. Otterbein's arrival in this country, and a little more than twenty years previous to the inauguration of a movement, exactly similar in spirit, under his labors, in Lancaster county, Pa. There were present at the convention Christian brethren who stood in the Lutheran, German Reformed, Mennonite, Brethren, and Tunker churches. Some other bodies were also represented.

Zinzendorf entered heartily into the spirit of the convention, for it was essentially Christian, and truly United Brethren. It was the spirit which had animated the general conference of the apostles and elders at Jerusalem; controlled the Waldenses and Albigenses in the most trying periods of religious history; ruled in the councils of the Bohemian Brethren; drawn together, into a well-organized body, the Unitas Fratrum at Fulneck, and long years after the fugitives who built Herrnhut. As was to have been expected, the Count soon became the leader of the movement. The first convention was dissolved in peace and brotherly love; and, during the winter and spring of the same year, six other conventions of a similar character were held. At the third, an organization, denominated, "THE CONGREGATION OF GOD IN THE SPIRIT," was consummated.

In doctrine, those who entered this union were distinctively Arminian. They were particular in insisting upon the universality of the atonement; and, hence, they soon came into conflict with those ministers of the Reformed church who were Calvinistic in faith. With respect to Christian experience, they occupied the high Scriptural ground, that no one can be a true Christian without a change of heart; and holiness of heart was deemed an essential qualification for membership in the household of faith. In practical life, they cultivated the fruits of the Spirit, such as love, joy, peace, meekness, and temperance. And they were not only interested in religion for themselves, but they longed for the salvation of a lost world. It was pre-eminently a missionary body. Zinzendorf, Bachtel, Antes, Spangenberg, and others, went out in the fraternal spirit of this union, and proclaimed, to all within their reach, a free, present, and full salvation to all who would repent of their sins, and believe on the Lord Jesus Christ. A bright day seemed about to dawn upon the unhappy German people of America. The wilderness and the solitary places were about to be made glad, and the desert to blossom as the rose.

Alas! these hopes were destined to early disappointment. As soon as the movement became formidable, the old high-church spirit arose up against it, and overthrew it.

Who would have thought it possible, and yet it was true, the church at Germantown, for whom the pious John Bachtel had labored sixteen years, cast him out of her communion. This was accomplished, after much trouble, in 1744.

And, unfortunately for this union movement, during the very year of its inauguration, Dr. Muhlenberg arrived in America. He was a good man; but, from his decided Lutheran stand-point, strongly opposed to the organization of a church to be composed only of true Christians. Being a man of talent, industry, zeal, and devotion to the cause, he succeeded in drawing away from the congregation many of the Lutherans who had been attracted toward it, and of closing up the way of the evangelists, who labored in the union, to Luther communities. We would not judge Dr. Muhlenberg harshly, but it does not appear that he possessed the spirit of Spener, or he could not have come into conflict with Zinzendorf. And it is a sad fact that, although he was a devoted Christian, and did a great deal of good, yet no revival of religion ever, so far as we can learn, occurred under his labors.*

---

* In the Memoir of his Life and Times, we have many notices of his labors similar to the following: "In the month of November, I

But the most determined opposition to this movement came from Michael Schlatter, of the German Reformed church. He was, evidently, a less spiritual man than Muhlenberg. Rev. John Philip Boehm, a prominent Reformed minister of long standing in America, had been a bitter opponent of the union from its inception, and, at an early period, published a treatise against it. It does not appear that he had ever experienced a change of heart, or that he insisted upon the necessity of such change as a condition of church membership. Immediately on the arrival of Mr. Schlatter, he accepted of Mr. Boehm as his counsellor, and at once set himself violently against the union. He was especially bitter

confirmed and admitted to the Lord's Supper, the young people whom I had instructed. There were twenty-six in number, chiefly adults, one of whom was a married man. They had committed to memory the questions on the plan of salvation with considerable accuracy. I earnestly labored to impress them with the proper import of what they had learned; and, without ceasing, admonished them to frequent prayer and the practice of what they had heard. * * The greater part also assured me, in personal conversations I had with them, that they have frequently been upon their knees in private, at home, and that they have experienced in their hearts the influences of the Spirit of God through the Word." Had Muhlenberg taught these people that they must not only go on their knees frequently at home, but experience a change of heart before they could be received into the church, how different would have been the history of the Lutheran church in America.

against the "crafty Herrnhuters," as he denominated the United Brethren. By his indefatigable labors he succeeded in closing up the way of access to the perishing German Reformed communities. Some good Reformed ministers went to the United Brethren; others confessed that they had erred in entering into the union, and withdrew from it; while a few, almost disheartened, determined still to wait for the redemption of Israel. Mr. Schlatter traveled a great number of miles, and baptized and confirmed very many people, but it does not appear, from any information we can gather of his life and labors, that he was ever converted himself, or that he was the means of the conversion of a single soul in America. He was frequently involved in difficulties with his own brethren, and, at length, turned his attention almost wholly to secular affairs. Around his death-bed no light appears to have shone.

A few years sufficed to narrow down the "Congregation of God in the Spirit" mainly to the limits of the United Brethren. But it was not, as we shall presently see, a failure. Indeed, it seems to have been a seed cast into the earth, which, after a few years, sprang up with vigorous growth. And in this case, as in many others, the wrath of man was made to praise God; for the unrelenting and most powerful enemy of the revival movement, into which Zinzendorf, Antes, and many others, had thrown their hearts, was the agent in bringing to this country a young man of piety and learning, who, in connection with others, inaugurated a movement similar in spirit to that which had been defeated, but far more powerful and successful, and which was carried forward, under his wise supervision, for nearly half a century. The commencement and progress of this movement will be the subject of the following pages.

PART SECOND.

CHAPTER I.

PHILIP WILLIAM OTTERBEIN.

If the reader will turn to a map of Germany, he will find toward its western side, bordering on Rhenish Prussia, the little Duchy of Nassau. It has an area of 1,751 square miles, and a population, mostly Protestant, of 430,000. Frankfort-on-the-Main touches it on the south-east, and Wisbaden is its capital and chief city. On the narrow neck of mountainous country which runs up between Westphalia and Hesse Cassel, not far from the Westerwald, is situated the little town of DILLENBERG. It contains two thousand five hundred inhabitants, and has a college, a hospital, an orphan asylum, and a ruined castle—a gray relic of the feudal age. In this village PHILIP WILLIAM OTTERBEIN was born, on the 4th day of June, A. D. 1726.

His parents were members of the Reformed church. His father, "the reverend and very learned John Daniel Otterbein," was for a while rector of a Latin school in Herborn, and afterward an affectionate and faithful pastor of congregations in Fronhausen and Wissenbach. He died in 1742. His mother, Wilhelmina Henrietta, was a woman of very superior understanding and piety. He had three brothers and one sister. The brothers all obtained a thorough classical and theological education, and devoted themselves to the sacred office. Gottleib, the eldest of the brothers, appears to have been a truly enlightened and deeply pious man; and after William had entered fully into the liberty of the children of God, and upon the work of reformation in America, he received from him warm-hearted sympathy and valuable counsel.

The charge of "Pietism" has been laid at the door of the Otterbein family; and the facts that have come down to us favor the supposition that it was one of the few precious German families in which the influence of the revival of the preceding century, promoted by Spener and others, was still cherished.*

---

* Gottleib Otterbein was the author of a work on experimental and practical Christianity, which was much prized by the pious.

It is but just to attribute no small share of the purity, strength, and beauty of Mr. Otterbein's character, as well as his remarkable success in the ministry, to the benign influences of the Christian home in which he was trained up. That he might be thoroughly furnished for every good work, his parents spared neither pains nor expense in his education; and, after he had completed the usual classical and theological studies required of candidates for the ministry, (which included Latin, Greek, Hebrew, Philosophy, and Divinity*) to the entire satisfaction of his seniors, he was solemnly consecrated to the sacred office. His ordination occurred in 1749, at Herborn,† on the Dille, a few days after he had reached his twenty-fourth year.

With a deep sense of the responsibilities of the ministerial office, Mr. Otterbein entered the pulpit of the Reformed church in his native town; and it was soon perceived that no ordinary measure of grace had been committed unto him. His sermons were remarkable for their plainness, spirit, and evangel-

* Spayth, p. 18.
† Herborn is the seat of a celebrated Calvinistic Seminary founded in 1584.

ical power; and they occasioned both censure and applause. His more pious friends, while in heart approving of both the matter and the manner of his discourses, advised him, nevertheless, to moderate his zeal, and to use greater caution in reproof, in order that he might avoid the displeasure of those in authority, some of whom had felt themselves too sharply reproved for their sins, by the young preacher.* But it was not in Otterbein's nature to swerve one hair's breadth from what he believed to be the line of duty; and the clamor raised against him only added point to his reproofs, force to his arguments, and fervor to his exhortations. He was not, at this period, in possession of the fullness of the blessing of the Gospel of peace, but he was pressing toward it; and it is evident that he was not only dissatisfied with, but grieved and alarmed at, the low state of religion in the Reformed church.

Unfortunately for Germany, the reformation left the church and state in close and unholy alliance,—an alliance which has always been disgraceful to religion; and it is a humiliating, yet undisputed fact, that both

* Spayth, p. 19.

have warred, but too successfully, against that civil and religious freedom with which the Creator has endowed every human being. At the beck of the church clergy, the magistrate has ever been ready to intimidate, restrict, arrest, and imprison God's true ministers; and the clergy, in return for such services, and for their fat livings, have, in almost all cases, taken sides with power and wrong, against the people and the right; thus misrepresenting and dishonoring the religion of the Bible.

And, in this case, although Mr. O. was a man of blameless life, and preached nothing contrary to the word of God, the "authorities were privately solicited to arrest his preaching, for a season," at least.* When his mother was informed of this fact, she said to him, "Ah, William, I expected this, and give you joy. This place is too narrow for you, my son; they will not receive you here; you will find your work elsewhere."

His mother believed that he was peculiarly fitted for the missionary work, and that God would open his way into some wide field of usefulness; but when and

* Spayth, p. 20.

where, she knew not. She was prepared, however, to make any sacrifice which might be demanded. Her solicitude was not that her son should secure a lucrative professorship, for which he was eminently fitted, or a rich and honorable living in the church, to which he might have aspired, but that he might, in the best possible manner, glorify God in the salvation of men. Noble Christian mother!

At the period under consideration, the Lutheran and German Reformed churches in America were almost entirely dependent upon the churches of the Fatherland for a supply of preachers; but, for a long time, no efficient measures were adopted to send out missionaries into the then wilderness land. The missionary spirit, if it existed at all, was at an exceedingly low ebb everywhere in the world outside of the United Brethren societies. Letters, however, were constantly returning to the parent country, from the more enlightened and pious in this, describing the sad destitution of the people, great numbers of whom were as sheep without a shepherd, begging the churches to send them pastors and teachers, and the means, in part, of supporting them. One of those affecting appeals, received by Mr. Gottleib Otterbein, was the immediate means of turning William's attention to the New World as the probable theater of his missionary labors.

Toward the close of the year 1751, Rev. Michael Schlatter, who had spent five years in America, as an exploring missionary, under the direction of the synods of North and South Holland, and who had made himself extensively acquainted with the wants of the German churches in this country, especially in Pennsylvania, returned to Germany, and went to the Palatinate for the purpose of procuring six young ministers for the American field.*

The way being so soon and so unexpectedly opened, Mr. Otterbein did not hesitate to respond to Mr. Schlatter's call, and, being accepted, he began immediately to make preparations to enter upon the work.

Dr. Schramm, superintendent of the Reformed church in Nassau, gave him the following letter of salutation:

LECTORIS SALUTEM!

Reverendus et doctissimus vir juvenis, Philippus Guilhelmus Otterbeinius, gente

---
* Schlatter's Life and Journal.

HISTORY OF THE

Nassauius, domo Dillenburgensis, S. Ministerii Candidatus, classis tertiæ hujus pædagogii præceptor, manuum impositione adsistentibus Cl. Arnoldo, professore atque primario cœtus Herbornensis pastore, et admodum reverendo Klingelhœfero ejusdem ecclesiæ secundario, ut vicariam in cœtu Ockersdorpiano præstaret opem 13 Junii, 1749, ordinationis a me impetravit axioma. Quod his ad ejus requisitionem testor, et dilecto meo quondam Auditori in peregrinas abiturienti oras, fausta quævis prosperumque iter ex animo precor, constantis mei adversus eum adfectus monimentum.

(Signans)   JOH. HENRICUS SCHRAMMIUS,
Theologia Doctor et Ecclesiarum Nassauicarum Superintendens
Herbornæ, III Calendas Martias, 1752.*

TRANSLATION.

THE READER, GREETING:—

The reverend and very learned young man, Philip William Otterbein, from Dillenburg, in Nassau, a candidate of the holy ministry, and a teacher of the third class in this seminary, received by me, assisted by Cl. Arnold, Professor and First

---

* The original copy of this letter was handed to Rev. John Hildt, by Mr. Otterbein, near the close of his life, and, by Mr. Hildt, placed in the Telescope office. We are indebted to Rev. J. Degmeier for the accompanying translation.

Pastor of the congregation at Herborn, and by the very Rev. Klingelhœfer, Second Pastor of the same church, on the 13th of June, 1749,—ordination by laying on of hands,—with the view of exercising his ministerial functions as vicar of the congregation at Ockersdorf. This I certify at his request, and recommend to all whom the present letter may interest, my much-esteemed former hearer, who is now about to emigrate to a foreign country, wish him a prosperous voyage, and subscribe this letter as a testimonial of my never-failing affection towards him.

JOHN HENRY SCHRAMM,
Doctor of Theology, and Supt. of the Church of Nassau.

{SEAL.}

Dated at Herborn, Feb. 28, 1752.

Steam navigation had not, at that period, rendered a trip across the ocean, as now, a mere pleasure excursion. Months were frequently consumed on the voyage, and owing to civil wars and other causes, the communication between the two countries was frequently interrupted for long periods. When the time, therefore, for the departure of her beloved William arrived, Mrs. Otterbein felt that the sacrifice was greater than she could bear. Ten years before, her husband had been called home; and, in all probability, the contemplated separation from her son in this life would be—as, indeed, it proved to be—final. As the appointed hour drew near she retired to her closet, and there poured out her maternal heart in prayer for grace to make the sacrifice, and for a blessing upon her son; and then, calmly trusting in God, she returned; and, taking him by the hand, and pressing that hand to her lips, she said: "Go, my son! The Lord bless thee, and with much grace direct thy steps. On earth I may not see thy face again; but go."* "With what strange and beautiful courage and grace can a mother's love bind its sacrifice upon the altar."†

Early in the spring of 1752, the six young men whom Mr. Schlatter had been commissioned, by the reverend synods of Holland, to employ, presented themselves at the Hague, for examination. Five of them were from Nassau, the other from Berg. Their names were Otterbein, Stoy, Waldschmid, Frankenfild, Wissler, and Ru-

---

* H. G. Spayth's His. U. B. in Christ. † Fathers of the German Reformed Church.

bel. The synods required that the candidates for the American mission should be "orthodox, pious, learned, of an humble disposition, diligent, sound in body, and eagerly desirous after, not earthly, but heavenly treasure, and especially the salvation of immortal souls;" and that persons of this description should be "examined thoroughly, by the deputies of the synods, as to their knowledge of theology, and of the Greek and Hebrew languages; and, being found qualified, they were to be furnished with

"1. An outfit from Germany or Switzerland to Pennsylvania, as it regards the person, books, and other necessaries.

"2. Besides perquisites, (*sic dicta jura stolac*) a yearly salary of fifty Belgic florins."

After a particular examination before the deputies, the candidates were all accepted and consecrated; and, in March, 1752, they sailed from the Hague. In the evening of July 27th of the same year they arrived safely in New York.* Shortly after, they proceeded to Philadelphia.

Wissler lived but a short period after his arrival; Rubel was located in Philadelphia, where he became involved in serious diffi-

* Schlatter's Life and Journal, pp. 231, 232.

culties, first with the synod, and afterward with his congregation, which resulted in the resignation of his charge and his withdrawal from the church; Stoy went first to Tulpehocken, and, becoming eventually involved in serious disputes with the synod or cœtus, he turned his attention partly to medicine, hunting, agriculture, and politics, and, being a man of talent and liberal culture, he exerted no inconsiderable influence in society; Waldschmid was located at Cocolico, and Otterbein at Lancaster.

CHAPTER II.

MR. OTTERBEIN'S MINISTRY AT LANCASTER.

In August, 1752, Mr. Otterbein entered upon the duties of a pastor at Lancaster, Pa. He had now reached his twenty-seventh year. The congregation at Lancaster was large and disorderly. Owing to frequent vacancies, and unenlightened and incompetent pastors, "loose ideas and practices had come to prevail, and various irregularities, especially in regard to order and discipline." To one who, like Mr. Otterbein, was seeking the fullness of the blessing of the Gospel, and striving to be conformed, in heart and life, to the law of Christ, such a congregation could not fail to be the occasion of great grief and annoyance, as well as a spur to indefatigable reformatory labor.

To the great work before him, he devoted himself with all the ardor of his soul. The six years which followed were fruitful of toils, trials, and conflicts, but also of great spiritual blessings; for, while he was employing all his resources to bring his people up to a purer and more scriptural mode of life, he was himself enabled, by grace, to enter into the complete liberty of the sons of God. For this blessing, his heart had long panted. Even before his departure from the Fatherland, his views upon the subject of vital, scriptural religion, were offensive to many of the Nicodemuses of the Palatinate.

"Except a man be born again, he can not see the kingdom of God," is a remarkably plain declaration, from the lips of Him who is the "Truth;" and experience uniformly testifies, that the human soul can never find permanent rest and peace until this change has been effected, and the Spirit of adoption has witnessed to the consciousness the dear relation of sons and daughters of the Lord, into which it introduces us. And yet, this plain and fundamental doctrine of the New Testament had been explained away or frittered down to a mere ceremony, or outward reformation, or abstraction, with most marvelous success, by Protestant divines, both in Europe and

America. Even masters in Israel, as in our Lord's day, when addressed upon the necessity and nature of the new birth, asked, with unbelieving ignorance, "How can these things be?"

Mr. Otterbein had not only felt the necessity of this change, but he had acquired a clear understanding of the nature and importance of the doctrine as taught in the inspired word. Hence, in his pulpit ministrations, he preached upon the subject in a manner which carried conviction to many hearts. Not long after he came to Lancaster, and immediately after he had preached one of his most searching discourses, a member of his congregation came to him in tears, bitterly lamenting his sins, and asked advice. Mr. Otterbein knew that this man was a sincere inquirer after the way of life, and yet, until he had entered into that way himself, he felt incompetent to direct him. But the visit of this penitent brought him to a crisis. Looking upon him sadly, yet tenderly, he only said, "My friend, advice is scarce with me to-day." The seeker went his way, and Mr. Otterbein repaired to his closet, and there wrestled, like Jacob, until he obtained the forgiveness of his sins, the witness of the Holy Spirit of adoption, and was filled with joy unspeakable and full of glory! Thus, after several years of earnest seeking for a higher spirituality, an awakened member of his own congregation, in tears, asking for advice, was made the means of causing him to press into the kingdom, as by violence.

The happy enlargement of Mr. Otterbein's spirituality, at Lancaster, enabled him to enter fully into the work of an evangelist, to point out clearly the way of salvation to others, to give "advice" to penitent sinners, and to sympathize with the spiritual children of God of all names and orders. How strange, yet it is true, from this important and interesting circumstance in his religious life may be dated a dissenting from him of some of his ministerial and other brethren in the church; and this difference increased as time advanced, and as he progressed in the knowledge and love of God, and contended earnestly, not so much for the formularies of the church as for the faith—the living, justifying faith, by which the soul is saved. ["Nach dem lebendigen, rechtfertigenden Glauben, der den Heiligen gegeben ist."]*

His preaching, during the six years of his stay at Lancaster, was not without excellent results. Many persons were awakened to a sense of their lost condition, and were happily converted to God. Among this number, honorable mention may be made of Frederick Shaeffer, who subsequently became a useful minister in the United Brethren church, and, to the close of his long life, stood firmly at his post in the cause of Christ and in the church.†

Nevertheless, irregularity and irreligion continued to such an extent that they occasioned him great "grief and annoyance," and "discouraged him in his work."

Those who have read the history of revivals and attempted revivals in the old German churches, know how very difficult it is to reform them, and to bring them up any where near to the New Testament standard in experience and order. At the end of five years of unceasing labor, Mr. O. was anxious to withdraw from the charge. But the congregation, notwithstanding its

* Spayth, p. 22. † Ib. 22.

refractory character, was strongly attached to him, and was unwilling to let him go. The cœtus, or synod, interceded for them, and he was at length induced to remain. However, he was unwilling to enter "into an engagement for any definite period; and, after setting forth the grievances which had rendered his ministry unhappy, and frustrated much of the good which might have been done, he demanded, as the condition of his continuance, even for a limited term, *the exercise of a just ecclesiastical discipline, the abolition of all inordinacy, and entire liberty of conscience in the performances of his pastoral duties.*" All this was promised by the congregation.

Entertaining doubts of a reform, and yet willing to make one more trial, Mr. O. drew up a paper, which is still preserved, in his own handwriting, in the archives of the church at Lancaster, and presented the same to his congregation, for their signatures. We quote this paper entire:

"Inasmuch as, for some time, matters in our congregation have proceeded somewhat irregularly, and since we, in these circumstances, do not correctly know who they are that acknowledge themselves to be members of our church, especially among those who reside out of town; we, the minister and officers of this church, have taken this matter into consideration, and find it necessary to request that every one who calls himself a member of our church, and who is concerned to lead a Christian life, should come forward and subscribe his name to the following Rules of Order:

"First of all, it is proper that those who profess themselves members should subject themselves to a becoming Christian church discipline, according to the order of Christ and his apostles; and thus to show respectful obedience to ministers and officers, in all things that are proper.

"Secondly: To the end that all disorder may be prevented, and that each member may be more fully known, each one, without exception, who desires to receive the Lord's Supper, shall, previous to the preparation service, upon a day appointed for that purpose, personally appear before the minister, that an interview may be held.

"No one will, by this arrangement, be deprived of his liberty, or be, in any way, bound oppressively. This we deem necessary to the preservation of order; and it is our desire that God may bless it to this end. Whosoever is truly concerned to grow in grace, will not hesitate to subscribe his name."

From this paper, it is evident that Mr. Otterbein, at that early period of his ministry, had adopted those views of what ought to be the personal religious character of each member of the church, and the order and holiness of the church collectively, which had been entertained by Spener, Menno Simon, John Huss, the United Brethren, the Waldenses, and, indeed, first of all, by the apostles themselves. But these views were not generally entertained by the churches of that period. On the contrary, the grossest irregularity and immorality abounded in the churches, without let or hindrance. And this was the cause of Mr. Otterbein's severest trials, his eventual separation from the Reformed church, and of the organization of an independent congregation in Baltimore.

Eighty of the male members of the church at Lancaster subscribed to the paper drawn up by Mr. Otterbein, yet the evils were not cured, and, toward the close of the year 1758, he resigned his charge. Honorable mention has been made of Mr. O.'s ministry at Lancaster, by those who have had no intelligent sympathy with the higher life into which he entered, and labored to bring the Reformed church. The author of the Fathers of the Reformed Church, before quoted, says that, "under his ministry, the old, small, wooden church, which stood in the back part of the graveyard, was superseded by a massive stone church, at the street, which was built in 1753, and only taken down in 1852, having stood almost a century. Internally, the congregation greatly prospered. Evidences of his order and zeal look out upon us, from the records in many ways; and enterprises, started in his time, have extended their results, in the permanent features of the congregation down to this day."

CHAPTER III.

MR. OTTERBEIN AT TULPEHOCKEN.

When Mr. Otterbein resigned his charge at Lancaster, he purposed to re-visit the Fatherland; but the winter, which had already set in, and the continuance of the war between England and France, induced him to defer the execution of this purpose to a more favorable period. "Meanwhile, he took charge, temporarily, of two congregations in Tulpehocken, Berks county, Pa., where he continued for two years."

Tulpehocken is one of the richest and most beautiful portions of Pennsylvania; and the period of Mr. Otterbein's labors there among the most interesting of his life. At Lancaster he had been richly blessed, but, at the same time, greatly embarrassed. There were elements in that congregation which could not be brought into obedience to Christ. At Tulpehocken there was less opposition, and a greater readiness to receive the truth; and more freedom of conscience and of action were accorded to the minister; and it was there that the outlines of the reformation of religion, which eventually separated him from the German Reformed Church,—a church which he venerated and loved,—became distinct and unmistakable.*

Not content with preaching on the Sabbath, he made it his constant business, during the week, to go from house to house, converse with the people, kindly and pointedly, upon the subject of personal religion; advise, admonish, or encourage, as their cases might require, and then read, sing, and pray with them. He was an admirable family visitor. Dignified, yet humble in his manners, with a discriminating judgment, a tender heart, and a countenance beaming with benevolence, he readily won his way to every heart in the family circle.

Preaching "from house to house" was a new measure in this country. Other pastors may have made occasional visits to the members of their charge; or, they may have gone into families to catechise the

* Spayth, p. 23.

children; but the visits of Otterbein, among the people at Tulpehocken, were of a totally different character. Like Paul at Ephesus, "day and night with tears, and from house to house," he labored to bring the people to Christ.

Another new measure, which he introduced at Tulpehocken, was evening meetings. At those meetings, his custom was to read a portion of Scripture, make some practical remarks on the same, and exhort all present to give place to serious reflections. He would then sing a sacred hymn, and invite all to kneel and accompany him in prayer. At first, and for some time, but few, if any, would kneel, and he was permitted to pray alone. This was in Pennsylvania, just one hundred years ago.

At the present period, when meetings for prayer are common in almost all churches, and when the voices of thousands and thousands are heard, in all our cities, at noonday prayer-meetings, it can hardly be conceived that, a century ago, such meetings were scarcely known, and that, when introduced, they were denounced as "irregular," "unchurchly," and "fanatical" assemblies.

It may be well to observe that, at that

period, there was not a single Methodist church in America; and that the reformation, under Whitfield, had made little, if any, impression upon the German population. This item of history affords us a glimpse of the low type of religion which prevailed, and the thick darkness in which the people were sitting, at the commencement of Mr. Otterbein's revival labors.

At the evening meetings referred to, after prayer, Mr. Otterbein would endeavor to gain access to the hearts of the people, by addressing them, individually, with words of tenderness and love. This was another new and important measure, which was regarded, by many, as an unpardonable irregularity.

As might have been expected, the good seed, thus sown and watered, was blessed of God, and soon began to spring up and bear fruit, for "He that goeth forth and weepeth, bearing precious seed, shall doubtless return again with rejoicing, bringing his sheaves with him." Mr. Otterbein's heart was cheered, at Tulpehocken, by the fulfillment of this precious promise. But, as the marked effects of these meetings began to appear,—as some who attended began to express a deep concern for the salvation of their souls, by weeping and lamenting their lost estate,—their propriety began to be called in question. "What does this mean!" said some, "the minister, and men and women kneel and pray, and weep, and call upon God, for Jesus' sake, to have mercy upon them! Who ever heard of such proceedings?" And yet these meetings were fairly introduced, never to be suspended, it is hoped, until all lands shall hear the glad tidings of salvation, and bud and blossom as the rose. Thank God, they were introduced; and, although the bitter reproaches of men, including some preachers and pastors, were cast upon them, they brought down richest blessings from heaven.*

How could the Protestant churches and societies, which were favored with the pure word of God in their own tongue, have overlooked the numerous references therein contained to social prayer? And yet we have seen that pastors, preachers, and people, not a few, were found, who did not relish these meetings for prayer, but op-

---

* Spayth, p. 24.

posed them as an innovation, and persecuted those who attended them.

In answer to these opponents, such passages of Holy Scripture as the following were introduced by Mr. Otterbein: "O come, let us worship and bow down; let us kneel before the Lord our Maker."—Ps. 95: 6. "Even them will I bring to my holy mountain, and make them joyful in my house of prayer; for my house shall be called a house of prayer for all people."—Isa. 56: 7. "For this cause I bow my knee unto the Father." "I will, therefore, that men pray every-where."—(Paul.) "Where two or three are gathered together in my name."—(Jesus.) "Which are the prayers of the saints."—Rev. 5, 8: 8, 13. Nevertheless, this *kneeling* in prayer, and these meetings, *especially* for prayer and religious conference, on week days and evenings, met with much violent opposition, and from none more decided and bitter than from those who, from their sacred and holy calling, should have been prepared to give them their hearty and undivided support.

Prayer-meetings, attended as they are, when conducted in the spirit of faith, and meekness, and pure love, by the Holy One, are a means of grace admirably adapted to bind the people of God together by the strong cords of Christian union, and to promote the blissful communion of the saints on earth. Prayer is one of the connecting links between the Creator and the creature, the Benefactor and the receiver, the Savior and the saved. It is the solace of the troubled spirit, dispelling the clouds that gather over it. It brightens the hope of future rest, and stimulates to a life of virtue and piety, and to acts of kindness to our fellow-men. Social, as well as private prayer, affords the sweetest and strongest supports amidst the trials and sorrows of life. In losses, in bereavements dark and desolate, when friends, and health, and wealth are gone, and comforts are fled, prayer, leaning upon hope, tarries with us, and affords substantial succor and relief.

"Prayer is the Christian's vital breath,
The Christian's native air,
His watchword at the gate of death,—
He enters heaven by prayer."

The prayer-meetings introduced by Mr. Otterbein at Tulpehocken, in 1758, afforded important aid to the blessed reformation which had been commenced among the people. "This is attested by witnesses on earth and in heaven; and it remains yet to be proven, that the reformation of the world can be prosecuted with any tolerable degree of success, or a church, however strong or well established, maintain its vitality, and continue to be a light in the world, and be instrumental in the conversion of sinners, in the absence of these meetings as a secondary means of grace."*

* Spayth, pp. 25, 26.

CHAPTER IV.

MARTIN BOEHM.

WHILE the work of reformation was advancing under the labors of Mr. Otterbein, at Tulpehocken, the Lord was preparing, in another place, and among another people, one of the chief instruments of the religious movement which is the subject of this history.

The apostles and evangelists were chosen from various occupations, positions, and professions. Peter was a fisherman; Matthew, a publican; Luke, a physician; and Paul, a learned doctor of the law. Some of these had the advantages of the finest mental culture which the best schools of their time afforded; others were ignorant and unlearned men; but all were endowed with excellent common sense. And it may be remarked, that all the great revivals of religion, which illuminate the pages of ecclesiastical history, have been effected by the blessing of God on the joint labors of educated and uneducated ministers. This statement will, we are confident, bear the test of facts, is in accordance with sound philosophy, and harmonizes with the inspired record.

We have just left a young man, with a university education, at Tulpehocken, visiting from house to house, holding prayer and conference meetings through the week, and, on the Lord's day, preaching a present and full salvation, in Jesus Christ, from sin, with apostolic power and unction. He was the St. Paul among the fathers of the United Brethren ministry. Before we proceed to notice more fully the circumstances under which the church of the United Brethren in Christ was eventually formed, we will give some particulars of the life and labors of MARTIN BOEHM, who was born and educated on a farm, and who may be termed the St. Peter among the fathers of the Brethren ministry.

Martin Boehm was born in Lancaster county, Pa., A. D. 1725, one year prior to the birth of Otterbein. His grandfather, Jacob Boehm, a native of Switzerland, was a member of the Reformed church. When a young man, and while traveling as a journeyman tradesman, he became acquainted with the Mennonites, and a convert to their doctrines, and, it is believed, also experimentally acquainted with Christ. The Mennonites, as we have seen from a sketch of their history, in Part First of this volume, were, at that period, among the most enlightened and spiritual people in Europe. Menno Simonis, who, but a short time previous to the conversion of Jacob Boehm, had closed his arduous life of evangelical toil, in doctrine and discipline, approached nearer the apostolic standard than either Luther or Calvin. Nevertheless, the Mennonites were the objects of a most relentless persecution. Lutherans, Calvinists, and Catholics alike regarded them with abhorrence, and killed them without pity.

The leaven of popery, alas! still worked in the bosom of the reformed churches, and, hence, the Mennonites, even in Switzerland, were hunted down with a ferocity which is almost inconceivable. "The favorite mode of punishing them, especially at Berne, was by drowning them. This manner of death was deemed the most appropriate, because it was only baptizing them in their own way."* The rivers and lakes, which abounded in Switzerland, often received the dead bodies of these devoted people. But, as the drowning of them only increased their number, the "council of Berne being embarrassed," as all bloody persecutors have been, resorted to measures less severe, and, "acting under the advice of the ministers," published, in 1533, an edict, announcing that they should be "left in peace, if they would *keep their belief to themselves*, AND MAINTAIN SILENCE; but that, if they continued to preach and keep up a separate sect, they should not be any more condemned to death, *but only to perpetual imprisonment on* BREAD AND WATER."

When Jacob Boehm's father was informed of his conversion to the faith of the Mennonites, he was, as we may well suppose, greatly exasperated; and he resolved that he should be thrust into prison. Before he was imprisoned, however, advised by an elder brother, he fled into Holland, where, under the shade of William of Orange, liberty of conscience and of worship were accorded to Christians of all denominations. Finding a

* De Haller, pp. 39, 69.

secure home in Holland, he married, and raised a large family, a part of whom emigrated to America, and, among the number, Martin Boehm's father, whose name was also Jacob.

But the great temporal prosperity which fell to the lot of the Mennonites, in Holland, was not favorable to their spirituality; and, at the end of two centuries, although a very high degree of morality was preserved among them, few, comparatively, enjoyed the light and liberty of the sons of God. Martin's parents were strict and conscientious observers of the rules of the Mennonite society; and he was, therefore, trained up under a religious influence, carefully instructed in the doctrine and discipline, and, in due time, by baptism and partaking of the Lord's Supper, was made a member of the Mennonite church.

Fully satisfied with his brethren and religious profession, he lived a blameless life; that is, without sinning knowingly, according to the light he then had, until the thirty-second year of his age. At that period it occurred that a preacher was to be chosen in the immediate society of which he was a member, according to the custom of the Mennonites, which is by lot.

"We will now give Martin Boehm's own account of his awakening and religious experience, as nearly in his own words as the idiom of the language will allow in translating.*

'When nominated, I had no desire that the lot might fall on me, and I earnestly besought my brethren to nominate some one in my place, better than myself. This, however, was not done, and the moment came when each nominee was to step forth and take a book. I stepped out, saying inwardwardly, Lord, not me. I am too poor. The books were opened, and the lot or token was mine! Believing, as I did, that this lot falls by divine appointment, I did not feel myself at liberty to refuse obedience to its decision, but felt constrained by my conscience to take upon myself the office of the ministry, and discharge it as best I could.

'According to our usage it was not expected from me to preach immediately thereafter, because our elder preacher was still able to preach; but it was my duty to assist him in preaching and exhortation as God would give me ability. I had been reading the Scriptures much, but now read them still more,

* Spayth, pp. 28, 29, 30, 31.

and with care, in order to impress their reading on my memory, so that I might have something wherewith to preach or exhort. Sunday came, the elder brother preached; and, in attempting to follow him by a word of exhortation, I failed, although for some two years past, I had been giving testimony at the close of the sermons, and frequently concluded the meetings. I continued reading. The next Sabbath I was requested to take part, and rose up, but could say little or nothing. I had charged my mind and memory with some Scripture passages, but, when wanted, could not bring them to my recollection. I prayed to the Lord to assist me in retaining his word, and strengthen me in my great weakness, that, to some extent at least, I might answer his call.

'Some months passed in this way, but it came not. This state began deeply to distress me—to be a preacher, and yet have nothing to preach, nor to say, but stammer out a few words, and then be obliged to take my seat in shame and remorse! I had faith in prayer, and prayed more fervently. While thus engaged in praying earnestly for aid to preach, the thought rose in my mind, or as though one spoke to me, saying, You pray for grace to teach others the way of salvation, and you have not prayed for your own salvation. This thought or word did not leave me. *My salvation,* followed me wherever I went. I felt constrained to pray for myself; and, while praying for myself, my mind became alarmed. I felt and saw myself a poor sinner. I was LOST! My agony became great. I was plowing in the field, and kneeled down at each end of the furrow, to pray. The word *lost, lost (verlohren),* went every round with me. Midway in the field I could go no further, but sank behind the plow, crying, Lord save, I am lost!—and again the thought or voice said, I am come to seek and to save that which is lost. In a moment, a stream of joy was poured over me. I praised the Lord, and left the field, and told my companion what joy I felt.

'As before this I wished the Sabbath far off, now I wished it was to-morrow. Sunday came: the elder brother preached. I rose to tell my experience, since my call to the ministry. When speaking of my lost estate, and agony of mind, some in the congregation began to weep. This gave me encouragement to speak of our fall and lost condition, and of repentance. The Sabbath following it was the same, and much more. Before I was done, I found myself in the midst of the congregation, where some were weeping aloud!

'This caused considerable commotion in our church, as well as among the people generally. It was all new; none of us had heard or seen it before. A new creation appeared to rise up before me, and around me. Now Scripture, before mysterious, and like a dead letter to me, was plain of interpretation; was all spirit, all life, (*alles geist und leben*.)

'Like a dream, old things had passed away, and it seemed as if I had awoke to new life, new thoughts, new faith, new love. I rejoiced and praised God with my whole heart. This joy, this faith, this love, I wished to communicate to those around me; but, when speaking thereof, in public or in private, it made different impressions on different persons. Some gave a mournful look, some sighed and wept, and would say, Oh! Martin, are we indeed lost?

'Yes, man (*der mensch*) is lost! Christ will never find us, till we know that we are lost. My wife was the next lost sinner that felt the same joy, the same love.'"

"It was a rich treat, to hear this father in Israel tell of his call to the ministry; how he shrank from it when proposed, and how it resulted in his finding Jesus, the lost sinner's friend, and the joy he felt when the burden of sin was taken away. Of this he loved to speak in his old age, and would recur to it with an animation peculiar to himself. To see his eyes light up, and his whole countenance assume, for the time, a youthful appearance, in contrast with his snowy locks and rich white beard, was a sight, which a pen dipped in liquid light could not describe: it had to be seen to be appreciated. 'Now I am,' he would say, 'a *servant* and a *child* of God. When this took place, I knew of no one who had felt and enjoyed the sweet influence of the love of God in the heart, but Nancy Keagy, my mother's sister. In our family connection, and in her immediate neighborhood, she was known as a very pious woman, and she was pious.'

"M. Boehm's call to the ministry, and his conversion soon after, took place in the year 1758.

"Between the years 1750 and 1760, numerous Mennonite families removed from the State of Pennsylvania, to what was then called New Virginia, and dispersed themselves through Frederick, Shenandoah, Rockingham, and Augusta counties. Owing to their scattered state, and the newness of the settlements, they were destitute of preaching generally; and particularly of their own choice. Of this they had little except what was afforded by preachers visiting them occasionally from Pennsylvania. In the year 1761, brother M. Boehm was called to Virginia, by some of his Mennonite brethren, who resided there. But previous to this call, some converts of the eminent George Whitfield had reached New Virginia, and had commenced preaching a present salvation. With others, some members of the Mennonite families became seriously affected, through the preaching of these 'New Lights,' as they were then called, for the want of a better name.

"Now here the Germans were in a dilemma, which, in their opinion, and according to the light they had, required the presence and advice of those in whom they had confidence; that is, their own preachers. Hence the call of Martin Boehm, at this particular time. To illustrate, we will select a case which will answer in place of many, characteristic of the state and views of religion among the Germans at that period.

"The daughter of a brother Keller had

become much affected, by hearing the 'New Lights' preach on one or two occasions. There, in that house of Bro. K.'s, you see a young person apparently in deep distress, although surrounded by kind parents, neighbors, and friends, who, in their turn, endeavor, by words and arguments, to cheer, chide, or, laugh the mourner into a pleasant mood.

"'Well,' said the kind father; for he was, in his way of thinking, a good man, and a good Christian in the Mennonite sense of the word, 'well, my child, what ails you? Are you sick? Do you wish to have a physician?'

"'No, dear father, no doctor; my heart is sick.'

"'Say not so, your heart is not sick.'

"'O my heart, my heart is sick. God is displeased with me. O my father, what shall I do? I am lost!'

"This agony of mind distressed the good parents much; but how the daughter could be sick at heart—why God should be displeased with their child, and why or how, this dear daughter could be lost, was in no way clear to them. Yet, evidently, she was suffering not unlike a criminal about to be delivered into the hands of justice, crying for mercy, often saying, 'Oh! is there no mercy for me?' The best and only reply she received was, 'You are not lost. God loves you. *Mercy*—what do you mean by mercy? You are not wicked—never was. You are a believer. Come, now, no more crying. Why? Wherefore do you weep?'

"This was repeated to her so often, that she finally sat in silence; and the fountain of tears either became exhausted, or refused to come to her relief. No one came to pray with her, and direct her mind to the blessed Savior.

"At this crisis Boehm arrived. After salutations had passed, and refreshments had been taken, Boehm, in conversation with Keller, inquired how matters stood in religion. Keller replied, 'Most of us are doing well, but some new doctrine has of late been preached by men here about, which has caused some disturbance among us.'

"'And what do those men preach?'

"'What they preach is rather more than I can tell you, but it is different from what we have ever heard. Our daughter, about two months since, was to their meeting, and has not been like herself since.'

"'And for two months she has been to no preaching?'

"'No, we could not think of letting her go, and have wished she had never heard those people; and, as we have written you, there are others of our people just like her, melancholy and dejected, and all we can get them to say is, we are lost (*verlohren*), we have no true religion; and for this reason we have sent for you, believing that they would be advised by our own preachers, and dismiss their gloomy thoughts.'

"'And where is that daughter of yours?'

"'Why,' answered the mother, 'there you see she is, and has not spoken a word to any of us to-day.'

"Boehm said he now moved his chair by her side, and sought to draw from herself the state and exercises of her mind. She listened to him for some time in silence, breathing at intervals a deep sigh. Soon the fountain of her tears was opened again, and she began to weep aloud, and said: 'Is it possible that you, a stranger, know what I have felt and suffered for weeks, and you believe that I am a sinner, that I am lost?'

"'Yes, I know this my daughter, but I know Jesus came to seek and to save that which is lost; and he is come to find you, and to save you to-night yet. Do you believe in Jesus?'

"'Yes, I believe Jesus Christ lives; but have I not offended him? Will he not come and judge the world and me? Oh, that he would but save me!'

"'Come,' said Boehm, 'we will kneel down and pray.' They kneeled down. The agony of Miss Keller was great. She cried, 'Lord, save, or I perish!'

"'Yes,' said Boehm, 'hold to that, he will save, and that speedily;' and so it was. She was blest, and all her sorrow was gone,— dissolved in joy.

"Seeing this, her mother cried out, 'Martin, Martin! what have you done? Why did you come? What will become of us now?'

"'Yes,' replied her husband, 'what will become of us? We, too, are lost!'

"That night was a night of mourning, and a night of joy for that house, for the morning light found them all rejoicing in the love of God!

"This scene proved a great blessing to Bro. Boehm. Before he left Virginia, many more were brought under the saving influence of the Gospel of Jesus Christ; and thus the families speaking the German language in that valley, saw the dawn of that light, which since then, and to this day, has shone with a peculiar splendor upon the people at large in that happy region, from whence clouds of witnesses have already passed into happier climes.

"As before remarked, Mr. Boehm's visit to Virginia was of great importance to himself. He there learned a lesson of experience from the good Master, which he could not so soon nor so effectually have learned at home; hence we can well fancy with what feelings, with what inspired thoughts and hopes he returned to his own. Timidity, and the fear of offending his elder brethren, he said, was much removed. He was confirmed in the truth and correctness of his own experience. He became satisfied that men every-where must repent, and that this repentance must be accompanied by a godly sorrow, deeply felt; and that there can be no rest, no peace, no hope, and no faith, without it. He further remarked, with much earnestness, that after his return, he felt 'an impression, or a presentiment that God would visit his people, and give them repentance unto life.' He had news to tell his friends at home, of what he had witnessed in Virginia; that there, too, he found and saw persons, some young, and some advanced in life, who felt themselves *lost*, some of whom had nearly despaired of obtaining grace and mercy, believing themselves the chief of sinners; that many had been blest, and had rejoiced in Jesus Christ their Savior, before he left. He could tell them how affecting their parting was,—what sympathy, what brotherly love, what melting of hearts!

"This year and the two years following, were years of joy to Mr. Boehm, while preaching repentance in the Spirit, and from experience. God was with him, and he did not preach without effect. The Spirit accompanied the word with power. Pungent convictions extorted the cry, LOST; and those convictions were followed by happy conversions.

"Sabbath preaching was not sufficient now to supply the wants of the many who were inquiring,—'What must we do?' Hence meetings began to be held on week days, and some by candle-light. This was another step toward the great reformation; and here we remark, as we pass, the similarity and likeness of the manner in which Otterbein and Boehm were led on by the Spirit, and providential circumstances as they presented themselves; and how each laid hold of those circumstances to promote the cause of God, and meet the wants of the people, who thirsted for salvation, and a deliverance from bondage, and from sin!"

CHAPTER V.

GREAT UNION MEETING—"WE ARE BRETHREN!"

WILLIAM OTTERBEIN and Martin Boehm were brought into the complete liberty of the sons of God, near the same period of time, and at places not far distant from each other. But they were members of churches very widely separated; indeed, no two churches in the world, perhaps, stood farther apart than the Reformed and the Mennonite. The Reformed, not a little puffed up with churchly pride, inherited from Romanism, looked upon the Mennonites with ill-concealed disdain; and, indeed, regarded them as no church at all, but as a sect,—a contemptible sect. The Mennonites, on their part, still cherished the recollection of the cruel wrongs and persecutions which their fathers had suffered from the Reformed church in Europe, and regarded that church, with its high sacramental notions, its paid and—too often—

proud ministry, and its loose discipline, as being little better than Romanism itself.

True religion, however, is a unit—"one Lord, one faith, one baptism"—and Otterbein and Boehm, so widely separated from each other by education, habits of life, and church relations, had each found the "one Lord," the one justifying and sanctifying "faith," and had received the "one baptism" of love and power. Alike they rejoiced in a present and full salvation from sin, which they faithfully proclaimed to others; and, therefore, that they might be perfectly united in the strong bonds of Christian fellowship, it was only necessary that they should be brought together and form an acquaintance.

As we have already seen, the blessing of God attended Mr. Otterbein's labors while he was at Lancaster; and, in a still more remarkable manner, after his removal to Tulpehocken. While at the latter place, he made frequent visits to other points; and wherever he labored, the people were moved, and many were awakened and brought into the kingdom of Christ. His influence, however, up to this period, was confined, principally, to persons who adhered to the German Reformed and Lutheran churches. Mr. Boehm, on the other hand, had found an open door, in places, among the Mennonites, many of whom heard him gladly, and welcomed him as a true preacher of that pure Gospel for which thousands of the primitive Mennonites had joyfully surrendered their lives. His influence was also extended to the Tunkers and Amish, German societies kindred to the Mennonites, among whom some converts were made.

Thus, two precious revivals of religion were in progress at the same time, in the same state, and among a people speaking the same language; and, thus far, they had flowed in separate channels. The time was near, however, when He who holds the rivers in his hands, should cause them to flow together, and, henceforth, to constitute but one stream.

A great meeting (grosze versammlung) was appointed, probably by Boehm, to be held at Isaac Long's, in Lancaster county, Pa.; and to it all Christians, of all sects and denominations, were invited. When the time appointed had arrived, the Lord's children, who were scattered abroad in various communions, moved by love, flocked together from far and near. There were in attendance members of the Lutheran, German Reformed, Mennonite, Tunker, and Amish, and, perhaps, of some other persuasions. By far the greater part of those who "stood on good ground," had been brought into fellowship with Jesus, through the instrumentality of Otterbein and Boehm, and were, consequently, rejoicing in their first love. It is more than probable, however, that some aged Christians were there who, twenty years before, had heard the word of life from such men as good Henry Antes and Zinzendorf, and had united with them in the "Congregation of God in the Spirit." Many of God's children were thus, for the first time, brought happily together in a worshiping assembly.

One may well suppose that, on such an occasion, a very high degree of interest would be manifested, especially in those who had, in heart, entered fully into the revival; and that self-examination and humiliation before God, and an unusual spirit of prayer for a Pentecostal baptism, would be excited.

At this meeting Otterbein and Boehm met for the first time. They were both in the vigor of manhood. Boehm was of small stature, wore his beard long, and was dressed in the plain Mennonite costume. Otterbein, on the contrary, was a large man, of commanding person, wearing the ordinary clerical dress. There was a striking contrast in the *personnel* of the two men.

"Boehm preached the first sermon, at the close of which, and before he had time to resume his seat, Otterbein arose, and, folding him in his arms, said, with a loud voice, 'WE ARE BRETHREN!'"

The effect produced by this touching expression of Christian fellowship and union, taking into account the ecclesiastical relations of the ministers, the character of the large congregation, the times, and the simple, stirring eloquence of the sermon just pronounced, can better be imagined than described. The scene would form a picture worthy the pencil of the most skillful artist.

Unable to repress their emotions, some in the congregation praised God aloud; but the greater part were bathed in tears, and all hearts seemed melted into one. The reader can not fail to be reminded of a union meeting of a similar character, and of like results, which marked the *renewal* of the United Brethren, at Herrnhut, in 1727.* And he will also call to mind the union conventions of 1741–42, brought together by the same spirit which animated the meetings inaugurated at Isaac Long's, and composed of similar ecclesiastical elements, gathered from the same region of country.†

This meeting, and the peculiar circumstances attending it under the harmonizing influence of the Spirit, which operated so effectually in uniting people, hitherto so widely separated, in one common and sacred bond of brotherhood, under the great Head of the church, free from party strife and feeling, gave rise to the application, for the fourth time, of the name, "UNITED BRETHREN," to which "IN CHRIST" was afterward added,—a name which the people, thus united, several years afterward, in official conference, adopted.‡

* Page 89.   † Page 111.   ‡ See Spayth, p. 41.

CHAPTER VI.

MR. O. AT FREDERICK.—GEORGE A. GUETHING.

Toward the close of the year 1760, Mr. Otterbein accepted a call from the Reformed church in Frederick, Maryland. While at Tulpehocken, he had made occasional visits to that charge, to supply, in part, the vacancy created by the resignation of Mr. Steiner. The Reformed congregation at Frederick was large, and remote from other portions of the church; and Mr. O. was induced to accept the call of the congregation, mainly because it had been difficult, on account of its location, to supply it with pastoral labor. His labors there, as in every other place, were attended by heaven's blessings. Rev. Dr. Zacharias, pastor of the same church in 1847, in a centenary sermon delivered that year, bears the following testimony to his moral worth, and pastoral faithfulness and success in Frederick:—

"During Mr. Otterbein's labors in Frederick, the church in which we now worship was built; also the parsonage, which has been the successive residence of your pastors ever since. Many other improvements, in the external condition of this congregation, were likewise made during this period; thus showing that Mr. O. was not only a very pious and devoted pastor, but was also most energetic and efficient in promoting the outward prosperity of the church.

"A few letters are still preserved in our archives, written by Mr. O. while at York, to members of this charge. From these letters, brief as they are, you may easily gather the spirit of the man. Though laboring now in another field, he remembered still, with affectionate kindness and concern, the people whom he had recently left. He mourned over their difficulties, and endeavored to profit them by imparting unto them his godly counsels, and offering up, in their behalf, his earnest prayers."

But earnest and successful as were Mr. O.'s labors in Frederick, they were not unattended with the usual difficulties and conflicts which awaited him during the whole of the period which succeeded his conversion at Lancaster, and preceded the establishment of an independent congregation in Baltimore. The catholic spirit which he exhibited, in extending the hand of fellowship to Christians of all denominations, and in fraternizing with "unlearned" and "irregular" preachers whom the Lord had raised up among the converted people, the searching character of his sermons, and the strictness of the discipline which he wished enforced, excited, at times, very great opposition to him in the church at Frederick, which, like too many of the Reformed and Lutheran churches of that period, was composed very largely of unconverted persons. At one period, the excitement became so great that a majority of the church determined on his summary dismission; and, to effect it most speedily, they locked the church door against him. On the following Sabbath, when the congregation assembled, his adherents, knowing that he had a legal right to the pulpit, were disposed to force the door; but he said to them—"Not so, brethren. If I am not permitted to enter the church peaceably, I can and will preach here in the graveyard." So saying, he took his stand upon one of the tombstones, proceeded with the regular introductory services in his usual fervent spirit, delivered a sermon of remarkable power, and, at its close, announced preaching for the same place, on the succeeding Sabbath. At the time appointed, an unusually large concourse assembled, and as he was about to commence the services again under the canopy of the heavens, the person who had the key of the church door, hastily opened it, saying, "Come in, come in! I can stand this no longer." But this was not the only, or the last instance in which the doors of Reformed churches were locked against him.

A man of Mr. Otterbein's zeal for souls could not confine his labors to a single town. The great destitution of the people impelled him to go out and proclaim the glad tidings wherever a door was opened. One of the places visited in his itinerant excursions was situated on the Antietam, a small stream which empties into the Potomac. At this place his labors were blessed in a remarkable manner, and he did not cease to visit it until near the close of his life. Perhaps no spot on earth became dearer to him than the Antietam.

Soon after the good work of evangelization had been commenced, a young man was converted there, and afterward introduced into the ministry, who deserves more than a passing notice in the history of the United Brethren in Christ. His name was GEORGE ADAM GUETHING. He was born in Nassau Siegerland Neiderschelde, Germany, February 6th, A. D. 1741. In his 18th year he emigrated to America; and, on the Antietam, he found employment during the summer, in quarrying stone and digging wells, and, in the winter, in teaching school. He was not a thorough scholar; yet he read Latin well, and his literary attainments were quite respectable. A short time after his settlement at Antietam, he was made acquainted with the Lord, and was filled with that divine love which, as a pure and quenchless flame, burned upon the altar of his heart until the very close of his life. Although quite a youth at the time of his conversion, it soon became evident that he was a chosen vessel of the Lord.

As long intervals necessarily elapsed between Mr. Otterbein's visits to Antietam, the people were encouraged to assemble themselves together, in his absence, for prayer and religious conference. At these meetings, the gifts and graces of Mr. Guething were called into exercise, with excellent results; and he was requested, still further to supply the lack of regular pastoral services, by selecting and reading a sermon on the Sabbath, when no preacher was present. With this request he complied; and, as he was a good reader, and entered into the spirit of the discourses, the people were gratified and instructed.

It was not long until Otterbein, who began to feel the pressing need of evangelical co-laborers, to aid in carrying forward the good work of reformation which was spreading in all directions, discovered that God had set his seal upon the ruddy-faced German youth, and he determined to bring him, at once, into the work. Believing that a man called of God to the ministry, should *preach*, and not *read*, sermons, he directed that one of the brethren, on the ensuing Sabbath, should remove the book from Mr. Guething's hands, and throw him at once upon his own resources, and the help of the Holy Spirit. Accordingly, at the appointed hour, as the young man arose to read, at the place marked, a brother stepped forward and took the book from his hands in a manner which gave him to understand what was desired in the place of a printed sermon. The result fully justified Mr. Otterbein's estimate of his gifts and talents. He addressed the people with touching simplicity and pathos, and brought tears from every eye.* From that day forward, preaching was the work of his life; and he became, in a few years, an influential and effective co-laborer of Mr. Otterbein and Boehm, in the great work which had been so well commenced.†

"The talent and ministerial graces of these three brethren, Otterbein, Boehm, and Guething, can not now be adequately estimated; it is beyond our ability to give the reader a perfect idea of them.

"Otterbein was argumentative, eloquent, and often terrible in the denunciation of sin. In the elucidation of the Scriptures, clear and thorough, few being his equal in these respects.

---

* These facts are gleaned from a MS. in the hand-writing of his son, preserved in the Telescope office.

† He was presented to the cœtus or synod, for admission, by Mr. Otterbein; and was received, and afterward regularly ordained, by William Hendel, sen., and Mr. Otterbein.

"Boehm was the plain, open, frank expounder of God's word; of ready utterance, having a clear and strong voice; and, being full of life and animation, he often carried his congregations before him as if they had been borne along by a resistless current.

"But Guething was like an early spring sun rising on a frost-silvered forest, which gradually affords more light and heat, until you begin to hear the crackling of the ice-covered branches, the dripping of the melted snow, as it were a shower of rain, and until a smiling, joyous day appears. So did Guething enlighten and melt the hearts of his congregations, by the word of truth, and so did the shouts of praise for redeeming grace follow floods of penitential tears. He was the St. John of this clover leaf, if the reader will allow the comparison; always

> 'Affectionate in look,
> And tender in address, as well becomes
> A messenger of grace to guilty men;'

of good parts, having a well-cultivated mind; in conversation cheerful, pleasing, and interesting; and every way a desirable companion. His winning manners and shining talents secured for him universal respect and esteem, good congregations, and what was much more important, access to the hearts and consciences of those who came to hear him. He would follow the sinner in his devious paths, showing the severity of God's holy law in a manner which made stout hearts to quail and tremble; and then, with feelings and language peculiar to himself, present to the stricken-hearted a loving Savior, and in tones so beseechingly sweet, that the effect was invariably a congregation in penitential tears. Here was the secret power which he possessed over an audience. All who ever heard him, saw it—felt it; he alone seemed to be unconscious of it. But love and a childish good nature, like the rays of an evening sun, resting quietly on his round face, was all that could be seen of the highly gifted mind, in the midst of sinners crying for mercy, or saints shouting for joy. Many were awakened under the preaching of brother Guething, in Pennsylvania, Maryland, and Virginia.

"But withal, he was not left without opponents in the course of his Gospel labors and journeyings. Having been brought up in the German Reformed church, that church was held dear in his affections, nor was this without a return from many members in that church, to whom his preaching had been made the power of God unto salvation. He likewise enjoyed the friendship and esteem of some of her preachers; but from that church came also some of his severest trials, by way of opposition to the work of grace and the conversion of the people. And as opposition or persecution which comes from those with whom we have been associated or united, in natural, social, and religious relations, cuts with a keener edge, and wounds deeper than when directed against us from any other source, Mr. Guething, when speaking of it, while the big tears dropped from his eyes, would say, 'For the hurt of the daughter of my people am I hurt. Oh! what a Savior we have, and yet the health of my people is not recovered!'

"Great meetings, such as were inaugurated at Isaac Long's, were held at an early day, in his immediate neighborhood, and so continued, from time to time, while he he lived, and long after the time of his earthly life. Otterbein was nearly always present at those meetings, until infirmity and age forbade attendance. Brother Guething's house was Otterbein's retreat,—his head quarters when out of Baltimore. Perhaps never loved two men better, nor for a longer period of time, than Otterbein and Guething loved each other. Brother Guething's was also the council house for the preachers, far and near. He was much looked to for counsel, for advice and instruction; and such was the love toward him, and the confidence in him, that his word had much of the authority of law, and his counsel was as the counsel of the ancients; and this was given on his part with such humility and tenderness of love, that the impression could never be forgotten nor effaced. But Brother Guething was a man, nor is it meant that he was faultless; but such as he was, God had raised him up for a great work. How faithfully he performed the work allotted to him, in the history of the Brethren church, was exemplified in the forty years of his illustrious life, spent joyfully in the service of his Divine Master."* We shall meet him frequently in the succeeding pages.

* Spayth, pp. 60, 61, 62.

CHAPTER VII.

OTHER LABORERS—CHRISTIAN NEWCOMER.

It is now time to direct attention to a very important measure, adopted subsequent to the great meeting at Isaac Long's,—a measure evidently sanctioned by heaven, but which brought upon Mr. Otterbein the severest censures, and some of his heaviest persecutions. It relates to the introduction of what has been termed, in modern times, a "lay ministry;" we prefer to designate it, *a God-called ministry.*

As already stated, although Mr. Otterbein was a settled pastor, yet he labored extensively as an evangelist; and, during the spring and autumn of each year, especially, he held, in conjunction with Mr. Boehm, many large meetings. Those meetings usually continued from Saturday until Monday; and they were the means of salvation to hundreds of souls. People far and near attended them; some to scoff, but many to hear and pray. Societies were generally organized at, or near the places where they were held, which demanded some kind of pastoral oversight. And cases like the following, frequently occurred. A truly converted man, living in the midst of a large community of unconverted church members, people and preacher alike blind,— hearing of a meeting to be held by the reformers, attends. To do so, he travels twenty or thirty miles. While listening to the word of God from the lips of Otterbein and Boehm, tears of joy run down his cheeks. His love, and faith, and zeal, are quickened. "O this precious Gospel," he says, "must be preached to my neighbors," and he entreats the ministers to appoint a meeting in his barn or woods. An appointment is made, and another society is formed. Another man is attracted to a great meeting by curiosity; but he is awakened and converted. He goes home, and tells his neighbors what God has done for him. The simple story disturbs the carnal slumbers of others, and at length a meeting for prayer is appointed, and a revival breaks out. A converted preacher must be obtained. because the "regular" pastor has never tasted redeeming grace, and bitterly opposes the work. Urgent calls are therefore sent to Mr. Otterbein or to Mr. Boehm. But these become too numerous. More laborers must be secured. The Lord of the harvest is entreated to send them forth; and he does send them forth.

It may be laid down as a truth, that a living church will always have a full supply of living ministers. Among the converts to Jesus of this period, and of the quarter of a century following, preachers of the Gospel were raised up who would have done honor to any church. Hence, when converts were found who were deeply pious, and had gifts, and who felt moved upon by the Spirit to exhort or preach, they were encouraged to go forward; and after they had been well tried and approved, a license to preach, signed by Mr. Otterbein and Mr. Boehm, was granted them. By this means the infant societies were strengthened, the numerous calls for evangelical preaching answered, and the word of the Lord published abroad.

One of the earliest and most successful of these early preachers, was CHRISTIAN NEWCOMER. He was born in Lancaster county, Pa., Jan. 21st, A. D. 1749. His father, Wolfgang Newcomer, was a native of Switzerland, but was brought to this country in his childhood. His parents were both pious members of the Mennonite society, in which were still to be found remains of that ardent piety which, two hundred years before, had blazed up gloriously under the labors of Menno Simonis. "I do recollect," says Mr. Newcomer, in his journal, "perfectly well, that I have seen them both on their knees, many a time, before the bed, offering up prayers or evening sacrifice to God, although in silence." * * "At a certain time I was present when they held a conversation respecting my grandmother. They said she was very sad and melancholy, in great doubts about the salvation of her soul, and in distress for fear of being lost; adding that she ought not to do so, but cast herself on the mercy of the Lord her God."*

This conversation made a deep impression on his mind. In a sketch of his experience he wrote:—"Ah!" said I to myself, "if such persons as my pious grandmother, (for I considered her a pious character,) do lament and are in distress on account of their salvation, what will become of me? how shall I appear before the great Judge of all the universe, to give an account of all that I

---

* We quote from his Journal, published in 1834.

have done? This impression lasted a considerable time."

At a later period he wrote:—"O! how many thoughts and dreams of judgment and eternity, disturbed my mind. I could see no way how I could be saved; reasoning with myself in this manner,—where so many are lost, and so few saved, thou also wilt be lost. This conclusion bore so heavily on my mind, as to almost distract me; being convinced of my sad condition, and knowing no way to make my escape, or accomplish a delivery. In the mean time, the grace of God continued to work powerfully in my heart. I formed resolution after resolution, to forsake sin and do better, but, alas! all availed not; before I was aware, sin led me captive again. Frequently did I endeavor to pray, in my ignorance of the plan of salvation; willingly would I believe and persuade myself that I was one of the happy number which are saved. I soon made the discovery, however, that I still continued in the captivity of sin and Satan, the terror of a sin-avenging God, and the fear of hell; and my own turbulent passions continued to sway their power without any perceivable abatement. I remember once being in a field at work, when the grace of God wrought such powerful conviction in my heart, that I went down on my knees in a hollow place in the field, crying to the Lord and saying, O! thou blessed Savior! I will cheerfully believe in thee, for thou art my Redeemer, and I am the purchase of thy most precious blood: but something within insinuated doubts, saying, how canst thou believe thyself one of the redeemed, when thou knowest thyself ensnared and held in captivity by sin? Alas! I did not know that I dared, or was permitted to come to Jesus Christ in my miserable and sinful state.

"The conviction of my guilt and sin still continued to harass my poor, though sin-sick soul, and it appeared to me that every individual could read my lost condition in legible characters in my countenance. O! how often have I expressed the wish that I never had been born; but as yet I was ignorant of the blessed Redeemer, the loving Jesus.

"Often did I dream concerning the day of judgment: especially did I dream once of standing on an extensive, open, and level piece of ground; on all sides, and in every direction, as far as the eye could pierce, there appeared a multitude of people; on a sudden the thunders began to roar in a most wonderful manner, and I thought the day of judgment at hand. In a moment I saw the Lord Jesus come down from Heaven in his glory—methought he seized me by the arm and drew me forcibly to him; with this I awoke, and instantly leaped out of bed; a ray of hope darted through my mind—perhaps, said I to myself, there is still mercy for poor, unworthy me.

"Sometime thereafter, a very heavy tempest arose one evening, in the western horizon; presently the whole canopy of Heaven was a black darkness;—tremendous thunder following, clap after clap, and the forked lightning illuminated the objects around me, making darkness visible:—this, said I to myself, is, perhaps, the day of judgment, of which I have lately dreamed. O! what anguish, fear, and terror, took possession of my heart; I walked from room to room, tried to read and to pray, all to no purpose: fear of hell had seized on me, the cords of death had wound about me; I felt as if wholly forsaken, nor did I know which way to turn;—all my prayers committed to memory, would not avail. O! Eternity!—Eternity! I exclaimed,—which way shall I fly?

The passage-door of the house stood open wide; I saw the rain pouring down, the lightning blaze, and heard the thunders roar. I ran, or rather reeled, out of the house into the yard a few paces, to the garden fence, and sunk on my knees, determined to give myself wholly and without reserve to Jesus, the Savior and Redeemer of mankind; submitting to his will, and to his will alone.

"Having, in this manner, humbled myself before my Lord and Master, unable to utter a word, a vivid flash of lightning darted across my eyes; at the same instant, a clap of thunder. O! what a clap!—as it ceased, the whole anguish of soul was removed; I did not know what had happened unto me; my heart felt glad, my soul was happy, my mouth was filled with praises and thanksgiving to God, for what he had done for me, a poor, unworthy creature. I thought if ever a being in this world had cause to praise the Lord, I was that creature. For several nights, tears of gratitude and joy moistened my pillow, and I had many happy hours. For some time I continued in this state of mind; my soul was happy when I arose in the morning; all nature had, in my eyes, put on a different appearance,—all things had become new, and I was enabled to rejoice all the day long." This change occurred in 1767, in the 18th year of his age. He adds:

"But by degrees I perceived an alteration in my mind; gradually I lost this pleasing sensation; fear returned again and took possession of my heart more and more; the confidence in God which I formerly was enabled to exercise, was lost; embarrassment and distress again occupied the place in my heart which they had for some time relinquished.

"In this situation I had a conversation with an elder or preacher of the Mennonite society, consulting him, and asking his advice. He counseled me to be baptized, to join the society, and take the sacrament. I took his friendly advice, and did as he had counseled me to do; but all this did not restore to me the joyful sensation or inward comfort which I had lost. True, I was not accused, nor did any person even insinuate any thing derogatory to my religion, but I knew and felt a deficiency of something within."

Subsequently he was married, and became engrossed in worldly affairs. Soon, however, he was again thoroughly aroused from his slumbers, brought in penitence to the cross, by a severe judgment of God, and once more, and with greater clearness than ever before, the Spirit witnessed to his spirit that he was a child of God. Referring to this return of peace to his soul, he says:—"In a moment the peace of God and pardon of my sins was manifested to my soul, and the Spirit of God bore witness with my spirit, that God, for Jesus' sake, had taken away the burthen of my sins, and shed abroad his love in my poor unworthy heart. O! thou glorious Being; how did my soul feel at the time? Only those who have felt and experienced the same grace, will be able to understand or comprehend what I am about to say. Yes, gentle reader, if, at the time, I could have called a thousand lives my own, I would have pledged them all, every one of them, to testify to the certainty of my acceptance with God. My joy, or rather ecstacy, was so great, that I was, in some measure, as one beside himself. Not to disturb those who were in the house, locked in sleep, I ran out into the yard to give utterance to my feelings. There I gave glory and hallelujahs to my Redeemer with a loud voice. My whole heart was filled with gratitude to God and the Lamb. Unto him be all the praise and glory for ever. Amen. Say not, dear reader, this is enthusiasm. Before this time, (but once) I did not know, nor did I believe it possible, to experience the pardon of sin in this life; but now again I was convinced of the reality, although at the time I never had yet heard this, what some will call, Methodist doctrine preached.

"Several weeks, I am almost ready to say, perhaps the most happy weeks of my life, passed away in this happy manner, my peace flowing like a river, and the love of God dwelling in my heart. I now felt a desire, yea, a something within, urging me to communicate this happiness to my fellow-creatures. I thought and believed it to be my duty to inform every individual of the loving-kindness of God, and especially of what he had done for my soul; but fear that I would be considered insane or a fool, prevented my performing this duty. Ultimately I determined to go to one of our preachers, who stood high in my estimation, and hold a conversation with him on the subject. I related to him, with all the fervor of a new convert, what the work of grace had accomplished in my soul. My heart was full of the love of God, and my expressions were, perhaps, rather fervent; therefore, he could not understand me. He thought me hasty; said that I had formed too stout an opinion in this matter, and might very easily be in error in believing such professed experience.

"When I had left him, and was again by myself, on my way home, the enemy of souls assaulted me with fearful doubts. Only see, whispered he to me, this man is a preacher, a pious character, and is ignorant of this work of grace in his soul, knows nothing of the certainty of his acceptance with God. Who art thou? how should you know more than this good man? would He bestow on you alone an experience of grace which, it appears, He withholds from other pious persons and religious characters? And yet I had imparted unto him not near all my exercises which I intended to communicate, because I soon discovered that he did not understand me. It was after dark in the evening; I had eight miles to walk. All the way I had to fight a severe combat with the enemy, being afraid I might have expressed the work of grace in my soul with too much ardor and assurance."

In this unhappy condition he passed several years, experiencing, alternately, great joy, and again passing days and nights in distress and agony of soul. He remarks: "I do sincerely believe, if I had been obedient to the call of God, I should have been saved much distress of mind. But the office of a preacher appeared to me too important, too great, and myself less than nothing."

While in this conflict of mind, thinking, like Jonah, of fleeing to a place of rest, he removed to Washington county, Maryland, where, in the good providence of God, he met with Otterbein and Guething. "Frequently," he wrote in his journal, "I heard them preach in my own vicinity, their preaching making lasting impressions on the hearts of their hearers. They insisted on the necessity of a genuine repentance and conversion to God, in the knowledge and pardon of sins past. Their preaching appeared to be owned and blessed of God. Many were awakened from their sleep of sin and death, were brought from darkness to light, and from the power of sin and Satan to God, found the pearl of great price, and adhered to, and followed the doctrine which they preached. These they formed into societies, and for the time being, were called by some, '*Otterbein's people.*' Whereas, these men preached the same doctrine which I had experienced, and which, according to my views and discernment, perfectly agreed with the doctrine taught by Jesus Christ and his apostles; therefore, I associated myself with them, and joined their society, and was blessed."

His doubts, in relation to the validity of his call to the ministry, were now all removed, and he was kindly pressed to make the effort to speak to the people publicly. He did so, beginning by the relation of his own experience. He says, in his journal:—

"I stammered this out as well as I had ability, and could not restrain my tears, beseeching the people to embrace in Christ the offered mercy. This had a good effect; many tears were shed, and convictions ensued. In this discharge of my duty, which I believe I owed to God and my fellow-men, a sense of the divine approbation rested on my mind."

"Thus, a door was effectually opened before him to preach the unsearchable riches of Christ; and he was, indeed, a chosen vessel of the Lord, as his subsequent labors most amply prove. Though, in some respects, less than Otterbein, Guething, or Boehm, nevertheless, take him as he was, we are justified in saying of him, that the grace of God was not bestowed on him in vain, for he labored more abundantly, journeyed more, preached more frequently, and visited more extensively. He was just the man, by nature and by grace, for his place. Tall in stature, of a commanding figure, and a keen visage, a voice moderately strong, and if, at times, interrupted for a moment by a slight impediment in his speech, it but hightened the effect of his preaching, drawing the attention of the audience only nearer to the speaker, affording him an opportunity to draw the Gospel *net* more effectually around them, and thus secure a larger draught. From first to last, and for many years, Mr. Newcomer made good proof of his ministry, in all things showing himself a pattern of good works.

In doctrine he was pure, grave, and sincere. He was successful in winning souls to Christ, and unremitting in his labors, being often and suddenly called upon to attend meetings appointed without his knowledge, to reach some of which, he had to travel one hundred and more miles. To do this required, on his part, much self-denial and sacrifice of domestic interests, which brought him often into great straits and sore conflicts. But he said he had promised to be obedient to God, and the brethren, so none of these things moved him from his purpose of preaching Christ. His burning zeal would give him no rest, in season nor out of season; neither in summer nor winter. He was sometimes heard to say, 'Well, this is hard, but the salvation of one soul outweighs it all; let me go.' Often he was compelled to make forced rides, to expose his person in the most inclement season of the year, and in the stages of high water; but none of these things could check him in his course." Mr. Spayth says: "When I was traveling Susquehanna Circuit, in the year 1812, in the depth of winter, of cold and snow, I had a meeting in Berks county. While preaching, Brother Newcomer's tall figure made its appearance at the door. I beckoned to him to come to the stand; but the room being crowded, he remained where he was, and, without leaving the door, closed the meeting with a very impressive exhortation, singing, and prayer. After the benediction, the audience began to disperse. Now was Newcomer's time; he shook hands with one, and then with another, addressing some by name; and exhorted all, both young and old, with a voice and visage as spiritual and holy as if he had just dropped down from the court of heaven. Many began to weep, and a gracious and powerful blessing was experienced. Thus, often, when it was thought that he was far away, he would drop in to meetings, unlooked for; but his advent was every-where and always hailed with joy, for God of a truth was with him."*

Such was Christian Newcomer, one of Otterbein's earliest and most efficient helpers, *raised up and put into the ministry on God's plan.* But, in the estimation of the High-churchmen of his day, he was an "*irregular*" minister, and his admission to

* Spayth, pp. 67, 68, 69.

the sacred office one of Mr. Otterbein's gravest offenses. But Mr. O. listened to the voice of God, and obediently followed it, and thus another important step in the reformation was taken.

CHAPTER VIII.

CO-LABORERS—HENDEL AND OTHERS, AND THE METHODISTS.

In November, 1765, Mr. Otterbein closed his labors at Frederick, and took charge of the Reformed congregation in York, Pa., from which he had received a regular call. At York he remained about nine years, inclusive of a year and a half, in 1770–71, spent on a visit to the land of his nativity. This was the last Reformed congregation of which he was ever pastor.

As we have seen, each year added to his influence and responsibilities, outside of the particular church of which he had the pastoral care; and, also, to the obstacles thrown in his way by the Reformed cœtus or synod of Pennsylvania, with which he was officially connected. In a succeeding chapter we shall see that, on his removal from York to Baltimore, in 1774, he virtually

dissolved his connection with the Reformed
cœtus, established a church independent of
the cœtus, and publicly and officially committed himself, and his congregation in
Baltimore, to the people who, soon after,
were regularly organized under the name,
"United Brethren in Christ." Toward this
consummation, things had been inevitably
tending from the period of his conversion,
but more directly and rapidly since the
union formed with Boehm, at Isaac Long's.

That we may thoroughly understand Mr.
Otterbein's history, and the circumstances
under which he became entirely separated
from the Reformed church, it is necessary
that we recur again to some facts already
adduced, inquire particularly into the character of the Reformed cœtus of Pennsylvania, and notice the rise of the Methodists in this country, and his relations with
them.

As to the masses of the members of the
Reformed church, it is evident that they
were unregenerate persons, knowing nothing
of the new birth or a change of heart.
Even Dr. Nevin admits that Mr. Otterbein
was driven into the measures he adopted,

"by the cold and dead temper which he found generally prevalent in the church.* The same was true of a majority of the members of the cœtus. They had not experienced the life of God in the soul, and hence could not sympathize with Mr. Otterbein, nor appreciate his labors; indeed, they were impelled, by the state of their hearts, to oppose, and, in many instances, to persecute him.

But this is only a partial view of the case. A small minority of the members, in many of the congregations, were truly spiritual people. This was the case at Lancaster, Frederick, York, Tulpehocken, Philadelphia, and elsewhere. Some of these had been converted in Europe; others under the labors of the spiritual men who went out under the direction of the "Church of God in the Spirit;" and others still, were the fruit of the labors of Mr. Otterbein, and those ministers who sympathized with him.

A minority of the cœtus were also truly converted men. Prominent among these was the distinguished DR. HENDEL, sen., whose sister Mr. Otterbein married. He was a native of the Palatinate; reached this coun-

* 28 Lect. on Heid. Cat.

try in 1764, and labored in Lancaster, Tulpehocken, and at Philadelphia, where he died of yellow fever in 1798. He was a man of profound learning and unaffected piety. With Mr. Otterbein he labored indefatigably to promote spirituality in the church. He was peculiarly gifted and powerful in prayer, and a great lover of prayer-meetings. John Christian Stahlschmidt says of him: "This man is one of the best preachers that I became acquainted with in America. He possesses much science and knowledge; and, without any sectarian or party spirit, he is, in heart, consecrated to the cause of true godliness."* Hendel and Otterbein were men of one spirit, and labored together in unity and love.

Next among the list of Mr. Otterbein's co-laborers and friends in the cœtus we must place DANIEL WAGNER. Mr. Wagner was born near Dillenburg, the home of the Otterbein family; and, when he was only two years old, his parents emigrated to this country. He was raised upon a farm, studied theology under Dr. Hendel,†

---

* Pilger-Reise zu Wasser und zu Land, p. 291. Quoted by Harbaugh, p. 127.

† Bishop Asbury denominates Mr. Wagner a pupil of Mr. Otter-

and entered the ministry in 1771. His pupil, Dr. Mayer, bears the following testimony to his character as a Christian and minister of Christ, all of which is corroborated by other witnesses:—"He was a holy man. Whoever had intercourse with him had abundant reason to know that in him 'the old man' was conquered. * * Especially did he love the souls of men, and travailed for their salvation. * * As a Christian, he was a true follower of his Lord and Savior. He did not consume himself in idle questions and disputations, or in sectarian zeal for words or opinions; for he felt that the kingdom of God is not in word, but in power. His piety was . . . lively, earnest, and full of feeling—the religion of the living, not of the dead. * * As a preacher, he had many excellencies. He received the word from God's mouth, and proclaimed it in his fear. Hence, his sermons were full of wisdom and power."* Such was Daniel Wagner, the steadfast friend and co-laborer of William Otterbein. He died in York in 1810.

bein. This seems to be an error. It is possible, however, that he did spend some time with Mr. O. during the period of his preparation for the ministry.

* Funeral sermon by Dr. Mayer.

JOHN CHRISTIAN STAHLSCHMIDT, also, deserves a place among the friends and co-laborers of Otterbein in the cœtus. While in his minority, residing with his father in Germany, about the year 1758, he was brought to an experimental knowledge of Christ Jesus. His uncle was a Pietist, and through his exhortations, and by the perusal of Jacob Boehm's "Way to Christ," he was strengthened and confirmed in a holy life. His father, being a Christian of the popular German type, was incensed at his new experience, and mode of life, and especially at his sympathy for the hated Pietists; and, although his son had now reached his nineteenth year, he whipped him with a rod until he extorted from him a promise that he would separate himself from the Pietists while he remained at home. Not being at rest under the tyranny of his churchly father, he fled to Amsterdam, Holland, where he became a sailor on a vessel in the East India trade. After many years, he returned home, was kindly received by his father, and engaged in business with his pious uncle. During all this time his love to Christ suffered no abatement. "Oh!" he would exclaim, "is there

here already so much peace, rest, and blessedness, in Jesus and his communion? What will once be ours in eternity?" Speaking of a wood near his place of business with his uncle, he wrote:—"Oh! how many blessed hours did I spend here, in sweet communion with my divine Savior! His love animated my whole heart. I often lived more in eternity than in time." In the year 1770, he came to America, and, at the residence of Rev. Mr. Stoy, he formed the acquaintance of Otterbein. In compliance with an invitation from Otterbein, he visited York, and remained with him six weeks, during which time he occasionally preached. By the recommendation of Mr. O., he went to Tulpehocken, to assist Mr. Hendel in his large field. With such spirits as Otterbein and Hendel he felt quite at home. After spending nine years in America, he returned to Europe. He was deeply interested in the reformation of religion which was in progress in this country, and, after his return to Europe, kept up a correspondence with Otterbein and Wagner. He died in peace in 1825. He was a steadfast and enlightened friend of Jesus.

These ministers, and some others of like spirit,* were the unswerving friends of Mr. Otterbein; and, although they were unable to control the cœtus, they exerted a good influence for the truth and for piety. But they were a cause of no little inconvenience and discomfort to those members of the cœtus who were hostile to evangelical religion. Otterbein and Guething, especially, were a source of constant agitation and grievance to the anti-evangelical party. Great efforts were made, from time to time, to purge out the evangelical element, and numerous and painful difficulties resulted therefrom. In some churches, the evangelical party were in the ascendency; in others the anti-evangelical party had entire control; and in a few cases they were

---

* Rev. ANTHONY HAUTZ, also, deserves honorable mention among the later friends of Mr. Otterbein, and of the United Brethren. He was a native of Germany, but came to Pennsylvania in boyhood. He studied theology under Dr. Hendel, and was licensed to preach in 1787. He preached in Harrisburg, Carlisle, and elsewhere in Pennsylvania, until 1804, when he removed to the State of New York, where he remained until his death at an advanced age. Dr. Helfenstine describes him as "tall, slim, meager, dark complexioned, with a large acquiline nose." Guething, Newcomer, and other Brethren preachers, were often invited to his church, and found in his society. In 1798, he attended a meeting in a Mennonist church, with Guething and Newcomer. Shortly after, these evangelists visited him at Carlisle, lodged with him, and preached at his church.

about equally divided. One case may be selected, out of many which are accessible, as an illustration of these remarks. Dr. Helfenstein relates the following facts concerning one of the oldest Reformed congregations,—the congregation which had, for many years, enjoyed the ministrations of Henry Antes:—"In the year 1790, my father, minister in Germantown, departed this life. An invitation was sent to Rev. Anthony Hautz, to visit that church. He did so. They gave him a call: he accepted it, returned home, and, shortly afterwards, gave them notice that he declined it. The reason he gave was, that, if the Rev. Helfenstein had his difficulties in the congregation, how could *he* be able to manage them? *The difficulties were the prayer-meetings that were at that time introduced into the congregation.* There was then a great revival in the church; numbers were awakened, and met together in prayer-meetings: to this there was great opposition, and caused much commotion in the congregation."

During the period of Mr. Otterbein's labors at York, other evangelical co-laborers made their appearance in this country; and, as Mr. O., true to the spirit of Jesus, received them as brethren, and became associated with them in the work of reformation, the breach between himself and the adverse party of the cœtus was greatly widened thereby. These new co-laborers were called METHODISTS.

In the year 1765, some Irish families, who had been members of Mr. Wesley's societies in Great Britain, settled in New York. Among them was Mr. Philip Embury, who had been authorized to preach, as a local minister, before his removal to this country. These emigrants, as is too often the case with Christians who remove to a new country, neglected the means of grace, became careless in regard to their soul's best interest, and were on the point of making shipwreck of faith entirely. Mr. Embury, the local preacher, had so far apostatized and forgotten the solemn responsibilities of a Christian minister, that he joined with some of his brethren in card-playing for a pastime.

Happily for these wandering sheep, a family of Hecks came over the following year. Philip and Barbara Heck were warm-hearted Christians, not easily moved away from the faith and hope of the Gospel. This was especially true of Barbara. Finding out, soon after her arrival, the sad state of things in the little colony of Methodists, her spirit was stirred within her; and when she ascertained where Mr. Embury and his brethren met to play instead of to pray, she made it her business to go in suddenly upon them, and, seizing the cards, she indignantly threw them into the fire; then, turning to Mr. E., she said: "You must preach to us, or we shall all go to hell together, and God will require our blood at your hands!"

This resolute conduct and stern rebuke of a woman of strong faith and deep piety, aroused Mr. Embury at once to a sense of his danger and duty; and, shortly afterward, he preached, in his own house, to a congregation of five persons, the first Methodist sermon delivered in America. A society was organized in 1766; and, in 1768, a good house of worship was erected. While the house of worship was going up, a letter was sent to Mr. Wesley, entreating him, in the most earnest manner, to send them a preacher. In this letter they say to Mr. W. and the conference, that, in case the means for the payment of the preacher's passage to America can not be raised in England, "*we will sell our coats and shirts to procure it.*"

Mr. Wesley was not slow in answering this earnest cry for help from the New World. Richard Boardman and Joseph Pillmore, volunteering their services, were first sent over. After these, came Robert Williams and John King, and others; and, in the year 1771, Mr. Asbury was authorized, by Mr. Wesley, to come over and superintend the whole work. Thus was Methodism, which has exerted a wide and powerful influence upon the religious history of America, established.

The Methodist preachers of this period were remarkably plain, humble, and zealous men. They were severe in their condemnation of pride in dress and vain display. Notes like the following are interspersed through Mr. Asbury's journal: "Here (at Richard Owing's) we had Dr. Warfuld, and several polite people, to dine with us. I spoke to the ladies about head-dresses; but the Doctor vindicated them, observing that religion did not consist in dress. I quoted the words of St. Peter." They were, generally, what are called uneducated men, and unsparing in their denunciations, not of colleges and of education, but of a "college-bred ministry." This brought upon them the charge of ignorance, and of opposition to learning. Passages like the following are found in the journal before quoted: "Before preaching in Kent county, one Mr. R., a church minister, came to me and desired to know who I was. He spoke great swelling words, charged me with making schism, and told me that I hindered the people from their work. I asked him if fairs and horse-races did not hinder them? He said, 'What did you come for?' I replied, 'To turn sinners to God.' He said, 'I can do that as well as you.' I told him I had authority from God. He then laughed at me, and said, 'You are a fine fellow, indeed!' I began to preach and urge the people to repent. After preaching, the parson went out, and told the people they did wrong in coming to hear me; and said I spoke against learning; whereas, I only spoke to this purpose, that, when a man turned from all sin, he would adorn every character in church and state."

With these men, Otterbein, Boehm, Schwope, Guething, Newcomer, and other

United Brethren ministers, formed an early and most cordial Christian fellowship. Mr. Asbury became acquainted with Mr. Schwope, and, through him, with Mr. Otterbein, in in 1771, the year of his arrival in this country; and he, ever afterward, cultivated their acquaintance, and embraced every favorable opportunity of enjoying their society. His love and veneration for Mr. Otterbein were great. At one time, he tells us, in his journal, he had, with Mr. O., "a blessed and refreshing time," and "spent the afternoon with him." This was in 1775. A year later, he says, "Returned, on Wednesday, to Baltimore, and spent some time with Mr. Otterbein. There are very few with whom I can find so much unity and freedom in conversation as with him." In 1784, he says: "Sunday, 20th, I attempted to preach at Newtown. I raged and threatened the people, and was afraid it was spleen. I found, however, that Mr. Otterbein had done the same a little time before." In 1813, not to lengthen these notices, he says—"A heavy ride brought us to Baltimore. I gave an evening to the great Otterbein. I found him placid and happy in God."*

---

* This was at the time when, according to Mr. Harbaugh, Otter-

In nearly all the communities where the German language was spoken, in the States of Pennsylvania, Maryland, and Virginia, the United Brethren preachers, as we have already seen, preceded the Methodists, and were in advance of them several years; and when the latter, under the energetic superintendence of Francis Asbury, pushed their way into the German settlements and towns, the Brethren were the first to receive them into their houses, to welcome them as ambassadors of Christ, and to afford them opportunity and facilities for preaching the Gospel, and extending among them the kingdom of Christ. This they did gladly, because the Methodists preached, with power and much assurance, a living Gospel,—a living and heart-felt religion; the very Gospel —the same religion—which they had experienced, and for which they had suffered no little persecution.

Many of the Brethren, it is true, understood the English language but imperfectly; yet they could see with their eyes, and feel in their hearts, that God was with the

bein was "silently mourning" over the great mistakes he had committed in "the heat of former enthusiasm" in the revival movement! Mr. Asbury did not find him in a penitential mood, however, but "placid and happy in God!"

Methodist evangelists; and when witnessed the conversion of souls under their ministry, their joy knew no bounds, and they regarded them as brethren in the Lord.

It is not surprising, then, that they should extend a hearty greeting to a body of English ministers, admirably adapted to the wants of the English-speaking people, who were holy, humble men, baptized with the same Spirit, and drinking at the same fountain with themselves, and who were raising up societies of zealous and devoted Christians. A mutual confidence and friendship ensued, which was of great advantage to the cause of religion, and the extension of the reign of grace. For a long period, Methodists and Brethren flowed sweetly together, and, in their public assemblies and great meetings, knew no difference. They preached and prayed, sang and shouted, together, and witnessed the most extraordinary outpourings of the Spirit of God upon many people, as the result of their united labors.*

Mr. Spayth, who participated in the scenes which he describes, says: "I confess it is hard for me to get away from

---

* Spayth, pp. 80, 81.

this sunny spot. The same love, I trust, still burns within my breast; and I can look back, and yet see, as if it were yesterday, the smile, the cordial shake of the hand, (hands now cold in death while mine tremblingly traces these lines) the hearty and joyous welcome, when Methodists and United Brethren met. Their voices, mingled in songs of praise, their hallelujahs often repeated, continue to ring in my ears; and, while I write, they thrill my soul afresh. Whenever my mind reverts to those scenes, an angel seems to whisper, it was then

> That the morning stars sang together,
> And all the sons of God shouted for joy.
>
> Then there was no iniquity in Jacob,
> Nor perverseness in Israel:
> The Lord his God was with him,
> And the shout of a king was among them."*

In all fundamental matters, the Methodists and the United Brethren in Christ

---

* "One of the elders who assisted at the consecration of Mr. Asbury was the Rev. Mr. Otterbein. Having enjoyed an intimate acquaintance with this pious and evangelical minister of Jesus Christ, and having full fellowship with him as a laborious servant of God, Mr. Asbury requested that he might be associated with Dr. Coke and the other elders, in the performance of this solemn ceremony." Dr. Bang's History M. E. Church, Vol. 1, p. 158. Mr. A. was ordained by Dr. Coke, Richard Whatcoat, and William Otterbein, Dec. 27th, 1784.

agreed perfectly. There were some things, however, which prevented the two societies, at the early period under consideration, from flowing into one. The Methodists were still under the dominion of the Episcopal church, and received from the ministers of that church the ordinances of Baptism and the Lord's Supper. Mr. Asbury appears to have been, for a number of years, a very strenuous Episcopalian, and sharply rebuked some of his co-laborers, who, unwilling to receive the sacraments at the hands of unrenewed clergymen, many of whom were the most bitter opposers of the revival, administered them themselves, or received them from ministers not in the fancied line of apostolical succession. One can scarcely repress a smile when he reads, in Mr. Asbury's journal, notes like the following: "Friday 24. Was much refreshed by letters from Maryland; but one of these letters informed me that Mr. S———e (Strawbridge, we suppose) was very officious in administering the ordinances. What strange infatuation attends that man!" With these Episcopal notions, the United Brethren could have no sympathy. During the first interview which Mr. Schwope had with Mr. Asbury, in 1771, this subject was discussed, Mr. Schwope vainly endeavoring to convince Mr. Asbury that Mr. Wesley did not do well in preventing Methodist preachers from administering the sacraments.

Close-door class-meetings were also objectionable to the United Brethren; and it appears that Mr. Wesley's rules respecting them were rigidly adhered to by the first Methodist preachers. They found it necessary, however, very frequently, to re-enforce themselves, in this unreasonable exclusiveness, by conference resolutions; because the love of Christ, which they possessed, protested constantly and loudly against it.

At a later period, however, Mr. Wesley made provision for the ordination of Methodist preachers, so that the first difficulty was removed; and, between 1809 and 1815, an arrangement was entered into, by which the second was partially obviated. This subject will come under our notice again, in a subsequent part of this history.

CHAPTER IX.

MR. OTTERBEIN AT BALTIMORE.

In the year 1774, we find Mr. Otterbein in the city of Baltimore, organizing a church which, in doctrine and discipline, was distinct from, and independent of, the German Reformed church.

He had now reached the forty-eighth year of his age, and the 25th of his ministry. Nearly twenty years had passed since he had entered fully into the light and liberty of the sons of God; and, during all that period, he had labored incessantly, in public and in private, at Lancaster, Tulpehocken, Frederick, Antietam, York, and at numerous other places, to promote, in the German Reformed church, and in other churches and sects, a revival of Bible religion.

And those labors had not been without fruits. The order and the morality of many congregations had been improved;

hundreds, and even thousands, had been truly converted to God; and a "new life had been brought into the church, at first as a grain of mustard seed, but later as a tree whose branches afford a grateful resting-place to many."*

Meetings for prayer and for religious conference had been established, and were kept up in numerous places in Pennsylvania, Maryland, and Virginia. These were attended by converted Mennonists, Lutherans, and German Reformed alike, and were conducted by laymen, unless a preacher might happen to be present. And, in thousands of families, the holy incense of praise and prayer, morning and evening, ascended to God.

The great meetings, so happily inaugurated at Isaac Long's, had been attended, from year to year, by the richest blessings. They had become an institution of no small value. Thither went up the people of God from all quarters and churches, as the tribes of Israel flowed together at the feast of Tabernacles.

The great truth, that a vital union with Christ is essential to religious life, had ob-

---

* Dr. Zacharias' Centenary Sermon, p. 15.

tained a firm hold in a large portion of the public mind. In many places it had become apparent to all that holiness of heart and life were essential qualifications for the sacred office, and for membership in the church of Christ. And many ministers, who bitterly opposed the revival, were, nevertheless, obliged, by the increasing light, to pay a stricter regard to decency, morality, and the outward forms of godliness, at least.

And last, but not least, the voice of God had been heard and obeyed, in the recognition of a ministry raised up among the converted people—a ministry composed of men of limited education, it may be, but of earnest piety, clear experience, and excellent sense—a ministry from the laboring people, and adapted to them.

These steps had been taken only in obedience to the clearest expressions of the will of Providence. Nothing had been hastily done. Nothing was further from Mr. Otterbein than a desire to wound the feelings of his brethren, or to occasion division or strife. And yet, such were the necessary results in many places. From the period of his conversion to the year 1774, and onward, opposition to the revival, and to its agents, was bitter and unintermitting. All the usual appliances which an ingenious and unscrupulous adversary has been able to invent were tried.

But none of these things had moved Mr. Otterbein. During all those years of conflict he had advanced steadily in the knowledge and love of God. All who mention him, whether friends or foes, speak with emphasis of the high state of spirituality he had attained—of his holy walk, heavenly conversation, and evangelical preaching. He had become fully enlisted in the revival movement, and firmly united with all who could give a reason of the hope that was in them. Ecclesiastically, he was connected with the German Reformed church, but, vitally, he was bound, by the strong cords of a common experience, and a sacred fellowship in Christ, to the "Brethren," who had, like streams rising in diverse directions, flowed into one channel at Isaac Long's.

Meantime a number of persons who had been converted under Mr. Otterbein's ministry at Lancaster, Frederick, York, and elsewhere, had removed to Baltimore, then a thriving young city. The Reformed church of Baltimore was under the pastoral care of J. C. Faber, whose ministrations were formal and unedifying, and whose life was offensive. The state of the congregation, viewed from an evangelical stand-point, was deplorable indeed. Discipline was neglected, and pastor and people were alike involved in sin. But there were in this church, as in many others, two parties; and, about the year 1770, the evangelical party sought to procure another pastor, for they could hardly hope for a reformation of the congregation without the aid of an enlightened spiritual guide.

Previous to this time, a young minister named BENEDICT SCHWOPE, from Germany, had commenced preaching in the neighborhood of Baltimore. He is mentioned by Mr. Asbury, in his journal, in a number of places, as a very pious, talented, and zealous German minister, in full sympathy with the revival movement, and with Mr. Otterbein. Mr. Asbury formed his acquaintance during the first year of his ministry in America, and always alludes to him, in his journal, in terms of warm affection and respect.*

This young man was the choice of the

---

* Asbury's Journal, Vol. 1, pp. 52, 96, 109, 149.

evangelical party, in the German Reformed congregation at Baltimore. But, being in the minority, which was unhappily the case with that party in too many congregations, they could not effect a change. "Like priest, like people." The majority of the old congregation adhered pertinaciously to Faber, and to his like, for many years. They had no notion of an evangelical minister.

Unable longer to live under the pastoral care of a man like Faber, the evangelical portion of the congregation withdrew, and established religious worship at another place in the city. Four years of ineffectual effort at a reconciliation and a re-union of the congregation ensued. In 1771, Faber resigned; but George Wallauer, a man of less character, was immediately chosen in his place. Meantime the seceding party were served by Mr. Schwope. At an early period efforts were made, by Mr. Schwope, and those with whom he labored, to induce Mr. Otterbein to remove to Baltimore. Mr. Francis Asbury, who had made that city his head quarters, and who had become warmly attached to Mr. Otterbein, wrote him urgently on the subject.* At length, *in direct violation of a resolution of the Reformed cœtus*, but in obedience to the voice of Providence, Mr. Otterbein resigned his charge in York, and removed to Baltimore.

The history of the struggle between the two parties in the old Reformed church at Baltimore; of the withdrawal of the evangelical party, and their often-defeated efforts at an amicable adjustment of the existing difficulties; of their resolution, as a last resort, to organize a new and independent church on Gospel grounds alone; and a statement of the doctrine and discipline of that new church, were briefly and plainly set down by Mr. Otterbein himself, in the Church Book of the new society. As that is a document of permanent interest, it must be inserted entire.

* See Asbury's Journal, p. 99

THE CHURCH BOOK OF THE EVANGELICAL REFORMED CHURCH.*
HOWARD'S HILL, BALTIMORE.
In the Name of the Triune God: Amen.

In the year 1771, there stood in the Reformed church in Baltimore, a preacher by the name of Faber; but, forasmuch as said Faber was not in fellowship with the Reformed preachers in Pennsylvania, i. e. he was not a member of the Cœtu Pennsylvanu, and likewise led an offensive life, a division took place in this church. In the month of October of said year, the said Reformed preachers met in Reading, Pa., where deputies from both parties of this divided church attended. Here it was resolved to dismiss said Faber, which was done.† Both parties agreed now, unitedly, to call a preacher from the cœtus, and to offer this call to Mr. Bluhmer: this was

---

* Translated from the original German MS., by H. G. Spayth.

† Rev. Mr. Schwope was charged as being the occasion of the strife in Mr. Faber's congregation, as was also Mr. Otterbein; and, complaints coming up before the cœtus, Revs. Gross and Gobrecht were appointed a committee to investigate the case, and adjust the difficulties. This committee reported favorably of Mr. Schwope, and against Mr. Faber. History of the Fathers of the German Reformed Church, Vol. II., p. 390.

done, but the call was not accepted by him. The cœtus now resolved to send to the Baltimore church, a preacher from among the four who, at that time, according to letters from Holland, were on their way, and now daily expected. In the meantime, there came to Pennsylvania W. Wallauer, whom the synod of Holland had not sent. The opposite party, without saying a word to the other party, contrary to the agreement and the resolve of the cœtus, brought him away, and received him as their preacher. But at the next cœtus, which was held in the year 1772, deputies from both parties attended; and the cœtus protested against Wallauer, and the conduct of his party, and declared that they could take no further notice of them. Scarcely any hope being now left of a reunion, the remaining members of this church found themselves under the necessity of looking about for another preacher, and of forming a church for themselves. A call was made to William Otterbein, who then stood in the Reformed church in York; but he refused because of the disorganized condition of the congregation; but, after repeated solicitations, he expressed a willingness to accept, provided the cœtus should give consent. At the next cœtus, deputies from both parties appeared again, and, be- more a final action was taken in the matter with Otterbein, a union took place, and William Hendel was proposed as preacher, to which the deputies of both parties con- sented. But, a few days after the return home of the deputies, the opposite party rejected the proposition, and all to which their deputies had pledged themselves. The division was now greater than at any for- mer period. The prospect of a re-union en- tirely vanished, and the members of this church, who had before addressed William Otterbein, saw the absolute necessity of forming a church for themselves; and they gave Otterbein a new call, which he finally accepted; and subsequently, in the year 1775, it was, by the cœtus held in Leb- anon, confirmed.

Article 14. After due consideration, the cœtus deems it proper (good) that Domine Otterbein continue in his pastoral office. From report, it appears that his labors are blest, and the opposing party cease the strife.

CONRAD BUCHER, Sec. pro tem.

CHURCH BOOK.

William Otterbein came to Baltimore, May 4th, 1774, and commenced his ministerial work. Without delay, and by the help of God, he began to organize a church, and, as far as it was possible for him, to bring it within the letter and the spirit of the Gospel. Such disciplinary church rules as were needful, were, therefore, from time to time, adopted, made known, and the importance of keeping them earnestly enjoined.

But the afflicting and long-continued war, and the dispersion, on account of the same, of many of its members into the interior of the country, prevented those rules from being written in a book for their preservation.

But through and by the goodness of God, peace and quietness being restored, and the gathering together of former members, with a considerable addition of new members, the Church finds herself, at this time, considerably increased. Therefore, it is unanimously concluded and ordained, by the whole church, to bring the CONSTITUTION and ordinances of this church into the following form, which we hold as agreeing with the word of God; and for their permanency and perpetual observance, herewith record and preserve.

By the undersigned preacher and members which now constitute this church, it is hereby ordained and resolved, that this church, which has been brought together in Baltimore, by the ministration of our present preacher, W. Otterbein, in future, consist in a preacher, three elders, and three deacons, an almoner and church members, and these together shall pass under and by the name—The Evangelic Reformed church.

2d. No one, whoever he may be, can be preacher or member of this church, whose walk is unchristian and offensive, or who lives in some open sin.—(1 Tim. iii.: 1–3. 1 Cor. v.: 11–13.)

3d. Each church member must attend faithfully the public worship on the Sabbath day, and at all other times.

4th. This Church shall yearly solemnly keep two days of humiliation, fasting, and prayer, which shall be designated by the preacher; one in the spring, the other in the autumn of the year.

5th. The members of this church, impressed with the necessity of a constant religious exercise, suffering the word of God richly and daily to dwell among them,— (Col. iii.: 16. Heb. iii.: 13:—x: 24, 25)— resolve that each sex shall hold meetings apart, once a week, for which the most suitable day, hour, and place, shall be chosen, for the males as well as the females: for the first, an hour in the evening, and for the last, an hour in the day time, are considered the most suitable. In the absence of the preacher, an elder or deacon shall lead such meetings.

(*a*.) The rules for these special meetings are these: No one can be received into them who is not resolved to flee the wrath to come, and, by faith and repentance, to seek his salvation in Christ, and who is not resolved willingly to obey the disciplinary rules, which are now observed by this church, for good order, and advance in godliness, as well as such as in future may be added by the preacher and church Vestry; yet, always excepted, that such rules are founded on the WORD OF GOD, which is the only unerring guide of faith and practice.

(*b*.) These meetings are to commence

and end with singing and prayer; and nothing shall be done but what will tend to build up and advance godliness.

(*c.*) Those who attend these special meetings but indifferently, sickness and absence from home excepted, after being twice or thrice admonished, without manifest amendment, shall exclude themselves from the church, (*versamlung*.)

(*d.*) Every member of this church [who is the head of a family] should fervently engage in private worship; morning and evening pray with his family; and himself and his household attend divine worship at all times.

(*e.*) Every member shall sedulously abstain from all backbiting and evil-speaking, of any person, or persons, without exception, and especially of his brethren in the church.—(Rom. xv.: 1–3. 2 Cor. xii.: 20. 1 Peter ii.: 1. Ja. iv.: 11.) The transgressor shall, in the first instance, be admonished privately; but, the second time, he shall be openly rebuked in the class-meeting.

(*f.*) Every one must avoid all worldly and sinful company, and, to the utmost, shun all foolish talking and jesting.—(Ps.

xv.: 4. Eph. v.: 4–11.) This offense will meet with severe church censure.

(*g.*) No one shall be permitted to buy or sell on the Sabbath, nor attend to worldly business; not to travel far or near, but each spend the day in quietness and religious exercises.—(Isa. lviii.: 13, 14.)

(*h.*) Each member shall willingly attend to any of the private concerns of the church, when required so to do, by the preacher or Vestry; and each one shall strive to lead a quiet and godly life, lest he give offense, and fall into the condemnation of the adversary.—(Math. v.: 14–16. 1 Pet. ii.: 12.)

6th. Persons expressing a desire to commune with us at the Lord's table, although they have not been members of our church, shall be admitted by consent of the Vestry, provided that nothing justly can be alleged against their walk in life; and more especially when it is known that they are seeking their salvation. After the preparation sermon, such persons may declare themselves openly before the assembly; also, that they are ready to submit to all wholesome discipline; and thus they are received into the church.

7th. Forasmuch as the difference of people and denominations end in Christ,—Rom. x.: 12. Col. iii.: 11)—and availeth nothing in Him but a new creature—(Gal. vi.: 13-16)—it becomes our duty, according to the Gospel, to commune with, and admit to the Lord's table, professors, to whatever order, or sort, of the Christian church they belong.

8th. All persons who may not attend our class-meetings, nor partake of the holy sacrament with us, but attend our public worship, shall be visited, by the preacher, in health and in sickness, and on all suitable occasions. He shall admonish them, baptize their children, attend to their funerals, impart instruction to their youths; and, should they have any children, the Church shall interest herself for their religious education.

9th. The preacher shall make it one of his highest duties to watch over the rising youth, diligently instructing them in the principles of religion, according to the word of God. He should catechise them once a week; and the more mature in years, who have obtained a knowledge of the great truths of the Gospel, should be impressed with the importance of striving, through divine grace, to become worthy recipients of the holy sacrament. And in view of church membership, such as manifest a desire to this end, should be thoroughly instructed for a time, be examined in the presence of their parents and the Vestry, and, if approved, after the preparation sermon, they should be presented before the church, and admitted.

10th. The church is to establish and maintain a German school, as soon as possible; the Vestry to spare no effort to procure the most competent teachers, and devise such means and rules as will promote the best interests of the school.

11th. That, after the demise or removal of the preacher, the male members of the church shall meet, without delay, in the church edifice, and, after singing and prayer, one or more shall be proposed by the elders and deacons. A majority of votes shall determine the choice, and a call shall be made accordingly; but, should the preacher on whom the choice falls, decline the call, then, as soon as possible, others shall be proposed, and a choice made. But here it is especially reserved, that, should it so happen that before the demise or removal of the preacher, his place should already have been provided for, by a majority of votes, then no new choice shall take place.

12th. No preacher shall stay among us who is not in unison with our adopted rules, and order of things, and class-meetings, and who does not diligently observe them.

13th. No preacher can stay among us who teacheth the doctrine of predestination, (*Gnadenwahl*) or the impossibility of falling from grace, and who holdeth them as doctrinal points.

14th. No preacher can stay among us who will not, to the best of his ability, CARE for the various churches in Pennsylvania, Maryland, and Virginia, which churches, under the superintendence of William Otterbein, stand in fraternal unity with us.

15th. No preacher can stay among us who shall refuse to sustain, with all diligence, such members as have arisen from this or some other churches, or who may yet arise, as helpers in the work of the Lord, as preachers and exhorters, and to afford unto them all possible encouragement, so long as their lives shall be according to the Gospel.

16th. All the preceding items (*punckte*) shall be presented to the preacher chosen, and his full consent thereto obtained, before he enters on his ministry.

17th. The preacher shall nominate the elders from among the members who attend the special meetings, and no others shall be proposed; and their duties shall be made known unto them, by him, before the church.

18th. The elders, so long as they live in accordance with the Gospel, and shall not attempt to introduce any new act contrary to this constitution and these ordinances, are not to be dismissed from their office, except on account of debility, or other cause: should any one desire it, then, in that case, or by reason of death, the place shall be supplied by the preacher, as already provided.

19th. The three deacons are to be chosen yearly, on New Year's day, as follows:

The Vestry will propose six from among the members who partake with us of the holy sacrament. Each voter shall write the names of the three he desires for deacon, on a piece of paper, and, when the church has met, these papers shall be collected, opened, and read, and such as have a majority of votes shall be announced to the church, and their duties made known unto them, by the preacher, in presence of the church.

20th. The almoner shall be chosen at the same time, and in the same manner, as the deacons, who, at the next election, will present his account.

21st. The preacher, elders, and deacons, shall attend to all the affairs of the church, compose the Church Vestry, and shall be so considered.

22d. All deeds, leases, and other rights concerning the property of this church, shall be conveyed, in best and safest manner, to this church Vestry, and their successors, as trustees of this church.

23d. Should a preacher, elder, or deacon, be accused of any known immorality, and, upon the testimony of two or three creditable witnesses, the same should be proven against him, he shall be immediately suspended; and, until he gives sure proof of true repentance, and makes open confession, he shall remain excluded from this church. The same rule shall be observed and carried out in relation to members of the church, who shall be found guilty of immoral conduct.—(1 Cor. v.: 11–13. 1 Tim. v.: 20. Tit. iii.: 10.)

24th. All offenses between members shall be dealt with in strict conformity with the precepts of our Lord.—(Math. xviii.: 15–18.) No one is, therefore, permitted to name the offender, or the offense, except in the order prescribed by our Savior.

25th. No member is allowed to cite his brother before the civil authority, for any cause. All differences shall be laid before the Vestry, or each party may choose a referee from among the members of the church, to whom the adjustment of the matter shall be submitted. The decision of either the Vestry or referees shall be binding on each party; nevertheless, should any one believe himself wronged, he may ask a second hearing, which shall not be refused. This second hearing may be either before the same men, or some others of the church; but whosoever shall refuse to abide by this second verdict, or, on any occasion, speak of the matter of dispute, or accuse his opponent with the same, excludes himself from the church.

26th. The elders and deacons shall meet four times in the year, viz.: the last Sabbath in March, the last Sabbath in June, the last Sabbath in September, and the last Sabbath in December, in the parsonage house, after the afternoon service, to take the affairs of the church into consideration.

27th. This constitution and these ordinances shall be read every New Year's day, before the congregation, in order to keep them in special remembrance, and that they may be carefully observed, and no one plead ignorance of the same.

28th. We, the subscribers, acknowledge the above-written items and particulars, as the ground-work of our church, and we ourselves, as co-members, by our signatures, recognize and solemnly promise religious obedience to the same.

WILLIAM OTTERBEIN, *Preacher.*

LEHARD HERBACH,
HENRY WEITNER, } *Elders.*
PETER HOFMAN,

PHILIP BIER,
WILLIAM BAKER, } *Deacons.*
ABRAHAM LORSH,

BALTIMORE, January 1st, 1785.

This record proves, beyond all question, that the church on Howard's Hill, Baltimore, organized, under the auspices of

William Otterbein, as the Evangelical Reformed Church, (*gemeinde*) was, and is, different and distinct from, and independent of, the German Reformed church. Let a few prominent facts lying on the face of this record be considered:

1. The church on Howard's Hill was "brought together by the ministrations of William Otterbein." Before Mr. O. went to Baltimore, a division existed in the old church, between the unconverted and the converted members; and, although the latter, unable to live under the ministry of either Faber or Wallauer, had withdrawn, and had been served in the meantime by Benedict Schwope, yet they had never been organized into a church. It was in May, 1774, that Mr. Otterbein, "without delay, and by the help of God, began to organize a church" in Baltimore.

2. The name given to this church was not *German* Reformed, but *Evangelical* Reformed. It is well known that *German* Reformed was the proper and official name of the denomination with which Mr. O. had been identified. The choice, therefore, of another name, while it would not, if standing alone, prove a purpose to organize

a church separate from, and independent of, the German Reformed, does add strength to other facts found in this record.

3. A Christian experience and a Christian life are indispensable conditions of membership in this church, as well as morality and general correctness of deportment; and provision is made for the expulsion of those who cease to strive after holiness of heart. This was a thing unknown in the German Reformed church of that day.

4. Class-meetings are instituted, the manner of holding them described, and attendance thereupon, regularly, sickness and absence from home excepted, made a condition of church membership. Have class-meetings ever been instituted in German Reformed churches? We all know that they have not only *not* been introduced, but that they have been discountenanced and ridiculed. But this church, regarding the building up of each other in the most holy faith, as the primary object of their union, did not only make careful attendance upon these meetings the duty of both men and women, but they ordained that *no preacher unfavorable to class-meetings should ever serve them as a pastor.*

5. Not only secret, but *family* prayer is enjoined. Morning and evening each head of a family in the Otterbein church was expected to call his family around the family altar, and offer up the sacrifice of prayer and praise. Was the like duty enjoined in any German Reformed church in America at that period?

6. All worldly and sinful company was to be avoided, and foolish talking and jesting was made a ground for severe church censure.

7. The peculiar doctrines of Calvinism were not to be introduced. "No preacher can stay among us who *teacheth* the doctrine of predestination, or the impossibility of falling from grace, or who *holdeth* them as doctrinal points."

Ulric Zwingle was the founder of the German Reformed church, and he taught the doctrine of absolute predestination, as well as Calvin and the other reformers; but he did not impose it, as an article of faith, upon the church.* On the decease of Zwingle and Ecolampadius, in 1531, the chief direction of the Reformed church devolved upon John Calvin, whose influence

---

* Dr. L. Mayer, in History of all Denominations.

over it was commanding. The Heidelberg Catechism, which contains the doctrinal system of the German Reformed church, was published in 1563. It embodies the doctrine of absolute predestination, and the impossibility of falling from grace, but designedly places these doctrines in the background, and expresses them somewhat ambiguously. Dr. L. Mayer says—"The catechism, in its general character, is Calvinistic; but the doctrine of election is placed in the background." This is a fair statement of the case. Any one who will closely examine that catechism, can detect the doctrine of election there, as taught by Calvin, but it is "placed in the background."

But the Otterbein church constitution suffers it not to remain even in the background,—allows it no skulking-place behind an equivocal phraseology—but *specifically condemns it*, and will not allow its pastor to *hold*, much less *teach* it. This fact proves that the doctrinal basis of the German Evangelical church, founded by Otterbein, in Baltimore, was not the Heidelberg Catechism. It may be well to bear in mind, in connection with this point, that the doctrines of predestination and falling from grace had been warmly controverted during the revival which originated the "Congregation of God in the Spirit." During that controversy, the revival party took decided Arminian ground, while the church party advocated absolute predestination and its accompanying errors.*

8. But this record not only institutes an order of worship unknown to the Reformed church, and specifically condemns some of its fundamental doctrines, but it omits all *allusion* even to the Heidelberg catechism. No one would suspect, from the perusal of this record, that such a symbol of faith existed. Nor is there any allusion, whatever, to the cœtus of Pennsylvania, the synods of Holland, or to the German Reformed church. Can any one account for

---

* When Count Zinzendorf came to Philadelphia, in 1742, he addressed a letter to John Philip Boehm, German Reformed pastor in the church at Philadelphia, asking permission to preach in a house owned jointly by the Reformed and the Lutherans. In this letter occurs this passage:—"But because I know you preach in the same church, and I am not inclined to the doctrine of absolute reprobation, as a doctrine which, in my religion, is confessedly held as wholly and fundamentally erroneous, I have thought it proper to inquire of you whether you have a right to present aught against my preaching there, since I do not wish to burden any one, or interfere with his rights." To this letter Mr. Boehm replied, "I will be understood as protesting, if any one should say that permission was given from the Reformed side, or from me, to Count Zinzendorf, to preach at the time and place belonging to us, *the Reformed*."—Fathers of the Reformed Church, Vol. 1, pp. 280, 281.

these omissions, except upon the supposition that this church was intended to be independent of the German Reformed church?

9. To place this case in a still clearer light, we will insert the substance of the regulations adopted in the *German* Reformed church, (the church served by Faber, Wallauer, etc.) a few years after Mr. Otterbein began to build this new and independent church,—regulations which seem to have been adopted under the impulse of desires for reform, stimulated by the success of Mr. Otterbein.

"All the members of the congregation shall regularly attend divine worship on the Sabbath; and, with the exception of poor persons, shall contribute to the support of the pastor and the congregation. All contentious persons shall not be regarded as church members. Those who fall into open sin shall be put away, and shall not be restored until they show sincere repentance and amendment of life, and declare their willingness to submit to the discipline of the church. Difficulties in the congregation that can not be adjusted, shall be referred to the synod. No foreign minister can preach in our church without the consent of the pastor and consistory, and he must acknowledge the Reformed confessions of Switzerland and Holland. As soon as we can build a new church, all children that are not sick shall be baptized in the church, and their names registered; sponsors may be admitted, but only such as have been baptized and are communicants. In catechetical instruction, the Heidelberg Catechism only shall be used. The Lord's Supper shall be administered twice during the year, and all the communicants shall visit the pastor on a certain day before the communion, so that he may become well acquainted with them, and have an opportunity to speak with them about their spiritual state."*

How marked the contrast between the regulations of this church and those adopted by the *Evangelical* Reformed church. No one could mistake the former for any thing but a German Reformed church, while no one, from the record, would even *suspect* that the latter belonged to that communion.

10. But items 14 and 15 place this question beyond all cavil. Mr. Otterbein, in

---

* Centenary Sermon by Rev. Elias Heiner, p. 20.

connection with Mr. Boehm, had established numerous societies of converted people in Pennsylvania, Maryland, and Virginia; and, in obedience to the clearest expressions of the will of Providence, they had encouraged and authorized "helpers in the work of the Lord," to go forth exhorting the people to repentance, and preaching the glad tidings of salvation. We have already furnished a sketch of one of those helpers, (C. Newcomer) and others will be noticed in due time. Now, says the record, —No preacher can stay among us who will not care for those various churches in Pennsylvania, Maryland, and Virginia, which churches, under the superintendence of William Otterbein, stand in fraternal unity with us, and who will not afford all possible encouragements to those exhorters and preachers who have arisen, or may yet arise, as helpers in those churches. To meet these provisions, the preacher in Otterbein's church, in Baltimore, must, of necessity, stand in full connection and communion with the preachers and churches of the United Brethren in Christ. No minister of the German Reformed church could or would comply with these rules.

These regulations, if we may except those which had, necessarily, a local application to the church at Baltimore, were regarded as the discipline of the United Brethren, in general; and, as such, were acceptable to all the churches, from and after the first conference, held in Baltimore, in 1789, up to the general conference, in 1815, when they entered, with little variation, under appropriate sections, into the book of Discipline. We like the spirit which pervades this document throughout. It breathes sincere piety and high-toned spirituality. It is a thoroughly evangelical church constitution. The Bible is its basis. From the second paragraph to the sixth, including the letter *g*, we have presented to us, in a concise and scriptural form, all that is most essential in constituting a Christian church, and the rules which should govern the members of a church, both in their individual and in their associated capacity. Written, as it is, in a sententious style, it must be read with care. In the original German it is one of the most compact and comprehensive productions of the pen. It bears the impress of a master mind; and, taken as a whole, and viewed in connection with the prevailing prejudices of the times, it does honor to its author.

The points insisted upon are, the purity of the ministry; the piety of members; prompt attendance upon all the means of grace; class and prayer meetings; observance of the holy Sabbath; union and co-operation of ministers; free grace; instruction and education of children; separation from the world; pastoral visitation, and whatever else is essential to the usefulness, spirituality, and perpetuity of a church. As to the age of the discipline of the United Brethren in Christ, we care nothing, because it matters not whether it be of but yesterday, or of centuries past; but it is important that it agrees, in letter and in spirit, with the Holy Scriptures.*

Mr. Otterbein's settlement in Baltimore was attended with evident tokens of the divine sanction. During nearly forty years of pastoral labor, he enjoyed uninterrupted peace and prosperity. The little wooden church, in which his congregation first worshiped, gave place to a larger structure, and that in turn to the spacious edifice which now stands on Conway street.

* Spayth, pp. 56, 57.

No man was ever more faithful in pastoral visitation. The poor, the sick, the widow and fatherless, the stranger, and the awakened sinner, were objects of unceasing attention. Giving himself wholly to his work, he had time for every duty. His congregations were usually very large, and profoundly attentive and solemn.

An educated German, who first heard Mr. Otterbein, in Baltimore, about the year 1800, and who was awakened under his preaching, and eventually himself introduced into the ministry, gives the following account of his first visit to the Evangelical Reformed church:

"Nearly half a century has passed since I became acquainted with Mr. Otterbein; and never will I forget the impression made upon my mind, when I first saw and heard him. It was on Good Friday, in the forenoon, when, by the persuasion of a friend, I entered the church where he officiated. A venerable, portly old man, above six feet in hight, erect in posture, apparently about seventy-five years of age, stood before me. He had a remarkably high and prominent forehead. Gray hair fell smoothly down both sides of his head, on his temples; and his eyes were large, blue, and piercing, and sparkled with the fire of love which warmed the heart. In his appearance and manners there was nothing repulsive, but all was attractive, and calculated to command the most profound attention and reverence. He opened his lips in prayer to Jehovah. Oh, what a voice!—what a prayer! Every word thrilled my heart. I had heard many prayers, but never before one like this. The words of his text were these:—'Thus it is written, and thus it behooved Christ to suffer, and to rise from the dead the third day; and that repentance and remission of sins should be preached in his name, among all nations, beginning at Jerusalem.' As he proceeded in the elucidation of the text and its application, it seemed that every word was exactly adapted to my case, and intended for me. Every sentence smote me. A tremor at length seized on my whole frame; tears streamed from my eyes; and, utterly unable to restrain myself, I cried aloud.

"On the following Sabbath I again went to Mr. O.'s church, when he took special notice of the young stranger, and gave me an invitation to visit him on the next day. I complied with the friendly request, with some reluctance, it is true, but was received with such unaffected tenderness and love, and addressed with so much solicitude for my salvation, that my heart was won."

The cœtus or synod of the Reformed church, shortly after Mr. O.'s successful establishment in Baltimore, re-considered and rescinded its action against his settlement there, and proposed to receive the new church under its care;* but, as the congregation had formed an instructive acquaintance with the unevangelical elements which usually managed to control its action, and as the synod, about the same time, received Faber into its fellowship, they never accepted of the proposition. They were free from the official annoyance and control of those who sought to check the revival of religion, and they chose to remain free.

Mr. O. had not, however, formally, withdrawn from the Reformed church, and his name was retained, even up to the period of his death, on the records of the synod. For more than a quarter of a century, he had served as a minister in that church,

---

* See resolution signed Conrad Bucher, quoted page 233.

with unsparing devotion, and had remained in her communion as long as a prospect remained of benefiting her thereby. But that hope, as we have seen, eventually vanished; and, although he had nothing to retract or recall of what he had said or done, and what he was still doing, the dissolving of those relations which, next to God, had possessed his heart, filled his soul with sorrow and anguish, at times, which knew no bounds: tears would fill his eyes, and, in big drops, run down his cheeks; and then again, as if he would lay hold on heaven for an answer, he would exclaim, "Oh! how can I give thee up!" There were, as we have seen, a number of devoted, evangelical men in that church, to whom he was bound by the strong ties of Christian love; and it seemed to him that a reformation of the church must be effected. In those dark hours of agony and wrestling in prayer, his best friends dared not attempt to console him, and his grief was fully known only to God. But, as his was the night of sorrow, his was, also, the joy of the morning. The Lord knows how to send comfort to his chosen ones. In one of those seasons of sadness and distress, the Bible opened, for the morning lesson, on the 49th chapter of Isaiah, beginning—"Listen, O isles, unto me, and hearken, ye people from far; the Lord hath called me from the womb; from the bowels of my mother hath he made mention of my name. And he hath made my mouth like a sharp sword; in the shadow of his hand hath he led me; and said unto me, Thou art my servant," etc.

He occasionally visited the cœtus, and neglected no opportunity of testifying his interest in the progress of vital piety in the Reformed church. Persecution, and even the spiteful expulsion of his bosom friend and co-laborer, G. A. Guething, never embittered his feelings toward her. After six years of absence from the synod, when that body met in Baltimore, toward the close of his life, a committee was appointed to wait on him, and request a visit from him. Bending under the weight of four score years, and leaning upon a long staff, which he carried to support him, he went with the committee. When he arrived, an opportunity was given him to speak. He arose and addressed the synod in a most feeling manner, and strove to impress the minds of the ministers present with the importance of experimental religion,—of the new birth, and the great necessity of preaching it to the people distinctly and plainly, as men who must give account to God. After he had taken his seat, Mr. Becker,* who, about that time, assumed the pastoral charge of the German Reformed church in Baltimore, arose and opposed the views he had advanced, and answered him roughly. Mr. O. heard him through with his accustomed meekness, and then, taking his cane and hat, he bade the preachers farewell, bowed, and retired, never to return again.

Mr. Otterbein's pulpit in Baltimore was open to the Methodists, and was occasionally occupied by the most distinguished bishops and ministers of that church. When absent on his frequent and long itinerant tours, his place was supplied by Gue-

---

* This was Christian L. Becker, a very popular man in the synod with the dominant church party. He was the man who made the motion, in 1804, for the expulsion from the synod, "without delay," of G. A. Guething. He was, for a long time, pastor in Baltimore, and Dr. Heiner thus sums up the result of his labors there. "Large audiences waited on his ministry, and his labors were highly appreciated. During his administration, he baptized (children and adults) 597, and confirmed 151; and yet the number of communicants does not appear to have increased. Many of the congregation were more delighted with the doctor's fine oratory, than they were pleased to attend to their duty at the Lord's table."—Cen. Sermon, page 30.

thing, Newcomer, Boehm, and others of the preachers who had been raised up as co-laborers in the reformation. Although some of those co-laborers were, in common phrase, uneducated men, and went into his pulpit with trembling, yet they were always received and honored, by the congregation, as duly authorized ambassadors of Jesus.

CHAPTER X.

THE CONFERENCES OF 1789-1791—DRAKSEL, PFRIMMER, NEIDING, AND OTHERS.

The protracted and bloody war of the Revolution, which resulted in the separation of the American colonies from Great Britain, and in the establishment of the Federal Republic, interrupted the progress of evangelical religion for a long period.

While the great body of the people favored the war, and were willing to shed their blood and exhaust their treasure to secure the independence of the country, there were many who preferred a continued subjection to the British crown, and lamented and opposed the measures of the Whig party: these last were denominated Tories, and the name has become odious to the American people.

But there was another party, which usually enjoyed the respect even of its enemies, on account of the sterling honesty, honor, and love of the right and of freedom, which characterized its adherents. It may be denominated the Peace Party. It was composed of those Christians who were opposed to wars, offensive and defensive, under all circumstances. These men could not, of course, engage in the martial contest for liberty or death. They were generally men of superior moral courage,— men who could face death at the stake— who could die calmly for the truth, but who could not fight for it with "carnal weapons."

The bitter contests of party, the levying of taxes and supplies, the drafting of fighting men, the marching and counter-marching of armies, the bloody battles, and feverish excitement and anxiety of the public mind, during the eight years' war, called away the attention of the people from that wisdom which is pure, peaceable, gentle, full of mercy and good fruits, whose ways are ways of pleasantness, and whose paths are peace. Many of the infant societies of United Brethren were scattered abroad, as sheep without a shepherd; and ministers and members were subjected to sufferings, and losses, and hardships, which no pen has ever recorded.

Nevertheless, after peace was restored, and the disordered elements had become settled, numerous societies of United Brethren were found among the German people in Pennsylvania, Maryland, and Virginia. Converts had been made to Jesus, large meetings held, prayer-meetings kept up, class-meetings attended, and some preachers added to the faithful band, in the midst of the national struggle.

From the year 1766 to 1789,—a period of twenty-three years,—the preachers who felt that they were United Brethren, and who were co-operating in the revival movement, met together as often as once a year, and, usually, at a great meeting, where, in mutual and brotherly counsel, they attended to such business as would properly belong to a presbytery, classis, or conference. As the number of laborers increased, and as applications for authority to preach, from those whom God had manifestly called and qualified for the work, multiplied, these informal conferences became more necessary and important. Mr. Otterbein usually presided; and his influence, especially upon the rising ministry, was salutary in a high degree.

At length, however, a formal conference was deemed necessary. The work had become so far extended that it became impracticable to attend to the necessary business of the church at the great meetings. Accordingly, the FIRST CONFERENCE, regularly convened, was held in Baltimore, in 1789. Fourteen preachers were recognized as members of this conference. Of these, seven were present, viz.: William Otterbein, Martin Boehm, George A. Guething, Christian Newcomer, Henry Weidner, Adam Lehman, and John Ernst. The absent members were—Benedict Schwope, Henry Baker, Simon Herre, Frederick Schaffer, Martin Kreider, Christopher Grosh, and Abraham Draksel. Owing to conscientious objections entertained by some of the Brethren, no record had been kept of the number of members or of societies.

Of the preachers who belonged to the first conference, MARTIN KREIDER was, Otterbein and Boehm excepted, the oldest minister in the society. He was a true Aaronite, a strong pillar in the church, where he stood faithful to his brethren, to all men, and to God, during a long life. He was the father of John Kreider, the sweet singer, the sound and laborious preacher, who, like his father, was faithful to the end of life.

CHRISTOPHER GROSH, another member of the conference of 1789, was greatly beloved and respected. He was a prudent counsellor, a peacemaker, and a preacher mighty in the Scriptures. For more than forty years, he was a co-worker with the Brethren, and, when full of years, was gathered with the elect of God.

ABRAHAM DRAKSEL was born in Lebanon county, Pa., in 1753. He was brought up in the Amish or Omish society.

This society has been regarded as a secession from the Mennonites. It derived its name from Jacob Amen, a native of Amenthal, in Switzerland, and a rigid Mennonite preacher of the seventeenth century. The principal difference between the Amish or "Hooker Mennonites," as they have been called, because they wear hooks instead of buttons, and the other Mennonites, consists in their greater simplicity of dress, and strictness of discipline. Like other Mennonites, they take no oaths; administer baptism to adults only; allow no fixed salaries to preachers; consider war, in all its forms, antichristian and unjust; allow all their members to exhort and expound the Scriptures in their assemblies, and suffer none of them to become a public charge.

Mr. Draksel, being an obedient and loving son of kind parents, and leading a strictly moral and, in the estimation of his Amish brethren, pious life, was, in his twenty-sixth year, encouraged to take part in preaching, which he did with such grace and ability as he had. Soon after he began to preach, however, he felt the need of a change of heart, and, through the grace of God, experienced that change. The love of Christ, which was to him a blessed reality, constrained him to preach it to his brethren; and, in the warmth and joy of his first love, he had hoped that the doctrine of the new birth, and the news of his own happy conversion, would be well received by them; but it was not so. That the kingdom of Christ did not consist in rigid outward rules, or forms, or ordinances, but in peace and joy in the Holy Ghost, they would not believe.

On the contrary, they were offended and

scandalized by the new and heartfelt experience and preaching of Draksel, and determined to silence him. After having admonished him the third time, without producing the desired change, either in his religious views or manner of preaching, they sent a special deputation of the elders of the society to announce to him the decision of his brethren, that he should be silent. When these elders had finished their work and departed, it appeared to him that angels came and ministered unto him, and he felt such comfort and peace in God as he had never before enjoyed.

Chosing to obey God rather than man, he continued to preach, and, in 1782, became associated with the United Brethren, with whom he labored forty-three years. In 1804, he removed to Westmoreland county, Pa., and settled his family near Mt. Pleasant, from which place he made frequent preaching tours into Ohio. He was an acceptable and excellent preacher, and a successful evangelist. By his labors and sacrifices, the good cause was advanced, and he will live long in the memory of the church.

"His countenance was an index to the

grace and purity that reigned in his heart. With his fine silvery beard, he resembled the patriarchs of old. Of sweet and humble spirit, a lover of hospitality, a lover of good men, he was a pattern of piety."*
At the age of three score and twelve years, his end was joy and peace. Such was Abraham Draksel, the silenced Amish preacher, and a member of the United Brethren conference of 1789.

HENRY BAKER was a man full of faith and the Holy Ghost. Of the others, we can not speak particularly. They were, however, of like spirit and character.

The SECOND CONFERENCE was held in Paradise township, York county, Pa., at the house of Brother Spangler, in 1791. Twenty-three preachers were recognized as members of the conference, whose names follow: —*Present*—Wm. Otterbein, Martin Boehm, George A. Guething, Christian Newcomer, Adam Lehman, John Ernst, J. G. Pfrimmer, John Neiding, and Benedict Sanders. *Absent*—Henry Weidner, Henry Baker, Martin Kreider, F. Schaffer, Christopher Grosh, Abraham Draksel, Christian Crum, G. Fortenbach, D. Strickler, J. Hershey, Felix

* Spayth, pp. 160, 161.

Light, Simon Herre, John Hautz, and Benedict Schwope. During the two years which had intervened between the first conference, in 1789, and the second, in 1791, nine preachers had been added to the society. Henry Baker and John Hautz, both men of earnest piety and zeal, had removed to the west; Baker to Tennessee, and Hautz to Kentucky. The fruits of their labors in those new fields were by no means inconsiderable. They were gathered, however, by other societies.

Of the members of the conference of 1791, J. G. Pfrimmer and J. Neiding deserve especial notice, as they were, for a long series of years, very active, prominent, and successful ministers.

JOHN G. PFRIMMER was a native of Alsace, an old German province on the Rhine, ceded to France in 1648. He was born in 1762, and was brought up in the Reformed church. He emigrated to Pennsylvania in 1788, where he soon became fully enlightened in relation to experimental religion, and was made a partaker of divine grace. Having received a good education, and believing it to be his duty to preach, he began, soon after his conversion, to exhort, and to preach

Christ and him crucified. His eminent fitness to preach manifested itself in the impressions which his discourses made upon his hearers; and, in view of his education, talent, grace, and commanding powers as a speaker, he was regarded as a great accession to the strength and influence of the rising church.

Being a man of strong intellectual powers, having a mind well stored with useful knowledge, and especially with Biblical lore, and possessing withal a peculiar nervous energy which sent a thrill through all his words, his sermons were not only original and instructive, but stirring and abiding in their impression. He brought things new and old out of the rich treasury of inspiration, applied the truth, with great force, to the consciences of men, and was always ready with an appropriate text,—a "thus saith the Lord"—to fasten it there with power.[*]

By his energetic and efficient labors, many heard and received the Gospel, and the word of God was multiplied and spread abroad through a large part of Pennsylvania; first in its eastern counties, then in

[*] Spayth, pp. 70, 71.

the Susquehannah valley, and subsequently in the counties of Westmoreland, Somerset, and Washington, west of the Alleghanies. He commenced his labors west of the mountains as early as 1800; and, in 1809, he followed the tide of emigration westward through Ohio into Harrison county, Indiana, where he finally settled, without, however, intermitting his itinerant labors. After his settlement in Indiana, he extended his travels eastward, sometimes as far as Pennsylvania and Maryland. He was a member of the general conference held in Ohio in 1825.

JOHN NEIDING was born in Berks county, Pa., in 1765, soon after which his father removed into the neighborhood of Harrisburg, Dauphin county, where John was raised. His parents were Mennonites, and he was, as a matter of course, trained up carefully in that society. Being of a serious turn of mind, and maintaining a good character, while quite a youth, he was received by baptism into the church.

When he had reached his twenty-fifth year, he was chosen, by lot, to be a preacher. At this period, and, indeed, for some time previously, he had been dissatisfied with his religious state, and was earnestly seeking for a clean heart and a token of God's love. His appointment to the ministry caused his desire for a clean heart, and a token, (as he expressed it) that he was a child of God, to become still more intense, and he prayed more frequently and fervently for these blessings which he knew were promised to all those who should come unto God, through Jesus Christ. He soon found, and was enabled to rejoice in, a knowledge of sins forgiven, in the witness of the Spirit, or token of love divine, and in the possession of a clean heart.

Having an experimental salvation from sin, he was constrained to preach it to others; and, with great earnestness, he began to declare the nature and necessity of the new birth. He insisted, with the warmth and confidence which a fresh and genuine experience inspires, upon the Savior's declaration to Nicodemus, "Marvel not that I said unto you, *ye must be born again.*"

This was more than his Mennonite brethren expected from him, and more, unhappily, than a majority of them were willing to receive. While preaching with much feeling, some time after his conversion, many in the congregation began to weep, and some to cry loud enough to be heard. This was too much for the old minister who sat near to him, and, taking Neiding by the arm, he said, "Oh! not so, brother! You press the subject too far!" To this he quietly replied, "I will press it still further. There is no stopping this side of heaven!"

Among all the brethren yet noticed, or hereafter to be noticed, Brother Neiding was the Nathaniel. He possessed an excellent spirit,—meek, gentle, just. Of them that are without, he had a good report. The virtues and graces requisite in an elder in the church of God, were all exhibited in his character; and the clear light of his beautiful and holy life, which shed a luster along his pathway, was never extinguished, nor ever suffered even a momentary eclipse.

As a preacher, he was able, by sound doctrine, to exhort and convince the gainsayers. His language was select and chaste, and his manner inimitable. He had a voice, clear and musical as a silver bell, at complete command. Every movement of his body, of his hands, and even of his fingers, was graceful, expressive, and calculated to impress the Gospel theme. To the sinner, that clear and musical voice rang a painful alarm through every avenue of his soul, and he could not forget it; but to the broken-hearted penitent, to the returning prodigal, to the wounded and disconsolate spirit, it sounded forth grace, mercy, and peace through Jesus, in tones as sweet and heavenly as if they had really descended from the celestial climes. As a builder of the church edifice, the materials in his hands were "gold, silver, and precious stones."

His popularity was necessarily great among the evangelical portion of all the churches; and he received and accepted numerous friendly invitations, to participate in the dedication of houses of worship, extended to him by Lutheran, German Reformed, and other churches.

"Yet, be it remembered,—nay, rather in charity let it be forgotten—that John Neiding was deemed "irregular" by the Mennonite church, and was thrust out, as had been Martin Boehm and Abraham Draksel."

In noticing his demise, it will be seen that he spent a long and useful life in the holy ministry. Entering upon the work in the morning of life, he endured the heat and burden of the day without shrinking from the heavy tasks which it imposed upon him; and when that day declined, and snowy locks covered his head, he labored on still with undiminished zeal; and the last hour and minute of his life he devoted to preaching Jesus. "His last sermons, and especially those preached at camp-meetings, are still fresh in the minds of those who heard them, and are among the sweetest recollections of their lives."*

* Spayth, pp. 73, 74, 75.

CHAPTER XI.

THE WORK ADVANCING—INCIDENTS—CONFERENCE OF 1800.

At the conferences of 1789 and 1791, and at the subsequent conferences, to all of which special attention need not be invited, the preachers who could devote their whole time to traveling, were assigned particular fields of labor, upon which they labored as itinerants. Others were appointed to hold great meetings, designated at the conferences, in different sections of the country, and to devote as much of their time to the work of evangelization as their circumstances would permit. All the preachers and brethren, under the judicious and kindly superintendence of Otterbein and Boehm, devoted themselves, with remarkable zeal and singleness of aim, to the one great work of extending and strengthening the kingdom of God.

The preachers, especially on their itinerant tours, suffered much from foolish prejudice, false and scandalous reports, and insane bigotry; and, until they became well acquainted, were generally regarded as "wolves in sheep's clothing," "false prophets," "enchanters," and as the "filth and offscouring of all things." It was no uncommon thing for Otterbein, Guething, Pfrimmer, Newcomer, Boehm, and the other early United Brethren, to have the doors of houses erected for public worship,—usually Lutheran, German Reformed, and Mennonite—locked against them. Of this they never made complaint. The world outside was large, and it was their field; and as they were favored with plenty of hearers, they were always ready to "hold forth the word of life" in grave-yards, groves, barns, school-houses, or private dwellings.

In a note in his journal, under date of April, 1795, Christian Newcomer says:— "This day I came, in company with Bro. Guething, to what is called Berner's church; but we were not permitted to preach therein; so Brother Guething preached in the grave-yard adjoining the church, to a numerous congregation, with remarkable power." Two weeks later, he writes:—"We held a meeting at a place called the Black Ridge church; here we were also refused permission to preach in the church, and Brother Guething spoke in the school-house adjoining."

The opposition of some of the churches referred to is not to be wondered at, when the usual effects following the preaching of the Brethren evangelists are considered. As an illustration, notice a meeting held in a church whose doors, happily, *were not* locked against them. This meeting was held in October, 1797. We quote from Newcomer's journal:

"A sacramental meeting was commenced in Redland, York county, Pa. The first sermon was preached by Pfrimmer; I followed. Sunday 22.—This forenoon, Brother Martin Boehm delivered the first discourse; I then spoke from Heb. ii.: 5. While I was speaking, a young woman suddenly arose from her seat and exclaimed, '*Oh! Lord, I am lost!*' This created a stir in the congregation, and *one of the trustees went down on his knees and cried for mercy!* Another woman commenced crying out to the Lord to have mercy on her. Her husband, hearing her, made his way to the seat, and there they both wept bitterly. Bless the Lord! To me, and to many others, this was a precious time. 23d.—This forenoon, we had our love-feast; the brethren and sisters declared, willingly, what God had done for their souls, and, when the meeting closed, they retired greatly strengthened and encouraged."

A woman crying out, in agony, "I am lost," husbands and wives weeping aloud over their sins, a church trustee on his knees, pleading for mercy, and the whole winding up with a love-feast meeting, in which the woman who cried, "I am lost," told how she had found Him who came to seek and save the lost,—in which the husband and wife rejoiced together in a new-found Savior, and the trustee related how that, up to that time, he had lived in sin and blindness, were things hardly to be countenanced in every church. We wonder not that many doors were locked by those who would not enter into the kingdom of heaven themselves, and who were disposed to hinder those that were entering.

Of a quarterly meeting held in Pennsylvania, in 1796, we have the following brief sketch in Newcomer's journal:

"8th.—This forenoon, Brother Guething spoke to the people with demonstration and power: I think not a few were convinced of their awful situation. In the afternoon, I spoke from these words:—"How shall ye escape, if ye neglect so great salvation?" On the 9th, we had a powerful time; many poor souls confessed openly that they had rebelled against their God, lamented that they had spent their best days in sin and folly, and cried for mercy. Among the rest, a woman came forward, leading her daughter by the hand, both crying. The mother said, 'Here is my child; for some time she has opposed her husband in religion, but now she is convinced of her error, and seeks an interest in your prayers.' The daughter cried, 'Oh! yes, pray for me, for I am forever lost!' Blessed be God, she, with many others, found mercy."

Many pages might be filled, from Newcomer's journal, with very condensed notices of the great and glorious meetings, usually of three days' continuance, held between 1785 and 1800. A few of these notices deserve a permanent record in these pages, as showing the spirit of the early Brethren, and the manifestations of the presence and power of God which attended their labors.

Of a three days' meeting, held not far from Martin Boehm's, in Lancaster county, Pa., we have the following notice:—

"May 21st, 1797.—This day the grace of God was powerfully displayed; several brethren delivered the word with energy and power. On the sacramental occasion, we had a melting time; many approached the table of the Lord with streaming eyes. 22d.—This forenoon, we had our love-feast; it surely was a great time; the brethren and sisters spoke freely and feelingly of the dealings of God with their souls, and many were filled with the dying love of Jesus, and some to overflowing; even my poor soul received a substantial blessing. Glory be to God and the Lamb forever!"

A few days later in the same year and month, a meeting was commenced near Lebanon. "Brother Crum preached the first sermon, when many hearts were tendered, and tears flowed in abundance. Sunday, 28th.—Before day this morning, I received a powerful blessing at the hand of God. I could not remain any longer in bed, but arose praising and shouting, giving glory to

God for all his mercies. Brother Boehm preached the first sermon this forenoon; Brother Crum followed. In the afternoon, I spoke from Ps. ii.: 5, 8. In the evening, we celebrated the dying love of Jesus. This was the last day of our meeting, and the best day of the feast. Many were so filled with the love of Jesus that, like the disciples on the day of Pentecost, they appeared drunken. My heart was not left empty; but how could it be otherwise, when grace flows so abundantly out of the well of salvation. All may partake; all may come and drink of the water of life freely, without money and without price.

"June 3d, 1797.—This day, the sacramental meeting at Antietam. Even at the beginning, the Lord was present in power. In the evening, we held a prayer-meeting at Brother S. Baker's. Several brethren from Baltimore were present: we had a good time. Sunday, 4th.—This forenoon, William Otterbein preached from Ephesians ii.: 1, 6: —'And you hath he quickened, who were dead in trespasses and in sins; wherein, in times past, ye walked according to the course of this world, according to the prince of the power of the air, the spirit that now worketh in the children of disobedience: among whom we all had our conversation in times past, in the lusts of our flesh, fulfilling the desires of the flesh and of the mind, and were, by nature, the children of wrath, even as others. But God, who is rich in mercy, for his great love wherewith he hath loved us, even when we were dead in sins, hath quickened us together with Christ; (by grace are ye saved) and hath raised us up together, and made us sit together in heavenly places in Christ Jesus.' O, how conclusively did he reason! How did he endeavor to persuade his hearers to work out the salvation of their souls! How did he try to convince all of the necessity of vital, experimental religion—of a thorough change of heart! The congregation was uncommonly large, and all seemed to pay the most profound attention." The sacrament was administered, and Draksel preached in the afternoon. "5th.—This day we had an exceedingly glorious time. A great number, both male and female, young people and hoary-headed sinners, were convicted, and some happily converted to God."

Space must be given for a notice of one more of those glorious gatherings of God's people. This was convened in Cumberland county, Pa., in the year 1800.

"Brother Neiding commenced the meeting. At night attended a prayer-meeting. The Lord was powerfully with us. Sunday, 25th.—This morning, Bro. Boehm preached with great power. In the afternoon, I preached from 1 Peter i., 19, with considerable liberty. Before the close of the meeting, several young persons, of both sexes, were brought under conviction, crying aloud, with streaming eyes, for mercy. We prayed with them for some time; and several found the pearl of great price in the pardon of their sins. 26th.—To-day, Bro. Boehm preached again, on the sufferings and death of our Savior, with extraordinary power. * * Every heart present was touched and tendered. Two young women cried out, 'Oh! Lord, what shall we do? We desire to be converted to God, and get religion.' They stated that their father was prayerless; that he cursed and swore, and said, if they joined these people, he would never let them come into his house. Others cried out, 'I am lost! I am lost, and undone! Pray for us! oh! pray for us!' In this manner, several hours passed away, the shouts of salvation following the bitter penitential cries."

The Brethren ministry of this period were of the apostolic stamp. They visited the sick, hunted up the lost sheep, found their way to the prisoner's cell and the felon's dungeon, sought out the destitute, visited from house to house, instructed the children, exhorted the youth,* and, in every way, exerted themselves to the utmost to save men from their sins, and build them up in the faith of the Gospel.

In this great work, they were encouraged and aided, not only by the newly-arrived Methodist evangelists, but by those spiritual men in the Reformed church, whom we have named, such as Hendel and Wagner;†. and men of similar faith and

* To-day, I came to Brother Pfrimmer's. About thirty children had assembled at his house, to whom he was giving religious instruction. Some were under conviction. I also spoke to them. Their hearts were sensibly touched. May the Lord convert them truly.—Newcomer's Journal, May, 1800.

† This day, October 8th, 1797, the church in this place (Shafferstown) was dedicated to God. Rev. Mr. Wagner delivered the first sermon. In the afternoon, Brother Guething preached with a great blessing. By candle-light, Rev. Mr. Hendel delivered a handsome discourse. The next day, Rev. Mr. Rohauser preached in the forenoon, Lochman and Williams in the evening, and Newcomer at night.—N. J., p. 32.

spirit in the Lutheran church, such as Staunch* and the elder Kurtz.

During the last decade of the eighteenth century, quite a number of very promising young ministers were admitted into the conference. These were the fruit of the revival of vital godliness among the German people. The number of members in the communion of the church can not be ascertained. No enumeration had been taken, and there was a very general disinclination to adopt any such measure. The ministerial force numbered thirty-one. Of these, several, as before observed, were young men, and a few only of the whole number were able to devote their whole time to the ministry of the word. Otterbein and Boehm, although still active and very laborious preachers, had each passed his threescore and ten; and Guething had nearly reached his threescore. Others of the ministers were venerable in years, and had seen hard service.

On the 25th of September, A. D. 1800,

---

* The Rev. Mr. Staunch invited us (Brother Draksel and myself) to return with him to his house. In the evening, a select company assembled, and we had much religious conversation, and a little prayer-meeting. This minister and companion are pious. May God bless them abundantly.—Newcomer's Jour.

the conference assembled at Peter Kemp's, in Frederick county, Md.

Preachers present—Otterbein, Boehm, Guething, Pfrimmer, Newcomer, Lehman, Draksel, Christian Crum, Henry Crum, John Hershey, J. Geisinger, Henry Boehm, D. Aurauf, and Jacob Bowlus.

Absent—Neiding, Schaffer, Kreider, Grosh, Abraham Mayer, G. Fortenbaugh, David Snyder, Adam Reigel, A. Hershey, Christian Hershey of Pa., John Ernst, M. Thomas of Md., Simon Herre, Daniel Strickler, John Senseny, Abraham Heistand, and I. Niswander of Va.

In this conference, although the number of ministers was not large, the various parts of the church were well represented, and it was a session of more than usual importance.

Before the business was introduced, Mr. Otterbein prayed, read a portion of Scripture, and delivered a short address. Each preacher then made a plain and definite statement of his experience, and of his purposes in regard to the service of God in the work of the ministry. All expressed a determination, notwithstanding the toils and trials, the persecution and poverty, that awaited them, to continue to labor for the honor of God, and the good of mankind.

Each minister was then examined separately, respecting his progress in the divine life, and success in the work. Especial prominence appears to have been given, in the examination, to the interior life of the ministry.

Up to this period, the church had passed under the name of UNITED BRETHREN, a name which had been previously borne, as we have seen, by three bodies of Christians, of similar spirit, drawn together under similar circumstances, one of which existed long prior to the reformation in the sixteenth century. And, indeed, when converted Mennonites, Lutherans, Reformed, Tunkers, and Amish, were drawn together at great meetings, like the one at Isaac Long's, and those which succeeded it, and when, by providential circumstances, they were compressed into an ecclesiastical organization, no other name seemed appropriate. Its adoption was a moral necessity. A similar providential union had made it a necessity at Fulneck, in 1457; and, at Herrnhut, two hundred and seventy years later. When Count Zinzendorf organized a union church at Herrnhut, in 1727, he was not to be blamed for appropriating the most suitable name; and the same apology, if what God orders and approves needs an apology, will hold good in the case of the United Brethren in Christ.

It was suggested, however, at the conference of 1800, and not without reason, that this name, when employed in wills, deeds, and other legal instruments, might give rise to legal difficulties; and, although a change in the name was not deemed expedient nor desirable, yet, to avoid misapplication and misunderstanding, the words, "IN CHRIST," were added. Hence, since 1800, the proper name of the denomination has been, "THE CHURCH OF THE UNITED BRETHREN IN CHRIST."

The next important item of business transacted, was the election of William Otterbein and Martin Boehm to the office of superintendent or bishop.

It must not be inferred, however, that, up to this period, the church had been without a superintendent. That office had been filled with eminent ability and faithfulness, by Otterbein, up to this period. He had been placed in that responsible relation, not by a formal vote of his brethren, but by the force of those providential circumstances which gave rise to the church—in other words, by the election of God. The care of all the churches had rested upon him; to him all eyes were directed for counsel; every preacher, without an exception, deferred to his judgment; and such was the veneration and affection with which he was regarded, and the confidence in his wisdom and prudence, that, if he said to one, Go, he went willingly; and to another, Come, he came gladly. It was deemed proper, however, at this conference, to elect two superintendents. The choice of the second fell upon Boehm, who, in influence and in usefulness, was second only to Otterbein.

On the forenoon of the second day of the conference, Otterbein preached from Amos iv., 12, and was followed by Boehm.

The day succeeding the close of the conference, a sacramental meeting was commenced, at which, on the Sabbath following, Mr. Otterbein discoursed from Rev. iii.: 7–12. How appropriate this text to the time and the occasion! "And to the angel of the church in Philadelphia write: These things saith he that is holy, he that is true, he that hath the key of David, he that openeth, and no man shutteth; and shutteth, and no man openeth: I know thy works: behold I have set before thee an open door, and no man can shut it: for thou hast a little strength, and hast kept my word, and hast not denied my name." "He spoke," says Newcomer, "with astonishing clearness and perspicuity, and appeared to be inspired with the gift of interpretation."

The measures adopted by the conference of 1800, gave a fresh impetus to the cause of religion. During the succeeding year, ten great meetings, some of which were distinguished by remarkable blessings, were held in different portions of the country. Conversions were numerous, and some of them singularly powerful. At Antietam, and at Abraham Mayer's, especially, grace triumphed, although, as usual, Satan raged and stirred up persecution against the laborers and the converts. At the former place, "father Otterbein," says Newcomer, "preached," on Sabbath forenoon, "with such power and grace, that almost every soul on the ground seemed to be pierced to the heart, * * and the attention of every soul was riveted to the spot. I spoke after him, but only for a short time, when the people broke forth in lamentations for mercy." The succeeding day is described as "a day of grace," "a Pentecost," a day of the outpouring of the Spirit, as in days of old.

In Virginia, the labors of the ministers and brethren were attended with the rich effusions of divine grace. At some of the great meetings, the people fell before the Lord like mown grass; and if the distress of the penitents was deep, and their cries bitter, so was the succeeding joy.

The preachers, for want of time, were hurried away from these meetings, their battle-fields, while yet sinners trembled, tears were falling fast, and mourners were crying, "We are lost!"

It often occurred that the parting hour was an hour of redemption to numerous broken-hearted mourners. The thought that the meeting must be closed, and the faithful ministers depart hastily to other fields of toil, but deepened the wounds already made, and, with holy violence and an agony of earnestness which few can understand or appreciate, they would lay hold on heaven and cry, "I will not let thee go!" "Lord, save, or I perish!" Preachers and people gather once more around them. All hearts are melted. One more prayer is offered. Faith grows mighty, almost omnipotent. Heaven is opened again. The Holy Spirit descends. A shout breaks forth, of "Glory! glory! glory!" Then the evangelists depart, and go on their way to another meeting rejoicing.

> "On thy church, O, power divine,
> Cause thy glorious face to shine
> Till the nations from afar,
> Hail her as their guiding star.
>
> "Then shall God, with mighty hand,
> Scatter blessings o'er the land,
> And the world's remotest bound,
> With the voice of praise resound.
>
> "Lord, thy church hath seen thee rise
> To thy temple in the skies:
> God, my Savior! God, my king!
> Hear thy ransomed people sing.
>
> "When, in glories all divine,
> Through the earth thy church shall shine,
> Kings, in prayer and praise, shall wait,
> Bending at thy temple's gate."*

* Spayth, pp. 84, 85.

CHAPTER XII.

CONFERENCES OF 1801 AND 1802—GREAT MEETINGS—LOVE-FEASTS.

On the 23d of September, A. D. 1801, the conference again assembled at Peter Kemp's, in Frederick county, Maryland. There were twenty ministers present, whose names follow:—Otterbein, Boehm, Newcomer, Strickler, Guething, Peter Senseny, Neiding, Daniel Long, Mayer, Schaffer, Geisinger, John Hershey, Thomas Winter, L. Duckwald, Snyder, Peter Kemp, Matthias Kessler, Christian Crum, Abraham Hershey, and Thomas. Peter Senseny, Long, Winter, Duckwald, and Kessler, were new members. The names of the ministers who were absent are not given in the minutes.

The conference was opened with prayer and an address by Otterbein. He stated in the address, and dwelt upon the truth, *"that salvation comes alone through Jesus Christ, and that, if we are delivered from sin,* we must thank him only for it." The first day of the session was taken up in a relation of personal Christian experience, and a general statement, by the preachers, of the labors, trials, and success of the year. These relations and statements were of a very affecting and interesting character. The reports in relation to the progress of the cause in the different parts of the work, were highly encouraging. Success in winning souls had attended the labors of the ministers pretty generally, and the societies were in a state of prosperity. The second day's session was opened with reading from Revelation 14th chapter, and "prayer to Almighty God," (we quote the minutes) "that he may make us willing to preach the Gospel, and that he may enable us to live as we preach to others." The members of the conference were then all examined in relation to their moral and official character, and their usefulness in the ministry. When the question was asked, "Who belongs to the itinerancy?" the following brethren gave their names:—Christian Newcomer, David Snyder, M. Thomas, Abraham Hershey, Daniel Strickler, Abraham Mayer,

Frederick Schaffer, David Long, John Neiding, and Peter Kemp.

The following important resolutions were adopted:—

"1. Resolved, That each preacher, after preaching, shall hold a conversation with those who may be seeking the conversion of their souls, whoever they may be.

"2. Resolved, That the preachers shall aim to be short, and to avoid all superfluous words in their sermons and prayers; yet, should the Spirit of God lead them to lengthen their sermons, it is their duty to follow the divine direction."

To this second resolution was appended this simple and appropriate petition,—"Oh! God, give us wisdom and understanding to do all according to thy will. Amen."

It was also resolved that each preacher who could not attend the annual sessions of the conference, should give the conference due notice of the fact.

On the last day of the conference, Mr. Otterbein, as was his custom, preached a conference sermon, from Jude, 20th to the 25th inclusive. The reader will not be displeased to find the whole text quoted here:

"20. But ye, beloved, building up yourselves on your most holy faith, praying in the Holy Ghost,

"21. Keep yourselves in the love of God, looking for the mercy of our Lord Jesus Christ unto eternal life.

"22. And of some have compassion, making a difference:

"23. And others save with fear, pulling them out of the fire; hating even the garment spotted by the flesh.

"24. Now unto him that is able to keep you from falling, and to present you faultless before the presence of his glory with exceeding joy,

"25. To the only wise God our Savior, be glory and majesty, dominion and power, both now and ever. Amen."

The leading topics of this discourse were

1. The sanctity of the ministerial office.

2. The character of the men who should take upon them this office. They must be men of faith, of prayer, and full of the Holy Ghost.

3. The duties of the office.

4. Its great responsibilities.

While treating upon the responsibilities of the ministerial office, the force of his remarks were overpowering. Tears flowed from every eye, and preachers and people wept together. The impressions made by this sermon were not soon forgotten. Newcomer says: "The impression made upon my poor heart will, I trust, abide with me as long as life shall last."

The meetings, during the conference, were attended with the divine blessing, and a number of conversions to God occurred. Great unanimity and brotherly love prevailed throughout. On the third day, conference adjourned to meet the following October. The minutes are signed thus:—

MARTIN BOEHM.
WILLIAM OTTERBEIN.
GEORGE ADAM GUETHING.

The CONFERENCE OF 1802 met at the house of Brother John Cronise, in Frederick county, Md., not far from Peter Kemp's, October 6th, 1802. Otterbein and Boehm presided. The conference was opened with singing and prayer, by Boehm, followed by an address from Otterbein. The preachers were all examined, according to rule, as usual, and, to their comfort and joy, all were found to be walking in the path of duty. No circumstance occurred during the session, to interrupt the peace and harmony of the deliberations.

The only new name which appears upon the minutes, is that of William Ambrose, of Virginia. Two brethren were authorized to exhort, and Ludwig Duckwald and John Neiding received permission to "administer all the ordinances of the house of God, according to the Scriptures."

The question in regard to keeping a register of the names of the members in the church, again came up, and was discussed. A motion, favoring such a register, was lost by a vote of nine against three. A number of the members were, probably, neutral, as they did not vote at all.

The subject of prayer-meetings was also brought before the conference, and a resolution was passed, enjoining it upon preachers to establish and maintain prayer-meetings at every appointment where at all practicable.

Some proposals were made in regard to the collection of a fund for the relief of poor ministers. It does not appear, however, that any definite plan was fixed upon. The following resolution was passed:—

"Resolved, That, if any of our preachers

shall do any thing wrong, it shall be the duty of the preacher next (or nearest) to him, to talk to him, privately, in relation to the wrong. If he does not listen to him, or accept his advice, he shall take with him one or two more preachers; and if he does not listen to them, he shall be silenced until the next session of conference."

The following resolution was also adopted:—Resolved, That, in case one of our superintendents—W. Otterbein or Martin Boehm—should die, another minister shall be elected to fill the place. This is the wish of those two brethren, and the unanimous wish of all the preachers present."

From this resolution, it appears that, in 1802, the utility and importance of the office of general superintendent, or bishop, was duly appreciated by the venerable fathers, Otterbein and Boehm, and by their younger brethren.

The conference sermon was preached on the second day of the session, by Otterbein, from Heb. xiii.: 17. He was followed in an address by Boehm.

In the afternoon of the third day of the session, after the business had all been dispatched, and just before the adjournment, the conference listened to another address from Otterbein. "He exhorted us," says Newcomer, "particularly, to be careful to preach no other doctrine than that which is plainly laid down in the Bible; that nothing less than a new creature in Christ Jesus will be acceptable in the sight of God; that we should be ardently and diligently engaged in the work of the Lord; and, lastly, that we should love one another, and, for Jesus' sake, suffer and endure all things."

The preachers went to their fields of labor full of faith and the Holy Ghost. A few days after the conference, a quarterly meeting was held at Hoffman's, in Rockingham county, Va. Let the good Newcomer give us, in his own simple language, an account of this meeting:

"Brother Guething spoke with tender compassion; the people began to cry aloud. The meeting was held in a barn. When Brother Guething had closed his remarks, I arose, went among the people in the congregation, exhorting them to accept of the overtures of mercy. Presently a young man fell on my neck, crying and calling aloud: 'Oh! Mr. Newcomer, what shall I do?—what shall I do to be saved?' I replied, believe in the Lord Jesus Christ. Instantly, two others (who were brothers) fell on their knees, each crying, 'What shall I do? I am lost forever. Oh! Lord Jesus, have mercy on me.' A young woman fell down, crying for mercy: her sister, who was sitting beside her, with a child in her arms, instantly laid it on the floor, imploring the mercy of God. Next came the mother, also crying, 'Oh! Lord—mercy, mercy for myself and children.' The father also drew nigh, took the child up, to prevent its being hurt in the group, and stood alongside of his children and wife, with tears streaming down his furrowed cheeks. O, what a sight! The scene could not be beheld without emotion. The whole congregation began to cry and moan; the excitement became general. Presently one fell here, another there; a woman hanging on the bosom of her beloved companion; a daughter in the arms of her distressed mother: all crying for mercy. Never before have I witnessed the power of God in so great a degree, among so many people. We commenced singing and praying; and, glory be to God, many distressed souls found peace, and pardon of their sins, in the blood of the Lamb. The meeting was protracted till late at night. I went home with Mr. and Mrs. Meyer, a godly, pious pair; they entertained me very friendly.

"21st.—This day the congregation was still more numerous than the day before. Brother Guething spoke first, with great power, from 1 Cor. i.; v. 23, 24: I followed him. The power of God was again signally displayed, the love of Jesus shed abroad, and united all hearts in the bonds of brotherly love. At the administration of the sacrament, you could perceive all distinction of sects lost in Christian love and fellowship. Lutherans, Presbyterians, Mennonites, Baptists, and Methodists, all drew near the Lord's table, and united in commemoration of the dying love of the Redeemer. Many were not able to avoid shouting and praising God for his unbounded mercy and goodness. With difficulty, we parted from the people, but we were compelled to leave them, in order to fill our appointment at Mr. Hivener's, about ten miles distant."

"Nineteen great meetings were held during this year. The times selected for holding these meetings, were the months of May, June, August, September, and October. The holding of these meetings formed, as we have already seen, another link in the chain of reformation. It was a new measure, but one which was productive of much good, and resulted in the best of consequences. They afforded an enlarged field of action, and a wider spread of the knowledge of true religion; and a fit opportunity to enforce the practice of its moral precepts. Hundreds, and we may say thousands, by these means, came to hear, who, in the ordinary way of holding religious or divine worship, would not have been brought under the saving influence of this dispensation of life. Prejudices which had taken possession of the minds of many, accompanied by a sectarian spirit, were thereby more or less removed or shorn of their strength, and the best of all was, many experienced a change of heart. On the Sabbath day, the concourse of people was frequently such as to render the administration of the holy sacrament on that day impracticable. When this was the case, the love-feast and the sacrament were held on Monday. Those love-feasts in the early days of the rise of the church, were peculiar to the time, and characteristic of the progress of a glorious reformation, wrought by HIM who holds the seven stars in his right hand, and who said, 'Behold I have set before thee an open door.' The distinctive divisions, which embraced the German population and churches, (as stated elsewhere) consisting of Lutheran, German Reformed, Mennonite, and Tunkers, had, previously, and at this very period, little or no Christian fellowship or communion with each other as churches. But here at these meetings they were seen and found worshiping God together, from the four divisions. We say in those love-feasts, the Tunker, the Mennonite, and the high-churchman, were seen to rise alternately, and tell their Christian experience. Men whose heads had become silvered by age, with the middle-aged and the youth, testified, for the first time, that God had bestowed upon them his mercy, and had pardoned their sins. The simplicity, the earnestness, with which this testimony was delivered, could not fail to carry conviction with it. These witnesses showed how hard it was to give up all, in the midst of persecution, the derision of friends, and false comforts of pastors, and to persevere in faith and prayer, until the blessing came. Two or three cases we will state in words nearly, and we might say, word for word, as they passed.

"One arose and said, 'I was brought up in the church, I was catechised and confirmed, have been a member of the church for twenty years, and yet, now only do I know, by experience, the realities of religion.'

"Another said, 'I was raised a Mennonite, —was received into that society in my eighteenth year. I am now forty years old. I led a moral life, and was frequently told by my teachers, all was safe. But, six months ago, I found myself a poor lost sinner. Oh! I saw myself a great sinner, condemned by the word of God and the tribunal of my own conscience. My distress was great, but God has had mercy upon me, and blessed me. Christ died for me. I love the Lord, I love his people. Oh! come, you are all my brethren,—you Reformed, you Lutherans, you my Mennonite brethren, who have not yet experienced the love of God. I was like you; you know it: oh! come, seek Jesus.'

"And yet another arose tremblingly, and the tears were rolling down his face. 'Brethren, I came fifty miles to this meeting. I was raised in the church. I was catechised, and was praised for learning the questions and answers so well. I was confirmed, partook of the holy sacrament, was a member in the church, attended preaching faithfully, and paid the preachers. I was considered, by my neighbors and friends, a good Christian, although they knew I sometimes used profane language, with other conduct unbecoming a Christian. Some of the preachers who are now on the stand, came and preached in my neighborhood. I would not go to hear them myself. The man who invited them to his house to preach, had been a particular friend of mine until he had preaching at his house. He tried to reason with me, but I would listen to no reason. I said to him, you and I have been confirmed together, and are members of one church, what do you want with preaching at your house? Is the preaching we have not sufficient? I hope you are not going to forsake the religion of your forefathers. What do you mean by saying we must be converted, and pray to be saved? This is a new religion; I want none of it. Why should *I pray?* The preacher prays for me, and I pay him for it. I was angry, and left him.

" 'But it so happened that some of my family went to hear the Brethren preach. One evening, news was brought me, that my son was praying for mercy. Now, my wrath, for a time, knew no bounds; but I hoped I could soon cure him of it. I invited our preacher to visit us, believing he would soon talk my son out of his praying notions. But he referred the preacher to the Bible, and the promise he had made in confirmation, which he had not kept, and could not keep, except God would give him a clean heart, and renew a right spirit within him. The preacher became thoughtful, and left; I followed him out to the gate. Well, what do you say of my son? 'Oh, it is best not to talk with him about religion at this time. He had better not read much in the Bible or Testament. Give him money, and keep him out of the way of those preachings and prayer-meetings,' &c., &c. But my son continued praying, and I kept my wrath. I now began to hate my neighbor, and wished those preachers and all of them were dead. I cursed them in my heart. Some time after this, the word was circulated that a big meeting was to be held at my neighbor Miller's. We were cautioned, from the pulpit, not to go near it, nor to hear, lest the false prophets which should come in the last time, might deceive us, and I resolved not to go. But when the time for the meeting came, on Sabbath morning, I thought I might safely go and hear a false prophet, for I had never heard one preach. I determined to be on my guard, and to keep just in hearing distance. When I first saw the preachers on the stand, my anger was somewhat raised against them. After preaching, however, I felt calm, and addressed a friend, saying, why, these men are like other men, only they would make one feel like a guilty sinner in the course of their preaching.

"'Monday morning, from a mere desire to see the end of this meeting, I went again; and, when one, and then another, rose up to tell their experience, I was surprised to hear men and women stand up in the congregation, and speak and talk about Jesus. But while some were telling how they had sinned against God, how they had been awakened and alarmed, how they had wept and mourned, and how the Lord had blessed them, and how they hoped to meet their Christian friends in heaven, this cut me to the heart. I went home, and what I had heard and seen in that meeting followed me night and day. Mourn and pray—meet friends in heaven—can I say so? No. Next day, when my wife looked at me, I thought she said to me, 'In heaven!' my son, too, I thought, said, 'In heaven!' and the wind, which blew sharply that day, seemed to whisper, 'In heaven!' My peace was gone; I saw and felt that I was a great sinner; and what to do, I knew not, or I did not want to know. I consulted our preacher again, and all the comfort which I received from him was, 'You had no business at that meeting, you were cautioned not to go, and now if you be foolish enough to make shipwreck of your faith,' (which, however, he hoped I would not do) 'I have cleared my skirts of your blood. You and those preachers may see to it.'

" 'But, said I, if the half is true of what I heard at that meeting, then I have no

religion; my own heart condemns me. But
you are our preacher, and you should know
best.

"'He replied, 'You have a religion, and
you promised to live and die in this faith
and this religion; what do you want with
another religion?'

"'I 'don't want another religion; I asked
you, Mr. Pastor, (*Herr Pfarrer*) what I
should do; I am a sinner, and feel condemned. Many at the meeting said they
had experienced great distress of mind, but
God had blessed them, pardoned their sins,
and they were happy; but I am unhappy—
miserable. Tell me, am I in no danger?
am I not lost?

"'He gave a deep sigh, but said, 'We are
all poor sinners in this world.'

"'I felt a desire to open the Bible, and
the first verse I read was, 'Come unto me
all ye that are weary and heavy laden, and
I will give you rest.' Light sprang up in
my mind, fear vanished; I felt, and now
feel, joy and peace in my Redeemer.'

"Many others related their Christian experience in few words; but the shortest
was both interesting and instructive. In
the administration of the sacrament, distinc-

tion of sects and churches appeared, for the time, to be lost in Christian fellowship and love; and, as one, they were seen approaching the Lord's table as sons and daughters of one Father—even our Father in heaven, and celebrating the dying love of Jesus Christ, the glorious Redeemer.

"These meetings, however long they have been in use in the church, have not lost in interest and vitality to this day. They have been most signally owned and blessed as a means of grace, by the great Head of the church; and there is no doubt but that there are many in heaven who have dated their conviction and conversion to them."*

"Oh! great is Jehovah, and great be his praise,
  In the city of God he is King;
Proclaim ye, his ransomed, in heavenly strains,
  On the mount of his holiness sing.

The joy of the earth, from her beautiful hight,
  Is Zion's most glorious hill;
The Lord in her temple still taketh delight,
  God reigns in her palaces still.

Let the daughters of Judah be glad for thy love,
  The mountain of Zion rejoice,
For thou wilt establish her seat from above,
  Wilt make her the theme of thy choice.

Then say to your children—Our refuge is tried,
  This God is our God to the end;
His people forever his counsels shall guide,
  His arm shall forever defend.
MONTGOMERY.

* Spayth, pp. 88--95.

CHAPTER XIII.

CONFERENCES OF 1803–4. — PENTECOSTAL MEETINGS—THE BENEFITS.

In the year 1803, on the 5th of October, the annual conference assembled at David Snyder's, in Cumberland county, Pa. The following members were present:—Otterbein, Boehm, Newcomer, Snyder, John Hershey, Kemp, Mayer, Grosh, Christian Crum, Valentine Flugel, John Winter, Schaffer, Guething, and George Benedum.

"The conference was opened"—we quote the secretary's devout record—"by reading 1st Timothy, 2d chapter, singing and prayer, that our Lord and Savior may bless our assembling together, and that it may be to the honor of his name and our edification. O Lord! hear us, for Christ's sake. Amen." These minutes were probably written by Guething, as they were signed by Otterbein, Boehm, and Guething, and they bear the marks of a devout and spiritual mind.

The preachers were all examined, and their official character and usefulness inquired into particularly. Some of the resolutions at this conference will be interesting to the reader. We insert a liberal translation of them from the original German.*

"Resolved, That Daniel Strickler and Christian Crum call a meeting of the preachers in Virginia, to arrange their fields of labor. May God grant them wisdom and strength from above.

"Resolved, That the supplying of the fields of labor in Maryland be left to the preachers of Maryland.

"Resolved, That Martin Boehm and Christian Grosh be a committee to station the preachers in Pennsylvania.

"Resolved, That David Snyder, Abraham Mayer, and George Benedum, make their own arrangements in regard to their preaching places. May the Lord assist them. Amen.

"Resolved, That Christian Newcomer and Henry Crum unite with Christian Berger, to travel through the portion of country where he resides.

"Resolved, That those two brethren give

* Translation by Rev. J. Degmeier.

authority to Christian Berger to baptize, but nothing further at present.

"Resolved, That, after preaching, the preachers shall spend a short time with the awakened souls of their congregations."

These resolutions show that the work had extended so far that it was not practicable for the conference in Pennsylvania to arrange the work for the preachers in Maryland and Virginia; hence, the permission given those preachers to meet in separate conferences for this single purpose.

The resolution requiring the preachers to hold class-meetings or religious conferences with awakened souls, after preaching, is suggestive of the fact that those early ministers seldom preached a sermon which was not made the power of God unto the salvation of some souls. Conversions occurred continually at ordinary appointments; and sometimes eight or ten, or more, were awakened and redeemed at a single meeting.

The religious services, during this conference, were highly interesting. The first sermon was preached by Christian Grosh, from John iii., 1, on the first evening of the session. In the forenoon of the second day, a sermon, of remarkable power, was preached by Otterbein. He was followed by Boehm. After a session of three days, conference adjourned.

"On the 8th, a meeting commenced at Brother Shopp's. Father Boehm opened the meeting, and preached with great power. The word reached the heart; many were deeply affected. The slain of the Lord were found lying in every direction, lamenting and crying aloud for mercy. Many obtained peace with God in the pardon of their sins.

"Love-feast held on Sabbath morning. The brethren and sisters spoke very feelingly, and with great liberty, of the dealings and mercies of God. It was a refreshing season. Father Otterbein preached with great power and energy. The grace of God wrought powerfully among the people. A man fell suddenly to the ground, and cried for mercy; others were so affected, that they were unable to move from where they were sitting or standing; and, at the close of the meeting, some had to be led, and some carried away."

"A gracious revival of religion took place this year, 1803, west of the Allegheny mountains, in what is called the Glades, also in Westmoreland and Washington counties, under the preaching of Brother J. G. Pfrimmer and Christian Berger. Brother C. Newcomer, who visited those parts that year, writes under date of November 10th:—

"'Preached at John Bonnet's. I had not spoken long, before some of my hearers fell to the floor; others stood trembling, and cried so loud that my voice could not well be heard.

"'On the 11th, we had meeting at Schwope's, and here the power of God was displayed in a most marvelous manner. The whole congregation was moved, and seemed to wave like corn before a mighty wind. Lamentation and mourning were very general. Many were the wounded and slain. Some of the most stubborn sinners fell instantly before the power of God. The meeting continued the whole night, and some were enabled to rejoice in the pardoning love of God.

"'On Sunday, we had a Pentecost. From three to four hundred persons had collected; more than the barn, in which we had assembled for worship, would contain. The congregation was remarkably attentive to the word. Though it rained, those that had no shelter in the barn kept their stand in the rain. During the time of preaching, the exhibition of God's power for the salvation of the people was seen and felt. Many fell from their seats; some laid as if they were dead. The weeping, and crying, and praying, came from all parts of the congregation.' "*

Remarking upon the meeting at Schwope's, Mr. Spayth says: "From the time of this meeting, twenty years had passed away, when the writer had the happiness to become acquainted with brethren and sisters who, at that meeting, had espoused the cause of religion, and who were still faithful servants of the Lord. Some of these have I met in the far west, to which they had emigrated, and where they had raised the standard of the CROSS. And though years had fled away since that blessed period in their life, and being now far distant from the place where God had first spoken peace to their then troubled souls, their memory still lingered with delight around that happy scene. And more than this, we have seen some of them spend

* Newcomer's Journal.

their last hour on earth, heard their last prayer, and have seen them die in peace.

"What are the benefits and advantages which we may expect to reap from religious meetings, distinguished and marked by such effects upon the assembled multitude, through the preaching of the Gospel and the agency of the Holy Ghost, as we have just witnessed? We put the question again, and ask—and all who will may ask—with serious and candid reflections, what are the benefits, the advantages, the results? Let those most competent to judge, answer. Let those who have been the immediate subjects of this excitement, of this divine power, *answer*. Let those who have been benefited by the conversion of others, *answer*. Let the illustrious trophies of the blessed Gospel, in the hands of an itinerant ministry, *answer*. Let prayer-meetings, class-meetings, and love-feast-meetings, *answer;* above all, let the word of God, the song of the redeemed in heaven, and the fruitless remorse of lost souls, *answer!*

"In view of this momentous and sublime subject, few, indeed, if any, will be found, who will be so suicidal as to **desire** a church that is silent or rejects this part of the economy of grace, and whose ministration is performed, year in and year out, in the absence of sinners trembling because of sin, mourners weeping, and crying to God for mercy and pardon, and where the shout of the blessed of the Lord is never heard within her walls.

"That the Brethren church has been identified with a blessed work of grace, from the reception of the first ray of Gospel light, which she was permitted to reflect, and which has, from that period to the present day, continued to shine around her with increasing strength, her present position amply sustains; and, in a retrospect of the past, will be equally sustained by the best of testimony. From Newcomer's Journal, dated Glades, Somerset county, Pa., Nov. 19th, 1803, we will make some extracts which come in place here:

"'Preached this day at Michael Sterner's, to a numerous congregation. Rode to Zug's, followed by many of the persons whom we had addressed at Sterner's. Here we met with a still larger congregation. I gave an exhortation; the hearts of the hearers were immediately touched; all, young and old, began to cry and pray. A man fell to the floor, and lay a considerable time as if lifeless. Sunday, 20th.—This forenoon, the meeting was very dull. Addressed the audience from 1 Peter i.: 3, 4, 5. Brother C. Crum spoke also, and it pleased God to accompany the word with power, and many cried aloud for mercy. We dismissed the people, but they had no desire to depart. I addressed them again. We met again at candle-light, and the presence of the Lord continued with us. On every side the people fell to the floor. Among these was a youth of about thirteen years of age. Some were struck with awe, others flew into a passion, taking hold of their friends and carrying them out of the house, saying this was the work of the Devil. I endeavored to persuade them, with meekness, to let the distressed alone, to have a little patience, that God would bless their friends, and restore them to consciousness again; adding, if it is the work of the Devil, or the powers of darkness, your friends will curse when they revive; and if the work is of God, they will pray and praise the Lord. They had carried the youth up stairs, and there laid him on a bed, watching him with great anxiety.

When he came to himself, he began to praise the Lord, and exhorted all around him in so wonderful a manner, that a number of them came in distress, confessing, with tears, that they had sinned against God, and saying, 'What shall we do to be saved?' They sent for me to come and pray for them, for, said they, 'We are lost and undone forever.' And some of these also obtained mercy and pardon; and now they again, in turn, exhorted their friends to fly to the outstretched arms of sovereign mercy.'

"This year, conference was appointed to meet at the house of Brother David Snyder, Cumberland county, Pa., October 3d, 1804. But an epidemic prevailing to a great extent (such as had not been known) in Maryland, and in the vicinity where the conference was to sit, but five brethren came to attend, to-wit:—Martin Boehm, Frederick Schaffer, C. Newcomer, Abraham Mayer, and Matthias Bortsfield. The brethren thus met, examined the letters sent into the conference, and, no more brethren arriving, adjourned the meeting, after resolving that the next annual conference should be held at Brother Jacob Baulus', near Middletown, Maryland, on the Wednesday before White-Sunday, 1805.

"May 19th, a sacramental meeting commenced at the Antietam, (G. A. Guething's house) at which Father Otterbein was present, and preached on Saturday, from Isa. li.: 7, 8. On the Sabbath, Father Otterbein preached again, from Psalms lxxii., with his usual energy, perspicuity, unction, and power. Under preaching, and at the communion-table, tears of sorrow and of joy flowed abundantly, and the wells of salvation furnished a rich supply.

"Doctor Senseny, of Winchester, Virginia, died this year. Brother Senseny had been an early member of the Brethren church, and for some years, and up to the time of his death, an acceptable and useful preacher. His business was the medical profession, in which he was very successful, possessing much skill and talent for usefulness in that department. In his attendance on the sick, he had made it his constant practice to say a word to the patient, of Jesus, the great Physician of souls, and often was seen to kneel at the bedside of the sick, and pray fervently. His exemplary life, his humility, his love and kindness, his piety, and charity to the poor, secured to him the respect, esteem, and love, of all who came within the sphere of his acquaintance. His last illness was very brief. He had but a few days' notice of his approaching death. Surrounded by a dearly-beloved family—wife, and sons, and daughters,—and dear brethren in the church, and wealth, and friends, he met this sudden call of his divine Master with Christian resignation, and was enabled to leave this world with joy and peace, saying, 'Lord Jesus, I come!' "*

* Spayth, pp. 98—104.

CHAPTER XIV.

A GLANCE AT THE CONFERENCES, FROM 1805 TO 1812.—FIRST CONFERENCE IN OHIO.

ON the 29th of May, 1805, conference convened at Jacob Baulus', in Frederick county, Maryland. Twenty-one preachers were in attendance. The minutes say:— "The preachers resolved, by the grace of God, to engage, with more earnestness than ever before, in the work of the Lord. Oh, Lord, help thou us, thy poor and unworthy servants, for thy name's sake."

Otterbein and Boehm were re-elected superintendents or bishops. This election would have been held at the conference of the preceding year, had not the prevalent sickness, noticed in a previous chapter, prevented a full attendance of the members of conference. It is evident from this that the brethren intended, from the first, that the election of superintendents should, providence favoring, occur quadrennially.

It was arranged, as we learn from the minutes, that Newcomer should travel the following year, through Maryland and a portion of Pennsylvania, and that Christian Crum should travel through Virginia; and it was agreed that each of these brethren should receive, for his support, per annum, the pittance of 40 livres. It was resolved that George Adam Guething be present at the great meetings appointed in Maryland, and, also, on the east side of the Susquehannah in Pennsylvania. It was recommended that Hagerstown be regularly visited by the Brethren preachers. One resolution we quote entire:—"Resolved, That the preachers who preach only where they like, or choose, shall receive no compensation for their services, and that it shall be the duty of such preachers to pay over to the conference the money they receive in this way, for the benefit of the traveling preachers." "Permission was granted to Brother Duckwald and Christian Berger to baptize, administer the Lord's Supper, and to solemnize marriages." All the business which came before the conference was attended to with perfect harmony of feeling. This was the last conference attended by Otterbein.

He had now attained his seventy-ninth year, and Boehm his eightieth. More than forty years before, these faithful servants of God had met, in the prime of life, at the great meeting at Isaac Long's, and had embraced each other as brethren, and from that period up to the conference at Jacob Baulus', as often as once a year, they had been associated together at conferences, or at great meetings, or at both, to preach, exhort, and to counsel in regard to the work of reformation among the people. Together they had witnessed the most astonishing displays of the grace and power of God. A faithful body of co-laborers had been raised up around them. The good seed had been sown in nearly all those portions of Pennsylvania, Maryland, and Virginia, where the German language was spoken; and, also, in the new settlements west of the Alleghanies; and it was producing an abundant harvest. Now, for the last time, these two venerable evangelists have sat together in the conference of their brethren; and, for the last time, their trembling signatures are recorded, side by side, on the conference minutes.

The conference of 1806 was held at Bro.

Eberhart's, in Frederick county, Md. It convened on the 21st, and adjourned on the 24th of May.

The question was asked at this conference, "Are all the preachers united in love?" The answer given is worthy of record:—"We are," said they, "not only united among ourselves, *but we also love all our fellow-men, whoever they may be.*" Joseph Hoffman and Christian Crum were appointed to travel the ensuing year; a letter was written to the brethren in Pennsylvania; the next conference was appointed to be held in Pennsylvania; great meetings were announced in various portions of the work, and brethren appointed to take charge of them.

In 1807, the conference met in Pennsylvania, at Christian Herre's. Martin Boehm presided. The session was short, and, as usual, peaceful. Work was laid out, at this conference, for Abraham Niswander, Christian Smith, David Snyder, Abraham Mayer, John Hershey, Frederick Schaffer, John Neiding, Joseph Hoffman, and Christian Newcomer; and authority was given Isaac Niswander and Abraham Mayer to administer all the ordinances of the house of God.

The conference of 1808 **met** in Virginia, May 25th, at Abraham Niswander's. The following ministers were in attendance:— Christian Newcomer, Joseph Hoffman, David Snyder, Isaac Niswander, Peter Kemp, William Ambrose, Ludwig Duckwald, Christian Crum, Frederick Duckwald, Abraham Mayer, Jacob Baulus, John Hershey, Geo. Adam Guething, and George Hoffman.

After an examination of the moral and official character of the preachers, little appears to have been done, except to arrange the labor for the ensuing year. It was— "Resolved, That those who desire to receive license to preach among us, shall be examined at a great meeting; and, if favorably reported, two of the elders shall grant them license for one year, at the end of which time they shall appear before the conference, for examination. In case they can not appear at the conference, their license may be renewed at a great meeting."

Again the conference convened at Christian Herre's, in Lancaster county, Pa., May 10th, 1809. The members present were— Martin Boehm, Christian Newcomer, Abraham Mayer, Adam Reigel, Isaac Niswander, Frederick Schaffer, Christian Smith, John Hershey, Matthias Bortsfield, Joseph Hoffman, Abraham Hershey, George Benedum, George Adam Guething, David Long, Christopher Grosh, Christian Hershey, David Snyder, and John Snyder. The subject of a union or co-operation with the Methodists, occupied much of the time.

Conference met June 6th, 1810, in Frederick county, Md., at the house of John Cronise. Sixteen preachers were present; and letters were read from Otterbein, L. and F. Duckwald, F. Schaffer, and other absent brethren. The church at Baltimore had had the subject of a closer union with the Methodists under consideration, and sent a letter to the conference in relation thereto. Provision was made at this conference for a more careful superintendence of the circuits. The elder preachers were required to visit all the appointments, on all the fields of labor, twice during the year, if at all practicable.

A letter, from the Methodist conference, was received, considered, and answered, in a fraternal spirit.

On the 13th of July, 1787, the Continental Congress, sitting in New York, adopted An Ordinance for the government of the Territory of the United States *north-west of the Ohio*, which concludes with "six unalterable articles of perpetual compact," the last of which declares that "there shall be neither slavery nor involuntary servitude in the said territory, otherwise than in punishment for crimes, whereof the parties shall be duly convicted."

The year following the adoption of this ordinance, the first permanent settlement was made in Ohio, at Marietta. In 1789, another settlement was made six miles below Cincinnati; and, in 1796, some New Englanders established themselves at Cleveland. In 1802, Ohio formed a constitution, and was admitted into the Union. The mighty march of emigration, which, in half a century, has resulted in the establishment, in the north-west, of a mighty empire, was now fairly commenced.

As early as 1803, some United Brethren, seeking homes for themselves and their children, penetrated into the forests of Ohio. Their first settlements appear to have been made in the Miami Valley, near Germantown and Dayton. A society, and, probably, the *first* United Brethren society in the State, was organized at A. Zeller's, near Germantown, in 1806. During that year, some persons were converted at Mr. Zeller's house, who are still living, and who, for more than fifty years, have been following on to know the Lord. Among the first preachers who emigrated to the Miami Valley, we find the names of Andrew Zeller—afterward a bishop of the church, Daniel Troyer—still alive, and bending under the weight of almost ninety years, and Thomas Winter—now a member of the Reformed church.

About the time that the Zeller, Kemp, Troyer, Sowers, and other Brethren families, settled in the Miami country, some preachers and members of the church emigrated to that rich and beautiful portion of the State which lies between Zanesville and Chillicothe. Among the preachers associated with the rise of the United Brethren in that part of the State, we find the names of Geo. Benedum, Abraham Heistand, and Dewalt Mechlin.

These early preachers found, in the new and rapidly-improving State, many open doors. The calls for preachers were numerous, the labor required severe, and the compensation exceedingly small.

The distance to the conference in the east was so great, however, that the brethren in the west could not attend it; and it became necessary, therefore, to organize a conference in Ohio. The conference in the east, having received communications from the west upon the subject, authorized Christian Newcomer to make a visit to the west, and to hold a conference. Accordingly, the FIRST CONFERENCE IN THE WEST met at Brother MICHAEL CRIDER's, in Ross County, Ohio, and was organized on the 13th of August, 1810. Fifteen preachers were present. Unfortunately, the records of the early conferences in Ohio have been lost; but, from brief notices of them in Newcomer's journal, as well as from the statements of some aged men still living, who attended those conferences, we learn that the Spirit of the Lord was with the Brethren, in their western homes, and worked mightily among them and by them. The conference in the west soon became a very influential portion of the church. The calls for preaching, in every direction, were numerous; societies were rapidly multiplied, and many preachers were raised up to aid those who had emigrated from the east. After 1810, conferences were held regularly in Ohio. The rise and progress of the church in the west, however, will come more particularly under our notice in a subsequent volume of this history.

The conference of 1811 met, May 23d, in Cumberland county, Pa. Twenty ministers were present, a number of whom were new members. Letters were received from absent brethren in Virginia, Maryland, and Ohio. The salary of a single preacher was fixed at $80 a year.

The conference convened at Antietam, May 13th, 1812. Twenty members were in attendance. Their names follow:—Christian Newcomer, Christian Crum, George A. Guething, Abraham Draksel, Abraham Mayer, Joseph Hoffman, Christian Smith, Isaac Niswander, David Snyder, Valentine Baulus, Jacob Baulus, Abraham Hershey, Lorenzo Eberhart, M. Thomas, Jacob Clymer, Christian Berger, Henry Heistand, Henry G. Spayth, Martin Crider, and Jacob Dehoff.

The examination of the members was attended to in a brotherly manner, and "the presence of the Lord was felt," says the secretary. He adds: "Thanks be to God through all eternity." The minutes of this conference were the last penned by the devout and holy Guething. His record begins with—"*Sanctify them through thy truth, thy word is truth! Do it, Lord Jesus, for thy own sake! Amen.*" And now, before laying down his pen, he writes: "Thanks be to God through all eternity!"

July 30th and October 29th were appointed as days of fasting, prayer, and thanksgiving, to be observed throughout the church. The work was placed under the care of superintendents or elders, who were assigned their districts, and were authorized to hold small conferences on the circuits, whenever necessary. It was determined that preaching be given by the itinerant preachers, at all the appointments, once in four weeks. The salary of a single preacher was fixed at $80 per annum; that of a traveling preacher, at $160, and traveling expenses. Henry Heistand and Henry G. Spayth were added to the itinerant list. Christian Newcomer was authorized to visit the brethren in Ohio, and to hold a conference there. "Lord give him grace," says the secretary.

Delegates were present at this conference with letters from the Baltimore and Philadelphia conferences of the M. E. church. They were kindly received; and it was "unanimously resolved that friendship and love shall be maintained between the two churches," and corresponding delegates were appointed.

The minutes give a list of all the ministers of the United Brethren in Christ who, at that time, were "authorized to administer all the ordinances of the house of God." Their names follow:—William Otterbein, G. A. Guething, Christian Newcomer, Christian Crum, John Hershey, Christopher Grosh, Abraham Draksel, L. Duckwald, John Neiding, David Long, Abraham Hershey, Christian Hershey, Abraham Mayer, William Ambrose, Isaac Niswander, D. Troyer, Geo. Benedum, Peter Kemp, Adam Reigle, Frederick Schaffer, Joseph Hoffman, David Gingerich, Christian Berger, David Snyder, and Christian Smith.

The faithful secretary closes up his long record with this prayer: "Oh! Lord God Almighty, bless thy work; grant thy Holy Spirit to all thy servants who preach thy truth; fill them with pure love, with zeal and wisdom; may they walk uprightly before thee, and honor thee in all their ways." A few days hence, and Guething was called home.

CHAPTER XV.

THE FRIENDLY CORRESPONDENCE.

The amicable relations and friendly correspondence which existed between the United Brethren in Christ and the Methodist Episcopal Church, have been frequently alluded to in the preceding pages; and, as it is a subject pleasing to dwell upon, honorable to both churches, and illustrative of the spirit of fraternal love and union which pervades all genuine revivals of true religion, we will devote a chapter to the subject.

The welcome which the first Methodist itinerants received from United Brethren ministers and people, on the commencement of their labors in this country, has been already noticed; as also the warm friendship and fellowship which existed between Otterbein and Asbury. The spirit of these leaders animated both societies. A few facts, showing the spirit manifested in those times, must be placed upon record.

In 1799, Newcomer was on a preaching tour in Virginia, in company with Brother Strickler. He makes this note in his journal:—"In Rockingham, we visited Brother Welsh, a Methodist preacher, and a most excellent man. He was delighted because of our visit. See how the love of God unites the hearts of his children."

Two years later, while traveling in the same state, Mr. Newcomer says:—"In Hagarstown, I met bishop Whatcoat. He communicated to me the glad tidings, that, at different places in America, powerful revivals of religion had taken place. 'And yet,' he added, 'I hope this is only the beginning;' to which I responded a hearty Amen."

On the 20th of October, 1801, Mr. Newcomer makes this note:—"This day I held a meeting at John Miller's. Here I met Nicholas Sneithen, a Methodist brother, lately from Delaware. He related to me glorious and wonderful news. It appears that the people are turning to the Lord by multitudes. The number of mourners, and such as are seeking salvation, are so great, that the preachers are worn down, through preaching and praying day and night. More than a thousand persons, some of them the wealthiest and most respectable part of society, have joined themselves to the Methodists. Unto God be all the glory." A few days after this, Otterbein and Newcomer, and Enoch George and Quinn, are found preaching, interchangeably, at Winchester, Va.

April 3d, 1803, Mr. Roberts, afterward bishop, preached in Otterbein's pulpit, in Baltimore. In the afternoon of the same day it was filled by Nicholas Sneithen. "This," says Newcomer, "was a blessed day to my soul." On the following day, Mr. Newcomer was invited to dine with a Methodist family. "The brother conducted me to his carriage, where I found his companion already seated. Both of them related to me, immediately, with childlike simplicity, what the Lord had done for their souls. I could not but love them with all my heart. We alighted at an elegant house, splendidly furnished. Every thing around it proclaimed its owner to be a man of wealth and distinction; and yet I found them to be true disciples of the meek and lowly Jesus. I was truly happy in their society."

On a Sabbath in May, 1804, Ezekiel

Cooper and Mr. Roberts preached in Otterbein's church, and, on the following day, Mr. Newcomer says:—"Otterbein, Roberts, Wells, and myself, dined together at Philip Greybill's. After dinner, we praised the Lord together, on our knees, for his manifold mercies."

At the great meetings, and especially at the camp-meetings, the spirit of Christian union was exhibited. Often did the brethren and preachers of both societies go up to the help of the Lord together. At a great camp-meeting in Pennsylvania, for example, in 1805, the Methodist ministers present were—Gruber, Ower, Cassel, Birch, Emmet, Steel, and Wells; the Brethren—Neiding, Newcomer, Snyder, Fordenbach, and Benedum. They all labored together, as if members of one church. "At this meeting, a great number," says Newcomer, "were happily converted to God."

In Mr. Newcomer's journal of this period and a number of succeeding years, we have constant notes like this:—"Brother Hershey spoke first, and Brother Strawbridge, a Methodist brother, followed." "Brother Young, a Methodist brother, followed me in the English." "At a sacramental meeting, at John Huber's, Brother Hoffman and Enoch George were present. We had a blessed time."

As early as 1803, the subject of a closer union between the two societies was broached in Baltimore, and, from that time onward, was a matter of frequent conversation and prayer at the large meetings, and on other occasions.

February the 12th, 1809, Mr. Newcomer makes this note in his journal:—"Brother Enoch George and myself lodged at Bro. G. Hoffman's. 13th.—We rode together to Brother Guething's, where we held a long conversation respecting a closer union between the English and German Brethren. After commending each other to the guidance and protection of God, we parted."

As a result of the conference at Guething's, Mr. Newcomer attended, in March following, the Methodist annual conference for the Baltimore district, which met that year in Harrisonburg, Rockingham county, Va. At this conference, a committee of five elders was appointed to confer with Brother Newcomer, and "ascertain whether any, and, if any, what union could be effected between the Methodist Episcopal church and the

United Brethren in Christ." On the 7th of April, this committee met. Of this meeting, Mr. Newcomer makes this note:—"We first entreated a throne of grace, for wisdom from above, and the blessing of the Most High, on the business about to be transacted. I am persuaded that all of us were seriously concerned, and had nothing else in view but the salvation of immortal souls, the furtherance of the good cause of our Lord and Master, in spreading his kingdom through our blessed country. We discussed many and different subjects, which I do not intend here to relate. Our transactions were concluded with prayer. The committee made their report to the conference. In the afternoon, I was invited to attend the session of the conference. The members, including the two bishops, numbered about sixty. After mature deliberation and discussion on their part, I received, from the conference, a letter, which I was to deliver to William Otterbein, in Baltimore. And it was further resolved, that a member of their body should be appointed to attend our next annual conference, as a delegate. Upon the reception of the letter by the United Brethren conference at Christian Herre's, a resolution was adopted by the conference, to give a brotherly answer to the letter, and, in the fraternal spirit of the Gospel, to open a correspondence upon the subject introduced. This letter was laid before the next Methodist conference, which convened in Baltimore in 1810. This correspondence and interchange of delegates continued for some years. The Philadelphia conference of the M. E. church also participated; and, eventually, a plan of harmonious action, in several particulars, was settled upon.

This treaty, if we may so style it, of amity and friendship, rested upon the conviction that societies, which were agreed in all the essential truths of our holy religion—which were alike in faith, experience, and practice, and which sustained a living itinerant ministry, should have some bond of union—some fraternal relations—other than those which had hitherto existed between them.

The terms of this union were few. Each church was left entirely distinct and separate, as before. The most important points related to the use of churches, and to class-meetings and love-feasts. Methodist houses of worship were to be open to United

Brethren, when not occupied by the Methodists; and United Brethren houses, in like manner, to the Methodists, when not occupied by the Brethren. The class-meetings and love-feast meetings were to be open, on both sides, to the members of both societies.

The letters of correspondence which passed between the two churches, have nearly all been preserved, and deserve a place in these pages.

THE CORRESPONDENCE.

HARRISONBURG, Va., —— 1809.

To the Conference of the United Brethren in Christ.

VERY DEAR BRETHREN:

We, the members of the Baltimore conference, being deeply sensible of the great utility of *union* among Christian ministers, as far as circumstances will permit, in carrying on the work of God, and promoting the interest of the Redeemer's kingdom, believing that you are friends, and brethren, engaged in the same glorious work with ourselves, have, after mature deliberation, thought proper to offer to you the following terms, in order to establish a closer and more permanent union among us:

1st. We think it advisable, for your own good, and prosperity, that each minister or preacher, who is acknowledged by the United Brethren in Christ, should receive, from their conference, a regular license, which may introduce them to our pulpits and church privileges, and thereby prevent impositions, as there are many who profess to be in union with you, that are not acknowledged by you. And we would further advise, that you favor each of our presiding elders with a list of the names of those ministers so acknowledged and licensed by you within the bounds of his district, that there may be no difficulties in admitting them to our privileges. And we would further observe, that all our traveling ministers and preachers have their names printed in the minutes of our annual conferences, and our local ministers and preachers have credentials of ordination, or a written license; and we hope that you will admit none to your privileges, calling themselves Methodist preachers, but such as have their names on the minutes, or licensed as above mentioned.

2d. As we have long experienced the utility of a Christian discipline, to prevent immorality among our people, we would earnestly recommend to you to establish a strict discipline among you, which may be a "defense on your glory." Our discipline is printed in your language, and we would recommend it to your consideration, to adopt it, or any part of it, that you in your wisdom may think proper, or any other form that you may judge best. And that under a discipline so established, you make use of every Christian and prudential means to unite your members together in societies among yourselves; by these means, we think, your people will become more spiritual, and your labors be more successful under the blessing of God.

3d. All those members among you who are united in such societies, or may hereafter be united, may be admitted to the privileges of class-meetings, sacraments, and love-feasts, in our church, provided they have a certificate of their membership, signed by a regularly licensed preacher of your church. And to prevent inconveniences, we wish you to furnish each of our preachers with a list of the names of all such members as may be in the bounds of their respective circuits, that they may know who are your members.

In order further to establish this union, *which we so much desire*, we have given particular instructions to our presiding elders and preachers who have the charge of districts and circuits where the United Brethren in Christ live, to admit your preachers and members, as above specified, to our privileges; and, also, to leave a list of the names of your preachers and members in the bounds of their respective districts or circuits, for their successors, that they may have no difficulties in knowing who you acknowledge as preachers or members.

Thus, dear Brethren, you may see that we sincerely wish to accommodate you as far as we can consistently with the discipline which binds us together as a spiritual people. We think that we have proposed to you such terms of accommodation as will meet your wishes; and, if carried into operation among you, we hope and believe a door will be opened for general usefulness among and with each other. We are persuaded that the great Head of the church will smile on us, and own our labors of love, and we shall be blest in seeing our children converted to God, and become useful members of that church which they may choose.

And now, dear Brethren, we commend you and your charge to God, praying that the Lord may be with you, and bless you, in your conference, and bless your honest labors to promote his glory and the interests of Christ's kingdom in the world.

We are, dear Brethren, your sincere friends and brethren in Christ.

Signed by order, and in behalf of the conference.

FRANCIS ASBURY.
WILLIAM MCKENDREE.

LANCASTER, Pa., May 10th, 1809.

To the Conference of the Methodist Episcopal Church.

MUCH RESPECTED BRETHREN IN CHRIST:

Being in conference assembled, and after taking into serious consideration all those points concerning a closer union between the United Brethren in Christ and that of the Methodist Episcopal church, as they have been proposed by an epistle from the late Baltimore conference, directed to us, as also, verbally, by two of your ministers, namely, James Hunter and James Smith, it does appear that the fundamental Christian doctrine, as held by both societies, is the same, the only difference existing between the two being in relation to some external church regulations.

Truly, it is to be lamented, that, not only in these latter days, but throughout the past centuries, by the setting up and obtruding of opinions, immense harm has been done; yet our conference does not mean, by this animadversion, to hint as though umbrage was taken, in view of your late epistle to us, but barely mention it as a matter of reflection. As to the first point proposed, concerning a written license to be given to our preachers, we must here inform you that we had already come to a conclusion as to that matter; but yet, till now, there were some among us who had not received a formally written license, but shall be supplied with them in future; and such as may refuse them, we wish you to look upon not as ministers ordained by us; for we do not intend to receive any professing to belong to your conference, except they have a certificate or license from the same.

This we conceive to be highly necessary, in order to prevent imposition from being practiced upon us.

In relation to the second point, concerning a token to be given to all our members, by our respective preachers, in order that they may find access to the Lord's Supper at protracted meetings, and the like, in your church, as above mentioned, we think it proper, and are perfectly willing to agree, with that order which becomes the Christian.

Concerning the third point, we would say, in respect to such as indulge in an unchristian course of conduct or conversation, that they shall remain deprived of Christian fellowship and communion as long as they remain impenitent and neglect to amend their ways. Thus, if we continue not to do unto others that which we would not wish done unto us, and thus, being guided by the influence of grace divine, we are confident that jars will soon subside, and contention die forever. Any further points to be considered, will be deferred to the sitting of our next conference. May the God of love deign to unite us still closer in the bonds of peace here, and throughout eternal ages.

Be assured of our sincere love, as fellow-laborers in the cause of Christ.

Signed by order, and in behalf of the conference.

MARTIN BOEHM.
GEORGE A. GUETHING.
CHRISTIAN NEWCOMER.

To the United Brethren in Christ.

DEAR BRETHREN:

We hereby acknowledge the receipt of the letter of the conference of the United Brethren, bearing date, May 10th, 1809, and are pleased to observe that you are fully sensible of the propriety of mutual letters of recommendation, both for preachers and members of the two societies, who may wish to participate in each other's privileges. We most earnestly encourage you to persevere in so useful a determination, and give it the fullest effect, as not only the two societies, but the church of Christ, and the cause of God in general, are interested in the detection of imposition among us.

Your determination to postpone the consideration of the subject of discipline until your next conference, makes it improper for us to resume that subject, presuming that you had sufficient reasons for so doing. We should have been highly gratified, if it had been consistent with your circumstances, to have given a final decision on the principles of the union which we proposed, and which we conceive is devoutly to be desired by the two societies. We are thankful to find that the spirit of Christian and brotherly love still prevails among you toward us, and do assure you that we reciprocate the affection, and hope never to do to you otherwise than we would have you do to us, and shall continue to receive, with an attention suitable to their importance, any communication which you may deem proper to forward to us.

Wishing you great peace in your own souls, great harmony in your conference, and great success in your ministerial labors,

We remain your brothers and fellow-laborers in the kingdom and patience of Christ.

Signed in the behalf of the conference.

JOSEPH TOY, Sec'y.

The reply of the Brethren is wanting.

Address to the United Brethren in Christ.

DEARLY BELOVED BRETHREN:

Having received your letter, etc., etc., we finally agree with you to give the right hand of fellowship, to preach the Gospel of a crucified Redeemer, and work together in spiritual peace and harmony, to bring lost sinners home to God, through repentance and holiness. And we further agree with you, that our preaching houses of public worship shall be open to all your preachers who have license from you. Likewise, it is our earnest wish that you should open all your public preaching houses to all our preachers that have written license from us. We also inform you that we have regulations upon record, to walk by, to direct our preachers to keep class-meetings, or to form classes at any place they think proper, etc. And, lastly, we give unto you the right hand of fellowship, and assure you that we shall always, as much as in our power lies, do unto you as we wish you to do unto us. We also crave an interest in your prayers, and assure you that it is our full desire to live in as close a connection with you as the nature of the case will admit, to bear with each other in love, and holding the same principles, and preaching the same doctrines, will not suffer smaller things, and only the shadows of religion, to separate us from each other.

An extract from the journal of 1810.

NICHOLAS SNETHEN.

An Address from the Baltimore Annual Conference, to the United Brethren in Christ.

DEARLY BELOVED BRETHREN:

We have received your affectionate letter, with hearty thankfulness, that the Father of our Lord Jesus Christ, the God of all peace and consolation, has inclined your hearts to unite in the bonds of the Gospel, to walk in love as Christ also hath loved us, and given himself for us.

We consider now, if we have not misunderstood you, that we are fully agreed in respect to the necessity of union, and a mutual endeavor to accomplish it. We have, therefore, directed and instructed all our presiding elders and preachers, whose business it may be to consult with the United Brethren, in their several districts and circuits, about the most expedient form of carrying the proposed union into effect. To our own forms of license and certifications, etc., we presume you can have no objections, as they have been of long use among us. If you have already a fixed form, we shall cheerfully accept it, and would only advise, that, if you have one yet to fix upon, you may bear in mind whether it will not be proper to be somewhat uniform in the formation of the license for your preachers, and the certificates for your members; but, should you see proper to vary in different places, our brethren are instructed to make no objections on that head, but merely to seek for information, and conform to your usage accordingly.

You will please, then, dear brethren, to accept from us the right hand of fellowship, and our assurances that all our preaching houses shall be open to your licensed preachers, as far as our power and advice may be extended, (for some of our houses may be under the control of trustees) and that our sacraments, love-feasts, and class-meetings, shall be open to your members who apply with such form of certification as you may judge proper, according to our proposals, sent to you from the Harrisonburg conference.

As soon as our presiding elders and preachers return to their respective districts and circuits, we shall consider this union as having fully commenced on our part. But we propose to keep open an intercourse between the two conferences, to improve and perfect the plan, as far as experience may furnish matter of improvement.

We hope to hear from you at our next annual conference; and we invite you to exercise the fullest confidence in us in your correspondence. Having given you this invitation, we take the same liberty. We hope you will not indulge, for a moment, a suspicion that we wish to interfere in your conference and church concerns. There will, constantly, no doubt, be many in both churches, not disposed to become privileged members; none of our regulations can have any effect upon such. But knowing, as we both do, the imperfections of human nature, we can not help foreseeing that offenses will come between the ministry and members of the two churches, who claim privileges. Now we think that some plan ought to be agreed upon for the settlement of all such difficulties. As nothing can now be done decisively, we beg leave to propose the following plan for consideration.

First—If any preacher or member of either church, claiming to be a privileged preacher or member in the other, shall be accused of any thing contrary to Christian prudence, or Christian conduct, by the church in which he may be a privileged preacher or member, the accusation shall be made to the conference or church in which he is in regular membership, who shall try and judge accordingly; but, in cases of this kind, if the difficulty be not settled according to the satisfaction of the conference or church-meeting bringing the accusation, his brethren shall advise and request him to desist from the use of the privileges, and to confine himself to his own proper conference or church.

Second.—No preacher or member, who shall have been excluded by one conference or church, shall be received by the other.

Third.—As often as may be convenient, a messenger shall be sent with any letter which shall be addressed from one conference to the other, with instructions to explain any difficulties.

We invite our beloved Brother Newcomer to a seat

UNITED BRETHREN IN CHRIST. 357

in our conference, as your messenger; and he is doubly dear to us as a messenger of such joyful tidings of brotherly love from you. "How beautiful upon the mountains are the feet" of all the messengers of mercy, love, peace, and good-will.

We have the happiness to inform you that we have enjoyed great harmony and love in our conference; and, by what we can learn of the state of religion at present, we have many tokens of good, and abundance of evidence that God is waiting to be gracious.

Wishing you peace and prosperity in the kingdom and patience of our Lord Jesus Christ, we remain your affectionate brethren in the bonds of Christian fellowship.

March 27, 1811.   JOSEPH TOY, Sec'y.

An Address from the United Brethren in Christ, to the Methodist Episcopal Conference.

DEARLY BELOVED BRETHREN IN CHRIST:

We have received your affectionate letter, bearing date, March 27th, 1811, by our Brothers Borg and Swertzwelder, with much joy and thankfulness, seeing, therein, that the God of love has united your hearts in peace and harmony with us, to unite more and more together in the bonds of the Gospel. We are certain, brethren, if we walk in the light, as children of the light, we shall, ere long, be of one heart and one mind. Seeing, likewise, blessed fruits of our union together, in a measure, already, and the glorious prospect before us, we do not hesitate a moment longer to give you the right hand of Christian fellowship. Again, we have now formed our membership into classes, as much as possible. However, there are a number yet among us who have not joined with us in this privilege, so long delayed by us: we earnestly hope that you will instruct your traveling preachers to bear with such as much as the order of your church will admit. We would further inform you that we have drawn up some regulations or discipline among us, and shall endeavor, more and more, to put them into effect among ourselves and our members.

Any preacher or private member expelled from your church, will not be received by us to the fellowship of saints in Christ; and we do hope that you will do the same, in relation to those expelled by us, at least, until sufficient reason be found of their repentance and good fruits.

We likewise hope that our mutual friendship and love to each other will be increased yet more and more, and that the intercourse, by letter, and messengers from and to each conference, may be kept up yearly, through which medium difficulties may be readily adjusted, and more especially as such messengers, or communications, will be joyfully received by us, and appreciated in the best possible way.

And, lastly, may the God of all peace and consolation, who has united our hearts together in the Gospel, spread his militant church, by us, from pole to pole; and, finally, when time is no more, make us, one and all, members of his church triumphant, to praise God and the Lamb forever. Remember us before the throne of God, is the earnest prayer of your affectionate brethren, wishing you peace and prosperity in the kingdom and patience of our Lord Jesus

Christ. We remain your affectionate brethren in the bonds of Christian fellowship.

Signed by order, and in behalf of the conference.

CHRISTIAN NEWCOMER.

May 25th, 1811.

An Address from the Methodist Episcopal Conference, assembled at Leesburgh, to the United Brethren in Christ.

TO THE CONFERENCE OF THE UNITED BRETHREN:

Grace and peace be multiplied unto you, through our Lord and Savior Jesus Christ. Behold how good and pleasant a thing it is for brethren to dwell in unity. May the holy leaven leaven the whole lump. We do most cordially and sincerely join with you in praying, that He who has united our hearts in the Gospel, may make us instrumental in assisting to spread his militant church from pole to pole, and, finally, when time is no more, make us, one and all, members of the church triumphant, to praise God and the Lamb forever and ever.

We have the happiness to inform you that we do not recollect when we had so gracious a sitting together. "Our peace surpasseth all understanding, and our joy is unspeakable and full of glory." We taste unspeakable bliss. "The power of the Highest overshadowed us, and the glory of God is in the midst of us." Hallelujah!

We have instructed our preachers to deal very tenderly with those members of your church who have not fully come into our measures of union, as far as the rules and orders of our church will admit, hoping and trusting that you will still do all in your power to promote and extend the spirit and practice of discipline among them, it being evident that our mutual success depends upon our union, wherever our lines of labor come together.

We agree with you in the advantage of correspondence and an interchange of messengers. Brother Newcomer was received by us, and we have appointed our Brothers Alfred Griffith and John Swertzwelder, as messengers to your next conference, with whom you may consult on any subject relative to the desired object of a final and perfect harmony.

We remain, dear brethren, your affectionate fellow-laborers in the bonds of peace.

NICHOLAS SNEITHEN.

March 26th, 1812.

An Address to the Conference of the Methodist Episcopal Church, assembled in Baltimore, from the United Brethren Church.

DEARLY BELOVED BRETHREN:

The members of the conference of the United Brethren assembled at George Adam Guething's, with the greatest satisfaction, mention the receipt of your address from Leesburgh. Our souls have been truly refreshed, particularly when we received the news of love, uniting our kindred souls. We will adopt the language of the royal Psalmist with you: "'Tis good and pleasant for brethren to dwell together in unity." We do cordially and sincerely pray that Jehovah may make us individually instrumental in spreading his blessed cause, and extending his militant church from the rivers to the ends of the earth. We rejoice with you, that the power of the Lord was in your midst; our hearts also burned with love, while consulting on the welfare of Zion.

We are truly thankful for the delicacy and tenderness intimated in your letter, as touching those members of our church that may not, as yet, be divested of certain peculiarities. But we humbly hope that the mists will, ere long, through the effulgence of Gospel day, be dispersed from every mind. We have, in many places, succeeded in forming class-meetings and extending discipline, and, as far as prudence shall dictate, we will pursue.

An interchange of messengers and correspondence will still be deemed a favor. Brothers A. Griffith and J. Swertzwelder were thankfully received by us, with whom we had the happiness to consult on the much-desired subject of permanent peace and harmony.

Brothers G. A. Guething and C. Newcomer were instructed as messengers to you. Finally, brethren, may the God of love and peace unite our hearts and efforts in the indissoluble bonds of Jesus' love, is the prayer of your fellow-laborers in the blessed Gospel of peace.

Signed in behalf, and by consent of the conference.
CHRISTIAN NEWCOMER.
Washington co., Md., May 13th, 1812.

The answer to this letter we have not been able to obtain.

To the Baltimore Conference of the M. E. Church, to be held in the City of Baltimore, March, 1814.

DEARLY BELOVED BRETHREN:

At this important period, while our national

tranquility is disturbed by the desolations of war, we rejoice to find that there is yet prevailing among you a growing disposition to spread our Redeemer's name among the people of the United States of America.

We received your affectionate address by the hands of your messengers, our beloved brethren, R. Birch and J. W. ———, and cordially unite with you in praying that our united efforts may be more and more successful in extending the victorious kingdom of the Lord Jesus Christ. And, brethren, this we believe we will not fail to accomplish, if we lay aside all national prejudices, and betake ourselves to more solemn fasting, humiliation, and prayer; and, in spirit, conversation, and public labors, more ardently endeavor to raise up a people for the Lord God of hosts in the midst of the earth.

Mingled as our hearers and members are throughout this widely-extended country, we are the more convinced that one spiritual interest should exist among us and lead us all on to put forth more powerful exertions to fill the world with the knowledge of our glorious and benevolent God.

We firmly believe with you, brethren, that pure, doctrinal truths, and Gospel discipline, dispel darkness from the mind, and correct the errors of the heart and life, and, through the efficacy of the Spirit, perfect us in the love of God. Endeavoring, as we are, to become united in establishing a real Gospel discipline among our people, we have it in contemplation, soon to have printed and circulated among our members, a system of rules which, though they may appear, .in some respects, imperfect, yet may serve for the commencement of a form of government for our people, which may, in process of time, be improved to such a state of perfection as may be to the benefit and happiness of future generations.

But, as we can not, at present, inform you in this letter, concerning the general form of the discipline we contemplate publishing, the bearers of this letter to your conference, our beloved brethren, Christian Newcomer and Valentine Baulus, will be fully qualified, and shall have power, to give you any information that may be necessary concerning the progress, in the discipline, we shall have made during the labors of the present year.

Desiring to continue a friendly correspondence with you, brethren, we wish you all success in the holy labors of the Gospel, hoping that we shall have an interest in your prayers and good wishes, while at the same time, we assure you, we will endeavor not to fail to pray to the God of all grace for you, and wish you all possible success in the good work of the Lord.

Signed in behalf, and by order of, the conference of the United Brethren in Christ, held in Lancaster county, May 6th, 1813.

CHRISTIAN SMITH, Sec'y.

The Philadelphia Conference to the United German Brethren, greeting.

DEARLY BELOVED BRETHREN:

We have been made acquainted with the friendly correspondence that has taken place between you and the Baltimore conference, tending to a happy union; and being informed by your messenger, Christian Newcomer, that it is your wish to enter into a like friendly correspondence with us, we, therefore, hasten to inform you that we are willing most cordially to embrace you as brethren in the kingdom and patience of Jesus Christ, and are ready to enter into the strictest union with you that the peculiar circumstances of the two societies will admit of, and have, accordingly, appointed two of our members, William Fox and William Foulks, to meet you at your next conference, to aid in the accomplishment of this desired object.

It was, dear brethren, the prayer of Christ, your Lord and our's, that his people might be one, and that for the most useful purposes,—that is, that they might be perfected in one, and that the world might believe, etc. We are, dear brethren, yours, in the bonds of a pure and peaceful conference.

Signed in behalf of the Philadelphia conference, at the annual meeting, in Philadelphia, 25th April, 1812.

WILLIAM S. FISHER.

The Conference of the United Brethren, to the Philadelphia Conference of the Methodist Episcopal Church, greeting.

DEARLY BELOVED BRETHREN:

We received your friendly address with much pleasure. We exult to hear that you are ready to enter into terms of union with us, as our brethren of the Baltimore conference have done, and pray that it may terminate in as happy a union, and we have no doubt but that it will, if you pursue the same charitable and friendly course toward us which they have taken. We wish, dear brethren, ever to do unto you as we would be done by. May the Lord unite our hearts in love, and help us to pull together in the yoke of Christ, that we may be as true yoke-fellows indeed; and may the kingdom of our Savior be mightily established in the earth by our united efforts. Brethren, pray for us. We have appointed our brethren, Christian Smith and David Snyder, as messengers to your next conference, with whom you may consult on any subject leading toward our contemplated union. We remain yours, dear brethren, in the bonds of the peaceful Gospel.

Signed by order of conference, May 12th, 1812.

GEORGE A. GUETHING.

Address of the Philadelphia Conference of the Methodist Episcopal Church, to the German Conference of the United Brethren in Christ.

DEARLY BELOVED BRETHREN:

Your friendly address by your brother and our's, and your messenger, Christian Smith, are received with pleasure. We beg you to be assured of our continued regard for you, and cordial desire of Christian union and communion, as far as may be consistent with the order and discipline of our respective churches. Our doctrines are fixed and established; our discipline is binding upon us, by the authority of the general conference; and we have long experienced and proved the great advantage of such regulations; consequently, to these, in our church communion of fellowship, we feel ourselves bound, by the most sacred obligations, to have an especial regard. And might we not, brethren, recommend them to your consideration, that you may prove all things, and hold fast that which is good? We have appointed our brethren, W. Hunter and H. Boehm, to present to you this address, and to assure you that your messengers and communications will always be welcome to us. We are pleased to find, by the reports from different and distant places, that our blessed Redeemer is still carrying on the work of spiritual peace and reconciliation, notwithstanding the commotions and revolutions in the world; and we hope the time is not far distant when the human race shall be united as the common workmanship of the common Creator's hand, and the common purchase of the common Savior's blood. We pray our gracious and holy Lord abundantly to bless you, and incline your hearts to supplicate for us before his throne. May you be divinely assisted in all your deliberations, and see the Lord's pleasure abundantly prospering in your hands, to the glory of our God and your God, through Jesus Christ, your Lord and our's.

Signed in behalf of the conference.

WILLIAM S. FISHER, Sec'y.

Philadelphia, May 1st, 1813.

———o———

This union was not destined long to flourish. The venerable patriarch in the M. E. church, Mr. Francis Asbury, who aided in forming it, and who rejoiced in it, went up to God on the 31st of March, 1816. Shortly after this, a prominent presiding elder, in his excessive zeal for Methodism, declared he would recognize the terms of union no longer, and that the members of the United Brethren church could have free access to Methodist love-feasts and class-meetings on one condition only, and that was, by joining the M. E. church. He began to violate the terms of agreement in H——, at a Methodist quarterly meeting in a United Brethren meeting-house! This was, surely, beginning judgment at the house of God.*

The Brethren, who have usually excelled in meekness and forbearance, if in little else, made no complaint;† and their meeting-houses, and class-meetings, and love-feasts, remained, as they are to this day, open and free.

* Spayth, p. 115.

† Rev. Jacob Baulus moved to Sandusky, O., at an early day, and, in the spirit of this union, opened his house for a Methodist quarterly meeting. The meeting was a good one. Some of his children were converted, and received into the Methodist society. When the time for love-feast came, Baulus was not permitted to enter the room! We received this from the venerable man's own lips.

CHAPTER XVI.

"THE SO-CALLED ALBRIGHTS."—ANOTHER PROPOSED UNION.

During the first decade of the present century, an ecclesiastical seed was cast into the earth, which, at the first, seemed to be indeed the smallest and least promising of all seeds; and yet, under the care of the Great Husbandman, it has become a tree of very respectable size, under whose shade many thousands of God's children repose. A brief sketch of this society, and of a proposed union with the United Brethren, will be in place in these pages.

Jacob Albright, the founder of "the so-called Albrights," was born in Pennsylvania, in 1759. His parents were members of the Lutheran church, and he was trained up in the religion of his fathers, which, at that time, was still, in too many places, a religion of the *church*, and not of *Christ*. In his thirty-second year, he was awakened to a full sense of his sins, and to the necessity of a change of heart. So great became his distress of mind, so deep his convictions of guilt, that he was ready to cry out in despair, "Ye mountains, fall on me, and, ye hills, cover me!" At length he says, "I fell on my knees, tears of bitter sorrow rolled over my cheeks, and a long, ardent, and inmost prayer ascended to the throne of grace, for mercy and the pardon of my sins. By and by, all anxiety and anguish of soul disappeared; happiness, and a joyous peace in God, filled my soul, God's Spirit bearing witness with my spirit that I had become a child of God. One happy sensation followed another, and such a heavenly joy pervaded my whole being, as no pen can describe, and no mortal can express."

Soon after this happy event, he united with the Methodist church, whose spirit and discipline he admired. His spirit was soon stirred within him, by what he regarded as the voice of God calling him to "go and work in the vineyard." The church to which he belonged authorized him to exhort; but, not appreciating his talents and call, or for some unexplained reason, did not encourage him to enter fully upon the work of the ministry. But so pressed was he in spirit, that, notwithstanding this discouragement, and his limited educational advantages, he surrendered all to Christ, and went forth preaching the Gospel to the German people. He was not, naturally, a graceful speaker, but he knew the way of life from experience; and, being honest, zealous, and persevering, and enjoying a large measure of the Spirit, he preached with good effect. Not receiving encouragement from the Methodists, with whom he had united, he separated himself from them, and, in A. D. 1800, about four years after he began to preach, he organized three societies or classes, of which he himself took the oversight.

During the whole period of Mr. Albright's ministerial life, he was the object of persecution. The growth of the societies under his care, was extremely slow. At the end of the second year, the whole number of members had reached but 20; in 1803, the number arose to 40. He had, by this time, however, obtained two helpers in the ministry; and, in November of this year, fourteen of the leading laymen of the societies he had organized, met, and solemnly ordained him to the ministry.* In 1804, the Association numbered 60 members, and another preacher was added. In 1805, five years after the organization of the first societies, the whole number of members reached 75. This year, however, a very successful preacher, George Miller, was added to the ministerial force, and the work began to move more rapidly. The first conference was held in 1807. It was composed of all the preachers, exhorters, and class-leaders, in the society; in all 28—8 preachers, and 20 class-leaders and exhorters. This conference decided that Mr. Albright should draw up articles of faith, and a discipline, for the Association, in conformity with the Scriptures; but, dying six months thereafter, he did not accomplish the work. The conference, however, elected Mr. Albright superintendent or bishop. The whole membership of the society, at this time, was 220. On the 20th of the May following this election, the good man closed his labors in the 50th year of his age.

Up to the period of Mr. Albright's death, it was still a question in his mind, whether the society would continue to be an inde-

* His. of Evangelical Association, p. 23

pendent organization. John Driesbach says: "About three months before his demise, * * I expressed to him my great desire that he would be able to draw up the projected articles of faith and discipline. His reply was: 'Brother John, if it is God's will for you to be and remain an independent organization, he will take care of you also in this particular; there will appear men among you who will accomplish what I am unable to do."*

At the second conference, held in 1809, G. Miller was instructed to publish the Articles of Faith and Church Discipline, as drawn up by himself; and this conference gave the Association the name—"*The So-called Albrights*,"—a name which was retained by the society until 1816, when "Evangelical Association" was substituted. The whole membership, in 1809, had reached 426. Up to the year 1813, the Association had worked hard, suffered much, and its increase had been very slow. At this period, it numbered 15 itinerant preachers, and about 800 members.

In April, 1813, Christian Newcomer, whose catholic soul would have bound all Christians together by the cords of love,

* His. of Evangelical Association, p. 43.

visited the conference of the then "So-called Albrights," for the purpose of promoting a union of the two churches. The subject was freely discussed by that conference. Mr. N. laid the discipline of the United Brethren before the conference, for examination, and it seemed to meet with general and cordial approval; and they delivered to him a written communication on the subject of union, to be laid before the United Brethren conference, which was soon to meet at Christian Herre's, in Lancaster county, Pa.

The conference met at Brother Herre's, and the subject of union with "the Albrights" was discussed, favorably considered, and a committee of four Brethren were appointed to meet a like committee appointed by the "Albrights," for the purpose of uniting, if practicable, the two societies. This committee consisted of the following persons: —*United Brethren*—Christian Crum, C. Newcomer, Jos. Hoffman, and Jacob Baulus: *Albrights*—George Miller, John Walter, John Driesbach, and Henry Niebel. The committee met near New Berlin, Pa., Nov. 11th, 1813, and, after spending several days in consultation, they separated, failing entirely to reach any satisfactory conclusion. The idea of a union, however, was not abandoned, and it was cherished with especial regard by Christian Newcomer and John Driesbach. Hence, we have, in Mr. Newcomer's journal, under date of April 3d, 1815, the following note:—"This morning, my poor soul is drawn out in prayer to God for sanctifying power. Oh, Lord! impart unto my soul thy nature and thy perfect love. I rode with Brother Henry Smith to Jacob Kleinfelter's, —the Albright brethren had their conference here. About 14 or 15 preachers had assembled. I made another attempt to effect a union between the two societies, but in vain."

Two years later still, another attempt was made at union. The subject had been discussed, at length, in the first general conference of the Evangelical Association, held in October, 1816. On the 14th of February, 1817, twelve ministers, six belonging to each society, met, in a social conference, at Henry Kumler's, once more to consider the question which had been before the two societies for four years. The names of the ministers composing this conference were:—*Of Evangelical Association*—J. Driesbach, H. Niebel,

S. Miller, John Kleinfelter, D. Thomas, and A. Ettinger. *Of the United Brethren*—C. Newcomer, J. Hoffman, Jacob Baulus, Abraham Mayer, Christian Berger, and Conrad Roth.

This conference also failed to effect a union, or to accomplish any thing toward it. "Yet," says Mr. Driesbach, "we prayed with and for each other, preached and exhorted alternately, bade each other God-speed in our operations, and pledged ourselves to treat one another as Christians and children of God." "Many members of both churches," continues Mr. D., "were displeased at the failure to effect a union, yet I believe it grieved none so much as it did Father Newcomer and myself." It is hardly necessary, after the lapse of nearly half a century, to enter into a discussion of the causes which prevented a union so much desired by some of the best men in both the rising churches. They related to the name of the denomination to be formed, the rights of local ministers, the example of washing feet, the itinerancy, and, it is alleged, without sufficient reason, we think, diverse views of a written discipline.*

---

* In the History of the Evangelical Association, p. 68, it is said

It was thought best to finish our notice of the friendly correspondence, and efforts at union, between the United Brethren in Christ and her sister churches, the Methodists and Evangelical brethren, although this has carried us a few years beyond the period of United Brethren history treated in this volume.

that the United Brethren "had not, at this time, a printed discipline, and its introduction was yet doubtful." This is a mistake.

CHAPTER XVII.

P. KEMP, JOHN HERSHEY, MARTIN BOEHM, AND GEORGE A. GUETHING—THEIR LAST TESTIMONY.

WE must now go back a little, and witness the departure, from the field of toil, of some of the most venerated fathers of the church. Between 1811 and 1814, the angel of death was busy among them.

"Brother P. Kemp died at his residence, near Fredericktown, Maryland, February 26th, 1811. He had been an early and efficient supporter of the rising church. His house, for many years, had been the preacher's home, and continued to be so long after his decease. Some time in the night, he was asked by a brother, whether the love of Christ was present with him? He answered, 'O yes! bless the Lord, I shall soon be with him." He began to sink slowly till, in the morning, between five and six o'clock, he expired in the arms of

Jesus, while the family and friends were engaged in prayer around his dying bed. Brother G. A. Guething preached the funeral discourse from Psalms viii.: 5.

"Eight days had scarcely passed from the departure of Brother Kemp, when the church was called upon to part with another of her beloved sons in the Gospel. Brother John Hershey departed this life at his home, near Hagerstown, Maryland, March 4th, 1811. Like Brother Kemp, Brother Hershey was long a loving and tried friend in the cause of that religion which he honored and adorned by his pious and upright manner of living in this world, as one who knew that, when this earthly house should be dissolved, he had a building of God, a house not made with hands, eternal in the heavens. Brother Hershey was a co-worker with Newcomer, Guething, and Otterbein. In him, the church lost a dear friend; but it has been, and is still, a consolation to know that his descendents have flourished in righteousness like the palm-tree, have stood by the Church in her trials, and have answered a father's prayer and legacy, bequeathed with his dying breath.

> "'The Church has wept
> In sadness o'er the loss,
> ———— in Christ they sleep.
> Who bore on earth his cross,
> And from the grave their dust shall rise,
> In Christ's own image, to the skies!'

"Brother Martin Boehm fell asleep in Jesus, March 23d, 1812. His days of illness were but few. For a person of his age, he had enjoyed remarkably good health. He was active, and able to ride a short distance, until within a few days of his dissolution. But death came, and it found him ready. Its icy hand diminished the vital flame gradually, and without much pain. No one thought him near dying when the hour of his departure came. He asked to be raised up in his bed, and said he wished to sing and pray once more before he left. His request was granted, and he sang and prayed in a clear and distinct voice! This done, he asked to be laid back upon his pillow. This was done, and behold he was no more on earth.

"His remains rest with others in the cemetery, near his meeting-house, which overlooks the old homestead,—a fit resting-place for such a saint."*

---
* Spayth, pp. 128, 129.

THE
REV. MARTIN BOEHM,
Died, March 23d, 1812,
Aged 86 years, 3 months, and 11 days.
HE PREACHED THE GOSPEL
Fifty-four Years.

In justice to his memory, to the church in whose origin he was so intimately concerned, and to the truth of history, we must pause at the grave of this venerable patriarch, to review an account of William Otterbein and Martin Boehm, which first appeared in the Methodist Magazine, volume 6, pages 210 to 249. This sketch purports to have been furnished to bishop Asbury, a short time previous to his death, by his friend, F. Hollingsworth, the transcriber of the bishop's journal: it has also been embodied in the History of the Methodist Episcopal Church by Dr. Bangs, and may be found in volume 2, pages 365 to 376. Here is the matter referred to:—

"Martin Boehm, of whom we desire to speak, as a professor of religion and minister of Christ, the labors and experience of his life may be pretty justly estimated by what we learn from himself, communicated in answers to certain questions propounded to him by his son Jacob, which we here transcribe:

"'*Ques.* Father, when were you put into the ministry?

"'*Ans.* My ministerial labors began about the year 1756. Three years afterward, by nomination to the lot, I received full pastoral orders.

"'*Ques.* What was your religious experience during that time?

"'*Ans.* I was sincere and strict in the religious duties of prayer in my family, in the congregation, and in the closet. I lived and preached according to the light I had,—I was a servant, and not a son; nor did I know any one, at that time, who could claim the birth-right by adoption, but Nancy Keagy, my mother's sister; she was a woman of great piety and singular devotion to God.

"'*Ques.* By what means did you discover the nature and necessity of a real change of heart?

"'*Ans.* By deep meditation upon the doctrine which I myself preached, of the fall of man, his sinful estate, and utter helplessness; I discovered and felt the want of Christ within, &c., &c.

"'*Ques.* Were your labors owned of the

Lord in the awakening and conversion of souls?

Ans. Yes; many were brought to the knowledge of the truth. But it was a strange work; and some of the Mennonist meeting-houses were closed against me. Nevertheless I was received in other places. I now preached the Gospel spiritually and powerfully. Some years afterward, I was ex-communicated from the Mennonist church, on a charge truly enough advanced, of holding fellowship with other societies of a different language. I had invited the Methodists to my house, and they soon formed the society in my neighborhood, which exists to this day. My beloved wife Eve, my children, and my cousin Keagy's family, were among the first of its members. For myself, I felt my heart more greatly enlarged toward all religious persons, and to all denominations of Christians. Upward of thirty years ago, I became acquainted with my greatly beloved Brother William Otterbein, and several other ministers, who, about this time, had been ejected from their churches, as I had been from mine, because of their zeal, which was looked upon as an irregularity. We held many large meetings in Pennsylvania, Maryland, and New Virginia, which generally lasted three days. At these meetings, hundreds were made the subjects of penitence and pardon. Being convinced of the necessity of order and discipline in the church of God, and having no wish to be at the head of a separate body, I advised serious persons to join the Methodists, whose doctrine, discipline, and zeal, suited, as I thought, an unlearned, sincere, and simple-hearted people. Several of the ministers with whom I labored, continued to meet in a conference of the German United Brethren; but we felt the difficulties arising from the want of that which the Methodists possessed. Age having overtaken me, with some of its accompanying infirmities, I could not travel as I had formerly done. In 1802, I enrolled my name on a Methodist class-book, and I have found great comfort in meeting with my brethren. I can truly say my last days are my best days. My beloved Eve is traveling with me the same road Zionward; my children, and most of my grandchildren, are made the partakers of the same grace. I am, this 12th of April, 1811, in my eighty-sixth year. Through the boundless goodness of God, I am still able to visit the sick, and occasionally to preach in the neighborhood: to his name be all the glory, in Christ Jesus.'

"To this, bishop Asbury adds, as a tribute of respect:—

"'Honest and unsuspecting, he had not a strange face for strange people. He did not make the Gospel a charge to any one; his reward was souls and glory. His conversation was in heaven. Plain in dress and manners, when age had stamped its impress of reverence upon him, he filled the mind with the noble idea of a patriarch.'

"The first remark we make on the foregoing," says Mr. Spayth, "is, that, as Father Boehm spoke but little English at best, the foregoing questions and answers were neither written nor spoken by him in English. It is true that he went to Virginia in 1761, but not as Jacob would have it understood, before he had experienced a change of heart, *but after that event.* As to the statement we have given of the cause of his going to Virginia, we are safe to vouch for its correctness, for we had it *from his own lips.* For some reason, or by some means, the statement given by Jacob, may be warped in the English version.

"The second exception we take, is, to the idea conveyed in the statement, that his name was enrolled on a Methodist class-book, in 1802. That his name was placed on the class-book referred to, is true, but the circumstances were as follows:—A meeting-house had been built on his land, principally by his aid, and that of his German brethren. Big meetings had been held at that place, at an early period of our history. We will take notice of one of those meetings, at Boehm's meeting-house, under date of October 17th, 1801. A sacramental meeting was appointed at this place: a great many people attended. Newcomer spoke first. The grace of God was powerfully present. Some were crying for mercy, and others praised God with a loud voice. At the evening meeting, the Lord displayed his power in a wonderful manner. Old and young were filled with joy: never, perhaps, was a whole congregation so happy. Sabbath morning was a happy and blessed time in love-feast. Brother D. Strickler spoke first; Neiding and Newcomer also addressed the audience. At candle-light, the house was very full. In a short time, all were again quickened, and gave glory to God, for hope of immortality, and a foretaste of celestial joy.

"At this meeting-house, the Methodists had formed a class, previous to the year 1802, under a liberal construction of their rules, and, hence, with the free assent of Brother Boehm. But this liberality was, some time after, withdrawn, and the restrictive rule, relating to class-meetings and love-feasts, was insisted on, and even the venerable Boehm was not excepted. Here was a dilemma. To admit Brother Boehm, the preachers said, was in violation of an express disciplinary rule; and to deny him the privilege in his own meeting-house, was hard, but the law is imperative and binding. Now comes the gist of the matter. Brother Boehm was entreated, *for form's sake*, at least, to allow his name to go on the class-book, nominally, as a private member, and all would be right. To this, for peace's sake, he consented, and nothing more.

"How far the law of kindness, of Christian friendship and hospitality, and of pure love, had to stand aside in this case, we leave to every one to say. As it was, it did not give the Brethren a moment's concern: nor would we here have taken any notice of it at all, had not the Methodist historian made it a subject of record. In conclusion on this topic, we remark, that Brother Boehm's relation to the Brethren church, was unbroken, from first to last, as has already been seen. This our annual conference proceedings sufficiently show. Thus, in 1800, in connection with Otterbein, he was elected bishop. He was prevented, by sickness, from attending the conference of 1801; attended conference in Maryland, in 1802; was re-elected bishop in 1805, and attended the conference in 1809, which was the last this devoted servant of the Lord enjoyed with his brethren in the church on earth. From this time to the time of his death, great age, with its accompanying infirmities, prevented him from attending an annual conference."*

At the conference of 1812, George Adam Guething appeared in reasonable health, and in remarkably good spirits. He took a very active part in the business of the conference, and signed, if he did not pen, the ex-

* Spayth, pp. 106—111.

cellent fraternal letter to the Philadelphia conference, which we have seen in a previous chapter.

Shortly after the conference, which had convened in his neighborhood, closed, accompanied by his wife, he went to Baltimore, to spend a week with his dearly-beloved Brother William Otterbein, whose infirmities confined him to the city. After reaching the city, he became somewhat indisposed. This induced him to shorten his visit. "Leaving the city for home, he put up at Mr. Snyder's, about thirty miles distant. Here his indisposition increased during the night. Early in the morning, he enjoyed a little rest, conversed with his companion and Mrs. Snyder about the Christian's hope, and the prospects of a glorious immortality. He became silent, and then said, 'I feel as though my end had come. Hark! hark!—who spoke? Whose voice is this I hear? Light! light! what golden light! Now all is dark again! Please help me out of this bed.' They did so. 'Now let us sing—

> Komm' du lang verlangte Stunde,
>   Komm' du Lebensgeist von oben;
> O wie soll mein froher Munde,
>   Jesu deine Treue loben ·

Wann mich deine Liebesmacht,
Dir zu dienen frei gemacht.'

TRANSLATION.

Come, thou long expected moment,
Come, thou Spirit from on high,
'Tis thy call, my Lord and Master;
How shall I express my joy,
When thy grace and power of love,
Bids me rise to climes above?

"He now sank on his knees, leaning against the bed, and prayed fervently, giving thanks to God for his abundant mercy toward him, his unprofitable servant. A prayer, this was, offered up at the very gate of heaven, and in it, mark you, there was no doubt, no fear, no desire for a longer stay on earth; but God the Father was confidently asked, for the sake of Christ Jesus, our Savior, to look upon him, to hear and accept this his petition, to receive his poor servant, and to take him to himself, for the sake of the great love wherewith he had loved him, and delivered him from all evil.

"He was helped into bed again, and, in about fifteen minutes, while his hands were calmly folded, his ransomed spirit fled."*

* Spayth, pp. 129—131.

"In condescending love, thy ceaseless prayer He heard,
And bade thee suddenly remove to thy complete reward:
Ready to bring thee peace, thy beauteous feet were shod,
When Mercy signed thy soul's release, and caught thee up to God.

"Redeemed from earth and pain, oh! when shall we ascend,
And all in Jesus' presence reign, with our translated friend?
Come, Lord, and quickly come; and, when in thee complete,
Receive thy longing servants home, to triumph at thy feet."

THE

REV. GEORGE ADAM GUETHING

ENDED HIS LABORS AND HIS LIFE,

June 28th, 1812,

Aged 71 years, 4 months, and 22 days.

HE SPENT FORTY YEARS IN THE

MINISTRY.

A venerable Methodist minister, Henry Smith, now in his 92d year, in a letter before us, concerning the early United Brethren ministers, pays the following tribute to Guething:—"I was acquainted with Rev. G. A. Guething, and my dear father loved him above all men, for it was under his preaching, at one of their (the United Brethren) great meetings on Antietam, that he gave his heart to God: and dear Newcomer used to say to me, 'Your father was converted in my arms.' He was a gifted, eloquent, and powerful speaker. His voice was fine and sweet, and his preaching found way to the heart as well as the ear."

CHAPTER XVIII.

CLOSE OF MR. OTTERBEIN'S LIFE.

Mr. Otterbein did not long survive his venerable and beloved co-laborers, Boehm and Guething. The year 1813 is marked with the closing period of his life. "His day had been long and toilsome; but the evening came, and with it calmness and undisturbed tranquility." "I gave an evening," says bishop Asbury, [the 22d of April, 1813] "to the great Otterbein. I found him placid and happy in God." The clouds had all departed, the sea was smooth, and not a ripple disturbed the passage of his bark through the "Golden Gate," into the heavenly port.

On the 1st of October, a little more than a month previous to his departure, he was visited by Christian Newcomer, who makes this note of the visit in his journal: —"Old Father Otterbein is weak and feeble in body, but strong and vigorous in spirit, and full of hope of a blissful immortality and eternal life." Mr. Newcomer adds:—"He was greatly rejoiced at our arrival; informed me that he had received a letter from the Brethren in the west, wherein he was requested to ordain me, by the laying on of hands, to the office of elder and preacher of the Gospel, before his departure, adding, 'I have always considered myself too unworthy to perform this solemn injunction of the apostle, but now I perceive the necessity of doing so before I shall be removed.'"

After some further inquiry, it was decided that Christian Newcomer and Joseph Hoffman, who had visited the city in company with Newcomer, and Frederick Schaffer, one of the earliest fruits of Mr. Otterbein's labors in Lancaster, who was then assisting him in the city, should be ordained; and the following day was set for the performance of the solemn ceremony.

On the morning of the 2d of October, the Vestry of the church, a number of the brethren, and Rev. William Ryland, an elder in the Methodist Episcopal church, together with the candidates for ordination, assembled at the parsonage. Mr. Otterbein was lifted from his bed and placed upon an easy chair; and it appeared that he had received an unction from the Holy One for the performance of this last public duty of his ministry.

He first spoke to the candidates for ordination, in a very spiritual and impressive manner, then fervently addressed a throne of grace for a blessing upon them; after which, being assisted to his feet, he laid his hands upon them, in connection with Mr. Ryland, solemnly repeating the ordination service. Certificates of ordination were then written in English and in German, which he signed and delivered to the brethren ordained.

We insert a copy of one of these certificates:—

Know, all men whom it may concern, that Joseph Hoffman is, this 2d day of October, 1813, in presence of the subscribers, leaders of the Congregation in Baltimore, by the Rev. Wilhelm Otterbein, in conjunction, and with assistance of William Ryland, Elder of the Methodist Society in Baltimore, by the laying on of hands, duly and solemnly ordained.

We desire and pray that his labors in the vineyard of the Lord may prove a blessing to many souls.

Given this 2d day of October, 1813.

(WITNESS.)   JOHN HILDT, Secretary.

WILLIAM BACKER   { SEAL }

BALTZER SCHAEFFER   { SEAL }

                                                 A True Copy.

GOTTFRIED SUMWALT   { SEAL }

JACOB SMITH   { SEAL }

                               WILLIAM OTTERBEIN.

On the following day, Brothers Newcomer and Hoffman took their departure. Otterbein exhorted them to faithfulness, told them that God would be with them, and carry forward the good work through their instrumentality. His last words to them were:—"Farewell. If any inquire after me, tell them I die in the faith I have preached." He had suffered for some time, from an asthmatic affection, and, as his end drew near, it became more distressing. The friends who gathered about his bed, on the 17th of November, 1813, saw that the time of his departure had come. The Rev. Dr.

Kurtz, an evangelical Lutheran minister, who had long been his warm friend and co-laborer, offered up, at his bedside, the last vocal prayer. At its close, Otterbein responded in these words:—"Amen, amen! It is finished."

He now appeared to sink away, and the friends who gazed upon the solemn spectacle of a dying father and prince in Israel, were pierced with grief. Rallying once more, he said, slowly and distinctly:—

"Jesus, Jesus,—I die, but thou livest, and soon I shall live with thee." Then, addressing his friends, he continued, "The conflict is over and past. I begin to feel an unspeakable fullness of love and peace divine. Lay my head upon my pillow, and be still."

For a few moments, stillness reigned in the chamber of death,—no, not of *death;* rather let it be called the portal of *life.* "See!" whispered one, "how sweet, how easy he breathes." The chariot of Israel had come, with its celestial coursers, and was waiting at the gate. A smile, a fresh glow, lit up his countenance, and behold it was death.

"He taught us how to live, and, oh! too high
A price of knowledge, taught us how to die."

His funeral solemnities were largely attended. Ministers and members of the various evangelical churches in the city crowded into the spacious edifice, which had so often resounded with his earnest voice, and paid an unfeigned respect to his memory. The funeral sermon was preached by Dr. Kurtz, who was with him in his last moments, from Matthew xx.: 8—"Call the laborers and give them their hire;"—a fitting theme to dwell upon, around the coffin of one who had been a laborer from the early morn of life till its setting sun.*

Four months after Mr. Otterbein's death, the Baltimore annual conference of the Methodist Episcopal church convened in Baltimore. On the last day of the conference, bishop Asbury, who was then venerable in

---

* One circumstance connected with Otterbein's death may not be unworthy of notice here. Brother A. Bruner, one of Otterbein's warmest friends, resided out of the city. Being sent for, at Mr. O.'s request, he came; but, having pressing business in New York, it was thought, by the physician, that Mr. O. would live until his return. While Mr. B. was in New York, he dreamed that he saw Mr. Otterbein fly up through the air, having seven lights in his hands, on which he awoke, and immediately looked at his watch. On his return to Baltimore, he ascertained that Mr. O. had died precisely at the time he had had his singular dream. He arrived just in time to meet the procession at the grave. The amiable and humble Bruner, who was himself a light, while on earth, has gone home. He died a peaceful and happy death, and has, long since, entered into rest.—*Spayth.*

years, and rapidly approaching the close of his life, preached, in Otterbein's church, a sermon on the death of Mr. Otterbein. This was done as a mark of respect for the memory of the sainted leader in Israel, and as a token of friendship and love to the United Brethren. United Brethren, Methodists, Lutherans, Presbyterians, and Episcopalians, thronged the house. The most eminent ministers of the M. E. church were present. Bishops Asbury and McKendree occupied the pulpit. The sermon was one befitting the occasion, and was spoken of, throughout the city, in terms of high praise.

Referring to the occasion in his journal, Mr. Asbury says:—"By request, I discoursed on the character of the angel of the Church of Philadelphia, in allusion to William Otterbein—the holy, the great Otterbein—whose funeral discourse it was intended to be. Solemnity marked the silent meeting in the German church, where were assembled the members of our conference, and many of the clergy of the city. Forty years have I known the retiring modesty of this man of God, towering majestic above his fellows, in learning, wisdom, and grace, yet seeking to be known only to God, and the people of God."

"Mr. Otterbein's remains were deposited in the city of Baltimore, and church-yard on Howard's hill. On entering the gate immediately in front of the church from Conway-street, the passage to the church leads through a small yard, called Otterbein graveyard. There the sainted Father of blessed memory sleeps alone, there being no other grave in that apartment. The grave is adorned with two plain marble slabs, the upper one resting on four pillars of marble, with the following inscription:—

HIER RUHEN DIE GEBEINE DES VERSTORBENEN WILLIAM OTTERBEIN. Gebohren 4. Juni 1726: Gestorben 17. November, 1813, Seines Alters 87 Yahre, 6 Monate, 13 Tage. "Selig sind die Todten, die in dem Herrn sterben; sie ruhen von hirer Arbeit und ihre Werke folgen ihnen nach."	HERE REST THE REMAIN OF WILLIAM OTTERBEIN. He was Born June 4, 1726: Departed this Life Nov. 17, 1813, Aged 87 Years, 5 Months, and 13 Days. "Blessed are the dead that die in the Lord, for they rest from their labors, and their works do follow them." In the Ministry 62 Years.

It has been truly said that "Mr. Otterbein was no partisan." A man of a more catholic spirit never lived. From first to last, nothing was further from his purpose, than to use his talents or his influence to occasion schism in any church, or to put himself forward as a leader; and although, under his guidance, and by his prudential measures, the work of reform and of revival advanced steadily onward, and acquired strength and stability constantly, yet "he would not be called chief."

"His character was pure. He was grave and serious, as became a minister of the Gospel. No light conversation, nor too free allusion to the divine Master or his attributes, ever escaped his lips." The supreme God,—infinite and eternal,—was with him, in word and thought, the profoundest object of reverence and subject of thought. His mind seemed filled with God, and was constantly exercised with the most reverential emotions.

In social intercourse, he was easy of access, especially to the seeker of religion; yet no one could approach him but with respect, or converse with him, without feeling the presence of a superior intellect and heart. Frank and simple in his manners, he always made conversation interesting, agreeable, and instructive.

As a Christian, Mr. Otterbein was eminently evangelical and practical. His faith wavered not, and his love never failed. His meekness forsook him not through evil report and good report. Persecuted through the most of his ministerial life, he endured it without a murmur or complaint. When denounced, by bitter, unconverted ministers, as an "enthusiast," a "false prophet," and a "fanatic," he could never find it in his heart to reply with severity; but he could, and often did, weep over their blindness and the blindness of their churches, quoting the Savior's language—"Oh! Jerusalem, Jerusalem!"

His humility was remarkable. Men of extensive learning, and of popular talent as public speakers, usually manifest a little itching for reputation; and, if they attain to eminence, are somewhat concerned about their posthumous fame: but Otterbein, profoundly learned though he was, never made the least display of it; and although, during the most of his life, he was without a superior in America, as a preacher, he had the lowliness of a child, and preferred all his brethren before himself. Educated thoroughly, and ordained regularly, in a sect-hating communion, he welcomed, as fellow-laborers in the Master's vineyard, unlearned farmers and mechanics who felt that they had *religion*, and a *call* to preach, and not much besides. He could embrace, in his catholic heart, the Mennonite Boehm, or the Amish Draksel, and cry out before all the people, "*We are brethren!*"

His benevolence was of the very highest order. He literally gave away all he acquired, and all he inherited. "His mode of living was of the most frugal kind, and that to the last days of his life. And wherefore? That he might have the means to contribute to the destitute; and his acts of charity were limited only by his means. Daily, Sundays excepted, did the indigent, and the common beggars of the city, knock at his door for alms; and they were never turned away, if the means to grant relief were in the good minister's possession. We give a case: A suit of clothing was much worn, and his friends sent him cloth for a new suit. Still the old garments were worn. When asked if his tailor had forgotten him, he wiped a tear from his eye, and pointed to some indigent persons opposite his house. After this incident, some of the friends frequently furnished him with certain kinds of cloth for distribution to the needy. His demise was an occasion of real sorrow to this class of people, who were not a few: heartily did they lament and mourn the loss of their earthly friend and patron.

> "With them his name shall live,
> Through long succeeding years,
> Embalmed—with all their hearts can give,
> Their praises and their tears."

In reproof, he was very plain and pointed. A fault-finding professor once visited him, who became garrulous in his complaints against his brethren. In the midst of his harangue, Mr. O. touched him on the shoulder, and said, "Stop, brother! I perceive that you have got into the Devil's office!" meaning that he had become an accuser of the brethren.

But it was as a preacher and as an evangelist that he most excelled. His manner of preaching was calm and collected. "Every word was distinctly uttered," and every sentence completed. He was clear, solemn, earnest, and always profoundly impressed with the solemnity and importance of his position as an embassador of Christ. His matter was, from first to last, CHRIST, and him crucified—CHRIST, our Wisdom,

Righteousness, Sanctification, and Redemption—CHRIST, the present and complete Savior, the Alpha and Omega, the all and in all. He excelled in depth of thought, in thoroughness of exposition, and in force of reasoning. When treating of redemption through Jesus, of the truth and power of the Gospel, and of the victory of faith, he was listened to with wonder and delight; "but when addressing impenitent sinners, every word seemed to weigh a talent, and every sentence to burn like fire:" yet, so deep and genuine was his sympathy for men, and his solicitude for their salvation, that he could not fail to win as well as awaken.

Christian Newcomer, who heard him preach at Antietam, in 1799, makes this note in his journal:—"William Otterbein delivered the first discourse. O, what a wonderful man he is to preach, and declare the counsel of God!" This was on Saturday. "Sunday, William Otterbein preached again with such power and unction from on high, that all present were much astonished."

At the age of seventy-five, Newcomer heard him again at Antietam. He says:—"Father O. preached, this forenoon, with such power and grace, that almost every soul on the ground seemed to be pierced to the heart. We had a large congregation, and the attention of every soul was riveted to the spot. I spoke a few words after him, but for a short time, when the people broke forth into lamentations for mercy."

When Mr. O. had reached his eightieth year, Mr. N. listened to a sermon preached by him in Hagerstown, Md. He exclaims, "O! what feelings penetrate my soul whenever I hear this old servant of Christ declare the counsel of God. In depth of erudition, and in perspicuity of thought, he is unique and matchless."

No minister could readily forget the sermons which he delivered at the conferences. At one of the last of the conferences he was able to attend, he preached with great plainness, especially to the preachers. The audience was profoundly impressed, and the preachers, after the dismission of the congregation, remained seated and silent, and their honest faces were wet with tears. C. Hershey, then a young man, for many years afterward a faithful preacher, and now a saint in glory, looked up and said, "Oh! my God, this man's word is heavy! Who is sufficient for these things?"

Rev. Dr. B. Kurtz, in a letter relating to Mr. O. and his co-laborers, says

"Otterbein, that true and living witness, whose memory I hold dear, and cherish in my heart of hearts, was still laboring in faith and patience, and with great success, when I commenced preaching the Gospel; but, a short time before my arrival in Baltimore, the Master had called him home. The pious part of the community still delighted in calling to mind his unctious sermons, his holy walk and conversation, and his wonderful success in winning sinners from the error of their ways, as well as in encouraging the weak, and building up believers. My uncle, Rev. D. Kurtz, a true man of God, was a co-laborer of the sainted Otterbein, on terms of intimacy with him, and preached his funeral sermon. He often spoke to me about him, and always indicated the profound regard and ardent affection he entertained for him. In Washington county, Md., and in the adjacent parts of Virginia, (where I spent the first sixteen years of my ministry) Otterbein was well known. He frequently visited that section, and every-where I met with living seals of his ministry. The devotion and enthusiasm with which those who had been converted under his preaching spoke of his power in the pulpit, of his spirit and holy conversation in personal intercourse, and of his untiring labors to lead sinners to Christ, was really refreshing, and filled my heart with love and admiration for that chosen and distinguished servant of the Lord. I knew a number of the early preachers who had been converted by Otterbein's instrumentality, and preached in company with some of them, on funeral and other occasions. They were all men of God, and, though not learned, like Otterbein, (who was a scholar as well as a saint) they were faithful, devoted, and eminently useful. If ever there was a true revival preacher, Otterbein was one."

The following paper, found among the manuscripts of bishop Asbury, containing questions by Mr. A., and answers in the hand-writing of Otterbein, will be of interest to the reader:

"To the Rev. William Otterbein.

"Sir:—Where were you born?

"*Ans.* In Nassau Dillenburg, in Germany.

"*Ques.* How many years had you lived in your native land?

"*Ans.* Twenty-six years.

"*Ques.* How many years have you resided in America?

"*Ans.* Sixty years come next August.

"*Ques.* Where were you educated?

"*Ans.* In Herborn, in an academy.

"*Ques.* What languages and sciences were you taught?

"*Ans.* Latin, Greek, Hebrew, Philosophy, and Divinity.

"*Ques.* In what order were you set apart for the ministry?

"*Ans.* The Presbyterian form and order.

"*Ques.* What ministers assisted in your ordination?

"*Ans.* Schramm and Klingelhœfer.

"*Ques.* Where have you had charge of congregations in America?

"*Ans.* First in Lancaster, in Tulpehocken, in Fredericktown in Maryland, in Little York in Pennsylvania, and in Baltimore.

"*Ques.* In what part of the United States have you frequently traveled, in the prosecution of your ministerial labors?

"*Ans.* In Maryland, Virginia, and Pennsylvania.

"*Ques.* How many years of your life,

since you came to this continent, were you in a great measure an itinerant?

"*Ans.* The chief of the time since my coming, but more largely since my coming to Baltimore.

"*Ques.* By what means were you brought to the Gospel of God and our Savior?

"*Ans.* By degrees was I brought to the knowledge of the truth while in Lancaster.

"*Ques.* Have you unshaken confidence in God, through Christ, of your justification, sanctification, and sure hope of glorification?

"*Ans.* The Lord has been good to me, and no doubt remains in my mind but he will be good; and I can now praise him for the hope of a better life.

"*Ques.* Have you ever kept any account of the seals of your ministry?

"*Ans.* None.

"*Ques.* Have you ever kept any account of the members in the society of the United Brethren?

"*Ans.* Only what are in Baltimore.

"*Ques.* Have you taken any account of the brethren introduced into the ministry immediately by yourself, and sent out by you? Can you give the names of the living and the dead?

"*Ans.* Henry Weidner, Henry Baker, Simon Herre, in Virginia: these are gone to their reward. Newcomer can give the names of the living.

"*Ques.* What ministerial brethren, who have been your helpers, can you speak of with pleasure, and whose names are precious?

"*Ans.* Guething, Weidner, Newcomer, and others.

"*Ques.* What is your mind concerning John Wesley, and the order of Methodists in America?

"*Ans.* I think highly of John Wesley. I think well of the Methodists in America.

"*Ques.* What are your views of the present state of the church of Christ in Europe and America, and of prophecy?

"*Ans.* In continental Europe, the church has lost, in a great degree, the light of truth. In England and America the light still shines. Prophecy is hastening to its accomplishment.

"*Ques.* Will you give any commandment concerning your bones, and the memoirs of your life? Your children in Christ will not suffer you to die unnoticed.

"No answer returned to this last question."

These answers are all characteristic of Mr. Otterbein. He has nothing to boast of, no high professions to make, and declines to answer the question concerning his burial and the "memoirs of his life." He never sought the praise of men, and had no dread of dying "unnoticed." The glory of God absorbed his whole thought, and was the only object of his ambition.

CHAPTER XIX

END OF THE FIRST PERIOD.—A RESUME.

WE have now reached the end of the first period in the History of the United Brethren in Christ. Nearly half a century has passed since Otterbein and Boehm met at Isaac Long's, at the great meeting where the people of God, of various persuasions, flowed together, and realized that they were United Brethren. We have seen how this union was consolidated and strengthened from year to year, how other societies were gathered in, and other ministers, of like faith, raised up and sent forth as heralds of salvation. We have contemplated the struggles of these evangelists to revive and reform the old communions with which they had been ecclesiastically connected, and how this had been but partially successful, and had resulted, in many instances, in their real or virtual expulsion from those communions. We have seen the infant churches struggling to maintain the faith during the long war of the Revolution; and, in 1789, we have looked in upon the first conference of ministers regularly assembled; and we have traced those annual conferences down to 1812. On the minutes, many names have been recorded which will become familiar to us in the succeeding pages of this work. And it has been our mournful, and yet pleasing, duty, to gather around the graves of the eldest fathers of the United Brethren ministry. We have seen Boehm, Guething, Otterbein, and others of the fathers, die; and, blessed be the God of all grace, they have died well! "Mark the perfect man, and behold the upright, for the end of that man is peace." "The path of the just is as a light, shining more and more until the perfect day." These Scriptures have been illustrated before our eyes in the history, and especially the closing history, of those venerable saints of God.

It may be well to take our leave of this interesting period of United Brethren history, by presenting a compréhensive view of the fathers, and of their labors, sketched by the pen of a discriminating cotemporary and co-laborer, who knew them well, and loved them as fellow-heirs of a like precious faith. In a discourse delivered on the death of Father Boehm, and shortly before the departure of Otterbein, bishop Asbury said:

"But our beloved brother, Boehm, who has gone to his high reward, was not the only laborer in the vineyard. Will it be hazarding too much to say that, in Pennsylvania, Maryland, and Virginia, there were one hundred preachers, and twenty thousand people, in the communion of the United Brethren? Many of these faithful men have gone to glory, and many are yet alive to preach to congregated thousands.

"Pre-eminent among these is William Otterbein, who assisted in the ordination which set apart your speaker to the superintendency of the Methodist Episcopal church. He is one of the best scholars and greatest divines in America. Why, then, is he not where he began? He was irregular. Alas, for us! the zealous are necessarily so, to those whose cry is, *put me into the priest's office, that I may eat a morsel of bread*. Osterwald has observed, 'Hell is paved with the skulls of unfaithful ministers.' Such was not Boehm, such is not Otterbein; and now his sun of life is setting in brightness: behold the saint of God leaning upon his staff, waiting for the chariots of Israel!

"I pause here to indulge in reflections upon the past. Why was the German reformation in the middle states, that sprang up with Boehm, Otterbein, and their helpers, not more perfect? Was money, was labor made a consideration with these primitive men? No; they wanted not the one, and heeded not the other. They all had had church membership as Presbyterians, (German Reformed) Lutherans, Moravians, Tunkers, Mennonists. The spiritual men of these societies generally united with the reformers; but they brought along with them the formalities and peculiar opinions of religious education. Some of the ministers located, and only added to their charge partial traveling laborers. It remains to be proven, whether a reformation in any country, or under any circumstances, can be perpetuated without a well-directed itinerancy. But these faithful men of God were not the less zealous in declaring the truth. * * *

Christian Newcomer, near Hagerstown, in Maryland, has labored and traveled many years. His heart's desire has always been to effect a union between his German brethren and the Methodists.

"I will not forget Abraham Draksel, a most acceptable preacher, in the west of Pennsylvania; Henry and Christian Crum, twin brothers, and twin souls in zeal and experience: these were holy, good men, and members of both societies. John Hershey, formerly a Mennonist—an Israelite;—he is gone to rest. Abraham and Christian Hershey, occasional itinerants, good men, busy and zealous. David Snyder: possessing gifts to make himself useful. Isaac Niswander: a good man, and good preacher. Most of these men were natives of Pennsylvania.

"The flame of German zeal has moved westward with emigration. In Ohio, we have Andrew Zellar and George Benedum, men of God, intrusted with a weighty charge, subjecting them to great labors.

"But our German fathers have lost many of their spiritual children. Some have returned whence they or their fathers came, and some have joined the Dutch Baptists.

"Our German reformers have left no journal or record, that I have seen or heard of, by which we might learn the extent of their labors; but, from Tennessee, where the excellent Baker labored and died, through Virginia and Maryland into Pennsylvania, as far eastward as Bucks and Berks counties, the effect of their ministry was happily seen and felt.

"We feel ourselves at liberty to believe that these German heralds of grace congregated one hundred thousand souls, that they have had twenty thousand in fellowship and communion, and one hundred zealous and acceptable preachers."

www.ingramcontent.com/pod-product-compliance
Lightning Source LLC
Chambersburg PA
CBHW030559300426
44111CB00009B/1038